Varieties of the Weird Tale

THE HIPPOCAMPUS PRESS LIBRARY OF CRITICISM

S. T. Joshi, *Primal Sources: Essays on H. P. Lovecraft* (2003)

S. T. Joshi, *The Evolution of the Weird Tale* (2004)

Robert H. Waugh, *The Monster in the Mirror: Looking for H. P. Lovecraft* (2006)

Scott Connors, ed., *The Freedom of Fantastic Things: Selected Criticism on Clark Ashton Smith* (2006)

Ben Szumskyj, ed., *Two-Gun Bob: A Centennial Study of Robert E. Howard* (2006)

S. T. Joshi and Rosemary Pardoe, ed.,*Warnings to the Curious: A Sheaf of Criticism on M. R. James* (2007)

S. T. Joshi, *Classics and Contemporaries: Some Notes on Horror Fiction* (2009)

Kenneth W. Faig, Jr., *The Unknown Lovecraft* (2009)

Massimo Berruti, *Dim-Remembered Stories: A Critical Study of R. H. Barlow* (2010)

Gary William Crawford, Jim Rockhill, and Brian J. Showers, ed., *Reflections in a Glass Darkly: Essays on J. Sheridan Le Fanu* (2011)

Robert H. Waugh, *A Monster of Voices: Speaking for H. P. Lovecraft* (2011)

Donald Sidney-Fryer, *The Golden State Phantasticks: The California Romantics and Related Subjects* (2012)

William F. Nolan, *Nolan on Bradbury: Sixty Years of Writing about the Master of Science Fiction* (2013)

Steven J. Mariconda, *H. P. Lovecraft: Art, Artifact, and Reality* (2013)

S. T. Joshi, *Unutterable Horror: A History of Supernatural Fiction* (2014)

Massimo Berruti, S. T. Joshi, and Sam Gafford, ed., *William Hope Hodgson: Voices from the Borderland* (2014)

Donald R. Burleson, *Lovecraft: An American Allegory* (2015)

S. T. Joshi, *The Rise, Fall, and Rise of the Cthulhu Mythos* (2015)

Robert H. Waugh, *The Tragic Thread in Science Fiction* (2017)

Lovecraft Annual (2007–)

Dead Reckonings (2007–)

Lovecraftian Proceedings (2015–)

VARIETIES OF THE WEIRD TALE

S. T. Joshi

Hippocampus Press

New York

Published by Hippocampus Press
P.O. Box 641, New York, NY 10156.
http://www.hippocampuspress.com

Cover art by Wallace Smith for *The Shadow-Eater* by
Benjamin De Casseres (1923).
Image and cover production courtesy of Kevin I. Slaughter.
Cover design by Barbara Briggs Silbert.
Hippocampus Press logo designed by Anastasia Damianakos.

First Edition
1 3 5 7 9 8 6 4 2

ISBN 978-1-61498-188-6

Contents

Introduction: Establishing the Canon of Weird Fiction

The very title of this essay may evoke some scepticism, for there are no doubt many who question the feasibility or utility of establishing canons of any kind. The thinking is either that some ill-defined but infallible entity called Posterity will be sufficiently adept, in its unconscious way, in sorting out the enduring from the ephemeral, or that the very notion of a canon is offensively elitist in its suggestion that a handful of self-appointed authorities know better than the cumulative votes of readers what should survive and what should be forgotten. It is difficult to reply in detail to these criticisms, but I can at least drop some hints.

The case for canon formation has been adequately made by Harold Bloom in *The Western Canon* (1994), and I will summarise and, in some sense, extrapolate from his arguments here. Bloom declares that canons will exist, whether anyone wants them or not, because there is only a limited amount of time in anyone's life to absorb the virtually unlimited number of literary, musical, artistic, and other aesthetic products of human civilisation; so that, unless one's absorption of these works is to be entirely random or arbitrary, some criterion—or, more likely, a series of criteria—must be established in order to make an intelligent selection of those works one chooses to consume and those one can justifiably bypass. Canons need not be exclusive, although by their very nature they will establish certain criteria that will result in the inclusion or exclusion of—or, at any rate, the setting up of a hierarchy for—a given work as compared to other works of its class. Canons are, and will always be, in flux, for there is no denying that a central, perhaps overriding, focus in the establishment of a canon is contemporary relevance. However intrinsically meritorious a given work may be, its place in the canon may rest chiefly on its continuing ability to speak to present-day concerns. Traditionally, the ability of a given work to be of relevance to widely differing temperaments, and to widely differing epochs, is a sign of enduring merit.

The proponents of literary democracy express a touching faith that the cumulative tastes and preferences of an unguided readership will infallibly result in the establishment of a canon that is unassailable by sheer force of numbers. But art is not a democracy; art is only an aristocracy of excellence. The extension of the notion of "one person, one vote" from the political sphere into the realms of art and intellect seems to me one of the most pernicious notions ever devised, for if carried to its logical extension it would mean that whichever aesthetic product attracted the greatest number of adherents would achieve supremacy. I have little doubt that, in any given week, more people watch *Survivor* on television than have ever read Homer's *Iliad* in any language over the past 2500 years; but I trust that brute fact will not be used to gauge the relative aesthetic merits of *Survivor* and the *Iliad*.

Our populist critics, pointing to the familiar examples of Shakespeare and Dickens, confidently assert that the popular author of today is the classic author of tomorrow. This facile claim is, however, quickly and irrevocably disproved by an actual study of literary history. In the nineteenth century, the most popular writers in English were not Dickens, Thackeray, or George Eliot, but rather writers on the order of Mrs. Mulock (Dinah Maria Craik), Marie Corelli, and Charlotte Mary Yonge—who, if they live on at all, live only as fodder for the history of popular taste. In her lifetime, Gertrude Atherton outsold Edith Wharton and Willa Cather, but few critics or readers today are likely to rank her above her prestigious contemporaries. One further assumes that the current popularity of Stephen King, Danielle Steel, and James Patterson over Toni Morrison and Gore Vidal does not suggest the aesthetic superiority of the former group of writers over the latter.

Where is all this leading? I trust it is now evident that popular taste, no matter how far it is chronologically extended, can never ensure the production of a canon that has any aesthetic legitimacy. This is because the mass of readers do not, and are in fact cannot, assess a work on its purely aesthetic merits; their criteria are almost always meretricious, resting on such factors as how much a given work may reflect transient social or political issues, whether it features "sympathetic" characters (i.e., characters either as bland and tiresome as themselves or overblown fantasy-figures whose wealth, beauty, and daring can serve as the focus of readers' wish-fulfilment fantasies), how pruriently titillating it can be (a time-honoured formula that accounts for the bestsellerdom of authors ranging from Robert W. Chambers to Judith Krantz), and the like.

I do not have the time to expatiate on why the aesthetic tastes of the mass public are, and has always been, so poor. One can point to the failure of the educational system in a country where, as surveys have repeatedly shown, nearly half the populace is functionally illiterate; but it strikes me that there are broader cultural factors at work in the United States. This country has, from its inception, never emphasised the acquisition of culture, seeing it as a useless frivolity that might associate us far more closely than we would like to the effete aristocracies of Europe; "knowledge" was interpreted solely as the acquisition of practical information designed to secure an income, or that led to concrete advances as in the sciences. The sentiment expressed by the aged Aaron Burr, in Gore Vidal's novel *Burr*, as he handed a set of Gibbon to a young disciple—"Take them; read them; become civilized"—remains to this day incomprehensible to most Americans.

It should also now be evident that critics and scholars must—and, as an historical and practical fact, do—take a central role in the formation of a canon. Readers' tastes are never entirely unguided; critics, scholars, editors, and publishers are vitally involved. The emergence of Herman Melville and Walt Whitman from the utter obscurity in which they were engulfed in the fifty years after their deaths are only two shining examples of authors who, almost entirely as a result of the diligence and enthusiasm of critics, now occupy an unassailable place in the canon. These examples could be multiplied many times over.

What is it about critics and scholars that differentiates them from the general readership? It is that the former exhibit a somewhat greater and more elevated degree of *critical judgment* than the mass of casual readers. Critical judgment—what, in the eighteenth century, was covered by the broad term "taste"—seems to me the defining characteristic of a critic. A critic's function is not merely to accumulate literary or biographical information (what Oswald Spengler, in reference to historians, termed "ant-industry" [1.41]); it is not to apply, in some mechanical fashion, a currently fashionable literary theory to a given work of literature, in a misguided attempt to turn criticism into an exact science. It is, preeminently, the application of taste and discrimination: the ability to sort the good from the bad, the enduring from the ephemeral, the sincere from the hackneyed, the complex from the superficial. There are, of course, those who maintain that the passing of evaluative judgments of this kind is foreign to the function of criticism; but if the root meaning of the word criticism—from the Greek *krinein* (to separate, pick, choose, distinguish, and, preeminently, to act as judge)—is taken into consideration, then it becomes clear that the act of evaluation is a central role of the critic.

Let me not be misunderstood. It would be as illegitimate to scorn popular writing uniformly as it would be to equate popularity with literary substance. Elitism has often been criticised because it is believed that the elitist critic refuses even to consider any artistic product that has the taint of popularity. But the true elitist is one who seeks only the best and has intolerance only for mediocrity, and the fair-minded elitist keeps in mind that the best can be found in a pulp magazine just as the mediocre can be found in the *Kenyon Review*. All I am urging here is that the number of copies an author sells is no reliable gauge of his or her literary merit; and, given the history of bestsellerdom over the past century or so, and the almost systematic failure of such works to achieve canonical status, a presumption against them is by no means unwarranted.

Is there, then, no virtue at all to "popular" literature? Are we to deprive ourselves of all "guilty pleasures"? The standard formulation made by popular writers themselves, along with the critics who act as their sycophants, is that they write "for entertainment only," and that this humble function should be recognised for what it is. But this seemingly simple formulation masks a surprisingly complex set of queries and quandaries. Who is being entertained, and how? Football games, crossword puzzles, and pornography presumably "entertain" a certain segment of the population; but there is no reason to accord these things any aesthetic status as a result. The fully developed critical judgment should prove impervious to the "entertainment" value of inferior work. I fail to see how it is possible to be entertained by hackneyed plots, slipshod writing, wooden characters, and a general absence of depth and complexity. There is not enough time in life for this kind of "entertainment." The skill that some popular writers exhibit in plot construction—in publicists' lingo, the ability to "keep the reader turning those pages"—ranks very low on the scale of aesthetic accomplishment. If it did not, then Michael Crichton or Erle Stanley Gardner would rank higher than Dostoevsky or Virgil.

What, then, are the legitimate criteria for the evaluation of literature, and specifically the evaluation of weird literature? The time-honoured elements—profundity, complexity of thought, adaptation of style to subject-matter—that have customarily been hailed as the marks of good general literature would appear to apply just as well to the weird. Each of these elements is notoriously difficult to define, and there can be legitimate dispute as to whether a given work embodies it, as compared with any other. Is *Dracula* a more "profound" work, aesthetically and philosophically, than *At the Mountains of Madness*? It would seem that only taste and judgment can even begin to settle the matter. The matter of style is also immensely complex, and immensely controverted. Lovecraft was notoriously accused of a "bad" style—

verbose, bombastic, esoteric, and flamboyant—as Poe was before him; but many of these criticisms (criticisms that are still being voiced, as the furore in certain quarters over Lovecraft's inclusion in the Library of America testifies) appear largely based on a blanket condemnation of material deriving from the pulp magazines (the only professional venue open to Lovecraft) and an exclusive admiration of the bare-bones spareness of the style of Hemingway, Sherwood Anderson, and their congeners. Conversely, certain other authors, ranging from Kipling to William Peter Blatty, have been criticised for their "low" or popular styles, when it could well be argued that this style uniquely suits their subject-matter.

The issue of philosophical depth in weird fiction has been the subject of some recent discussion, apparently as a result of my own emphasis on the point in *The Weird Tale*. I maintained in that study that the best weird fiction was "the consequence of a world view" (1) in that it sought to refashion the universe in accordance with the author's philosophical vision. I have apparently been criticised for reading weird fiction merely as veiled philosophy and not as an aesthetic product in itself, but I think this is a misreading, amounting almost to a caricature, of the view I expressed. I am fully aware that aesthetic criteria are and must be to the fore in the assessment of literature, weird and otherwise, and that the absence of a coherent philosophical vision is not necessarily fatal to aesthetic soundness. I may have erred in failing to detect a full-fledged philosophical vision in the work of M. R. James; I have lately come to believe that there is indeed such a vision, although I still believe it is not as inherently interesting, nor expressed quite as effectively, as in the work of the other authors (Arthur Machen, Lord Dunsany, Algernon Blackwood, Ambrose Bierce, and H. P. Lovecraft) whom I studied. I have since concluded that the general absence of a philosophical vision in modern weird writing may be the result of the concretisation of the weird as a definite "genre," in which certain tropes (the ghost, the haunted house, etc.) are used in a somewhat mechanical fashion without an underlying awareness of their philosophical ramifications. I do not believe I am wrong in finding a good deal of contemporary weird fiction somewhat thin and insubstantial not only in its absence of philosophical depth but also in any number of purely aesthetic deficiencies. If it is really the case that a philosophical vision only actuated the works of the writers I favoured in *The Weird Tale*, then I think it would be a sad admission of the general mediocrity of the field; but I am not yet ready to concede this point.

Lovecraft was keenly aware that weird literature, by reason of its non-mimetic nature, required a certain deftness of handling that did not pertain to ordinary realist literature, specifically in regard to the *convincingness* of the weird phenomenon:

> Inconceivable events and conditions have a special handicap to overcome, and this can be accomplished only through the maintenance of a careful realism in every phase of the story *except* that touching on the one given marvel. This marvel must be treated very impressively and deliberately—with a careful emotional "build-up"—else it will seem flat and unconvincing. Being the principal thing in the story, its mere existence should overshadow the characters and events. ("Notes on Writing Weird Fiction" 177)

There is some reason to believe that this formulation—especially in its emphasis on the *necessity* of "careful realism"—applies only to the kind of "supernatural realism" that Lovecraft himself mastered. Admittedly, supernatural realism is indeed a dominant mode of weird fiction, but it is evident that such a writer as Poe relied almost solely on a kind of frenetic witchery of style to effect the "willing suspension of disbelief" so critical to a weird tale's success. Clark Ashton Smith was somewhat less successful in this regard, although some of his work is so outré that it borders on fantasy. Lovecraft's devaluation of character development can also be seen to be somewhat self-serving, in that his "cosmic" approach, by conveying the awesome gulfs of space and time, deliberately emphasised human insignificance. More conventional literature of ghosts and vampires will lay greater emphasis on character, although there is conversely a genuine concern as to whether the use of such venerable tropes can retain convincingness in a sceptical age. It becomes problematical to classify such a work as Anne Rice's *Interview with the Vampire* (1976) as weird fiction at all, since, in spite of its skill in delineating the interplay of character, so little effort is spent in justifying the central supernatural phenomenon—the existence of vampires—that it really becomes a mainstream novel that happens to be founded on a supernatural premise.

Certain other criteria—or, rather, pseudo-criteria—can, I believe, be rejected at the outset. The recent politicisation of academic criticism has led some careless critics to maintain the aesthetic superiority of certain writers merely because they happen to be African American, or gay, or female, or endowed with other qualities that have minimal bearing upon the actual literary merits of their work. This bizarre misapplication of the otherwise sound principle of affirmative action into the realm of aesthetics will, I trust, soon be regarded as an intellectual aberration of our era. The value of such criticism in bringing to light certain writers who, because they were African American or gay or female or whatever, had been unjustly ignored is unquestioned; it is now time that these figures find their proper place in the canon without having to carry unwieldy sociopolitical baggage.

It does not seem that any single criterion for canon-formation can be utilised uniformly or indiscriminately. The criterion I would prefer to use—pure, abstract literary merit—must be tempered by other criteria: historical significance, widespread influence, and, yes, popular appeal. It is not entirely clear that these and other criteria can all work together; but the end result might, ideally, be a kind of historical snapshot of the relative importance that we, of the early twenty-first century, place upon the weird writing of the past two centuries.

The history of weird fiction is, to be sure, one of peaks and valleys. It seems to me vaguely disreputable that we owe the existence of the field to a piece of work so intrinsically inferior as Horace Walpole's *The Castle of Otranto* (1764). It is, of course, an unanswerable historical question whether, if Walpole's little novel had never existed, the field of weird fiction would have emerged in any event; but the plain fact is that it did emerge as a result of this shoddy piece of work. I am reminded of H. P. Lovecraft's warning to a correspondent who was looking forward to reading the novel after reading a summary of it in Eino Railo's *The Haunted Castle* (1927):

> Have you read *The Castle of Otranto?* If not, *don't!* Let the summary in Railo continue to give you a "kick", for the original certainly won't! Walpole was too steeped in the classical tradition of the early 18th century to catch the Gothic spirit of the latter half. His choice of words and rhythms is the brisk, cheerful Addisonian one; and his nonchalant and atmosphereless way of describing the most prodigious horrors is enough to empty them of all their potency. Thanks to the second-hand way in which you received it, you have become the first reader to get a genuine shiver from *Otranto* since the days of Sir Walter Scott! (*Selected Letters* 2.231–32)

The broader question raised by Walpole and the entire Gothic school of the late eighteenth and early nineteenth centuries is: Why do they continue to attract the attention of scholars and critics far out of proportion to their intrinsic merits? And why, moreover, does the standard quartet of Walpole, Radcliffe, Lewis, and Maturin (with a nod to Charles Brockden Brown, and Mary Shelley thrown in so that she does not get entirely co-opted by the science fiction field) continue to receive attention at the expense of more obscure toilers in the Gothic factory? I am not about to deny that these authors do in fact deserve their relative eminence over the Sophia Lees, Charlotte Dacres, and Francis Lathoms of the world; but if the significance of the works of this period is now largely historical or even sociological, there seems no reason to focus on the former and ignore the latter. And yet, I doubt that very many scholars of Gothic literature, aside from Frederick S. Frank or Maurice Lévy, have ever read any large proportion of the 422 Gothic novels in Frank's definitive listing. The plain fact is that the Gothic novels were a popular literary mode exactly analogous to the hundreds or thousands of works produced in the horror "boom" of the past few decades, and in both cases the great majority have deservedly disappeared, leaving only a few isolated islands of merit to face the relentless tsunami of oblivion.

Originators, then, do seem to retain an importance out of proportion to their merits; but I have a sense that scholars of the Gothic novel—assuming that at least some of them are interested in these works as instances of weird fiction, not merely for what they can tell about the cultural milieu in which they were produced—devote their energies to these works chiefly because a recognised canon of later weird fiction has not been established.

In a real sense, the true originator of our field was Edgar Allan Poe. Transforming already stale Gothic conventions by infusion of psychological insight and a highly compressed manner of utterance that resulted in the birth of the short story, Poe is the father of virtually all that came after him. By a bizarre coincidence, Joseph Sheridan Le Fanu was performing a roughly analogous transformation on the other side of the Atlantic, quite independently of Poe. Not as radical as Poe, and reforming rather than revolutionising Gothic modes of fear-production, Le Fanu over his long career laid the groundwork for the production of terror in both the novel and the novelette.

I am not entirely certain that any satisfactory account has been given as to why the weird tale proliferated so dynamically in the period 1880-1940—what Philip Van Doren Stern aptly labelled the "Golden Age" of the horror story. Purely literary considerations do not seem to provide an adequate answer: to be sure, the influence of Poe on Ambrose Bierce, H. P. Lovecraft, and many others is patent; but I am convinced that cultural factors played a significant role. For one thing, orthodox religious belief declined significantly among the intellectual classes during the later nineteenth century, as Darwin's theory of evolution appeared to provide the final element in the fashioning of an entirely secular conception of the universe. If Lovecraft is correct in asserting that supernatural fiction is "coeval with the religious feeling and closely related to many aspects of it" (*Annotated Supernatural Horror in Literature* 26), then a case could be made that a decline in religious belief would result in the augmentation of a need for *aesthetic* outlets for it. The atheist Lovecraft himself made just such a case: ". . . religion itself is merely a pompous formalisation of fantastic art. Its disadvantage is that it demands an *intellectual* belief in the impossible, whereas fantastic art does not" (*Selected Letters* 4.418). When God is removed from both the intellectual and the aesthetic landscape, the rationale for such entities as the ghost, the witch, and the werewolf—all resting at least indirectly upon a religious conception of the universe—is suddenly lost. Is it any wonder that such eccentric monsters as Lovecraft's Cthulhu, or the sand-entities that Algernon Blackwood evoked out of the hoary depths of Egypt, came to be? In any event, it is undeniable that such writers as Lovecraft, Blackwood, Arthur Machen, Lord Dunsany, M. R. James, and a host of others not only gave voice to the myriad terrors facing a rapidly changing Anglo-American culture (the terror of the untenanted wilderness, the terror of unholy antiquity, and, perhaps most poignant of all, the terror of the cosmic void suddenly emptied of its comforting and benevolent Creator), but also showed how weird fiction could be made to serve as the complex expression of the most intimate philosophical conceptions and a relevant commentary on social, cultural, and even political institutions.

I confess to a similar quandary as to why the weird tale (I exclude here the fantasy novel as splendidly embodied in Tolkien, Peake, and others) went into abeyance for nearly two generations after the death of Lovecraft. In the period from 1940 to 1970, only Shirley Jackson—who was far from considering herself a "horror" writer—and Robert Aickman could be said to have attained genuine eminence. Why did the "Golden Age" of horror writing collapse just at the time when the "Golden Age" of science fiction was in full vigour? Some attention, I believe, must be paid to market forces. Many academicians, comfortable in their tenured offices, appear to give short shrift to the plain fact that, in our capitalist society, the majority of writers are compelled to earn their living by writing; and that if the markets for their work are absent or insufficient, they will either turn to some other kind of writing or turn away from writing altogether. This appears to be exactly what happened to weird fiction after World War II. The pulp magazines, including *Weird Tales,* were in their dying agonies; the emergence of the paperback book did not help, because paperback publishers required voluminous sales to maintain profitability, sales that could only be achieved by more popular genres like the detective story, the romance, the western, and science fiction. A small press like Arkham House could hardly support even a single weird writer, let alone a cadre of them. It is no surprise that those American writers who had flourished in the pulps turned either to the mystery or suspense story (Robert Bloch) or to science fiction or fantasy (Fritz Leiber, Ray Bradbury, Richard Matheson).

The horror "boom" of the 1970s, 1980s, and 1990s seems to me much more a cultural, even a marketing, phenomenon than a literary one. The groundwork for the sudden popularity of such writers as Ira Levin, William Peter Blatty, Thomas Tryon, and Stephen King was prepared by the unending spate of horror films that had been regaling uncultivated viewers since the 1930s. Whereas Blatty and Tryon's work—especially the latter's—is far from lacking in substance, Levin is a prototype of the best-selling author endowed with provocative and suggestive ideas but wholly incapable of expressing them coherently. As for King, the fact that he is the most remarkable publishing phenomenon in our time is far from saying that he is the most remarkable literary phenomenon of the age. Once he had attained bestsellerdom, he quickly became a brand name who could be relied upon to generate the customary blockbuster sales with each new product, regardless of its merit or lack of it. King, however, is an unusual figure in that, although extraordinarily popular, he has also attracted a substantial amount of literary criticism, even from academicians. Some of this criticism may well be a product of academicians' fondness for literary slumming; and a recent trend in King criticism appears to suggest that his work is to be valued not so much for its literary substance as for its insights into contemporary American culture. I confess that, after an exhaustive reading of King's work, I can see little in this argument; I have never found any remark by King on American society or culture that could not have been made by a reasonably intelligent ten-year-old. The best that could be asserted is that King's work *unconsciously* has insights to offer into American popular culture; but the same could be said of television commercials or popular women's magazines, and no *aesthetic* value would accrue thereby.

I am on record as vaunting the literary merits of such contemporary writers as Ramsey Campbell, T. E. D. Klein, Thomas Ligotti, Peter Straub, David J. Schow, Dennis Etchison, and Norman Partridge over the best-selling quartet of King, Anne Rice, Clive Barker, and Dean Koontz. The latter certainly seem to have a high opinion of themselves, an opinion that does not seem entirely commensurate with the actual substance of their work; and some of them even make a virtue of their ability to reach a mass audience. Barker has stated axiomatically: "I'm writing popular fiction. . . . You get your material to the largest cross-section of people you possibly can" (Jones 104). But Barker does not seem to have thought out the utility or benefit of attracting mere numbers; in any case, it is by no means clear that he is in fact reaching a very wide cross-section of the public, as opposed to a relatively narrow—if numerically substantial—clique of readers who happen to enjoy his overblown word-bags of hypertrophic fantasy.

What, then, is the role of the critic of weird fiction? First, one should keep in mind that the mere act of teaching or writing about a given literary work carries with it the suggestion that, in that critic's judgment, the work is *worth* writing about; every critical act therefore sheds light on the critic's critical judgment. It may be tempting to delve into popular rubbish so as to place an article in a fashionable academic journal, but it carries the implication that the critic has no higher standard of aesthetic evaluation. Be careful, then, of what you choose to write about. And yet, if the opportunity presents itself, you should consider writing reviews and articles outside the tiny and insular realm of academic publications. One of the many lamentable trends in literary criticism during the past half-century is the near-total absence of what might be called "public criticism"—criticism intended to reach a wide audience of the *intelligent* literary public (not the *mass* public) outside the confines of the university. Criticism left exclusively in the hands of academicians who only write for one another, in an incomprehensible jargon that too often serves as a mask for poverty of thought and imagination, is a criticism doomed to irrelevance and insignificance. Conversely, criticism of weird fiction left entirely in the hands of uncritical devotees, or of writers whose personal or professional ties with other writers, editors, or publishers militate against the expression of honest and forthright views, is criticism of very little long-term value.

Secondly, the development of critical judgment in this realm must be made a desideratum. Wide reading of the weird fiction of the past two or three centuries will by no means guarantee the acquisition of critical judgment, but it would appear to be, at a minimum, a necessary prerequisite. It is precisely the absence of such wide reading that has condemned several histories of weird fiction to the intellectual dustbin: preeminent among these is Walter Kendrick's *The Thrill of Fear: 250 Years of Scary Entertainment* (1991), whose ignorance of recent developments in the horror field is deeply embarrassing. His laconic comment that "the best the twentieth century can do in that line is Stephen King" tells the whole sad story. David Punter's *The Literature of Terror* (1980), even in its 1996 revision, is not much better. The need to establish some kind of provisional hierarchy of post–World War II weird fiction—a hierarchy based not upon popular appeal but actual literary merit—is pressing.

Thirdly, do not be afraid to pass evaluative judgments. This is, as I have stated, a central and essential function in literary criticism. Well-informed readers will recognise that such an evaluative judgment is the expression of informed opinion and not the laying down of a dogmatic fiat; and the sum-total of such judgments, extended over years and generations, will form a complex mosaic that will in the end allow a canon to emerge. That canon may, will, and should evolve with the passing of time, but we as critics of the early twenty-first century owe it to subsequent generations of readers to voice our own judgments— tentative and non-prescriptive as they may be—on what we believe to be the best our field has to offer.

Works Cited

Frank, Frederick S. "The Gothic Romance 1762–1820." In *Horror Literature: A Core Collection and Reader's Guide*, ed. Marshall B. Tymn. New York: Bowker, 1981. 3–175.

Jones, Stephen, ed. *Clive Barker's Shadows in Eden*. Lancaster, PA: Underwood-Miller, 1991.

Joshi, S. T. *The Weird Tale*. Austin: University of Texas Press, 1990.

Lovecraft, H. P. *The Annotated Supernatural Horror in Literature*. New York: Hippocampus Press, 2nd ed. 2012.

———. "Notes on Writing Weird Fiction." In *Collected Essays, Volume 2: Literary Criticism*. Ed. S. T. Joshi. New York, Hippocampus Press, 2004. 175–78.

———. *Selected Letters*. Ed. August Derleth, Donald Wandrei, and James Turner. Sauk City, WI: Arkham House, 1965–76. 5 vols.

Spengler, Oswald. *The Decline of the West*. Tr. Charles Francis Atkinson. New York: Knopf, 1926–28. 2 vols.

Stern, Philip Van Doren. "Introduction." In *The Midnight Reader*. New York: Henry Holt, 1942.

I. The Golden Age

Some Notes on Ambrose Bierce

I. Bierce as Political Satirist

Virtually the entire work of Ambrose Bierce (1842–1914?) is satirical in origin and function, not excluding his gripping tales of the Civil War and his stories of the supernatural. In his political satires he employs fantasy, comic exaggeration, parody, and deadpan humour to convey his criticism of a wide range of American social and political institutions. These satires are of two separate but related types: one, a series of sketches purportedly written by a historian of the distant future looking back upon the nineteenth and twentieth centuries; the other, a group of tales set in imaginary realms whose customs, laws, and traditions bear striking resemblance to (and differences from) those of America in Bierce's day. Bierce would not be entirely satisfied if his readers were merely to appreciate the cleverness and imaginative richness of his satires; as the essays and editorials (most of them unreprinted since their original appearances a century and more ago) included in the second part of this volume indicate, his criticisms were heartfelt and of long standing. And because they broach some of the most fundamental, sensitive, and still unresolved issues of American political thought, they continue to command interest and attention.

Bierce's satirical sketches began to appear at the very outset of his literary career. After serving in some of the bloodiest battles of the Civil War, he made his way to San Francisco and, in 1867, started publishing in some of the city's local publications. By 1868 he was an irregular contributor to the *San Francisco News Letter*: several sketches and articles that appeared at that time were later gathered in his early volumes, *The Fiend's Delight* (1873) and *Nuggets and Dust* (1873). Many other items were never so collected, and only a careful study of Bierce's early stylistic mannerisms allows us to ascribe to him certain anonymous or pseudonymous works published in the *News Letter* prior to his assumption of that paper's editorship in December 1868. Five such items have been identified: a series of four "Letters from a Hdkhoite" published in April 1868, and "A Scientific Dream," published in November 1868. If these sketches are in fact by Bierce—both their style and their content seem unmistakably to be his—then the latter item is the first of his future histories, while the former is the first of that group of tales set in a fantastic land. A sixth item—"Across the Continent" (*News Letter*, 15 May 1869)—appeared when Bierce was the editor of the paper and was signed with the pseudonym "Samboles." Although he did not explicitly acknowledge the story as his, I believe that its attribution to him is secure.

It was not until Bierce migrated to England, where he lived from 1872 to 1875, that he resumed the writing of political satires. Amidst the enormous mass of journalism he produced during this period—including regular columns and contributions to the London papers *Figaro* and *Fun*, along with occasional appearances elsewhere—is a solitary item, "John Smith," appearing in *Fun* for 10 May 1873. Bierce included this future history, first published anonymously, in the first volume of his *Collected Works*.

Bierce returned to San Francisco in 1875. For two years he was literarily quiescent, but in March 1877 he resumed journalistic work. During his tenure with two weekly papers, the *Argonaut* (1877-79) and the *Wasp* (1881-86), he wrote only a single item that might be classed thematically among his political fantasies: "'The Bubble Reputation,'" a brief futuristic whimsy appearing in the *Wasp* for 8 May 1886. Bierce reprinted it among the "negligible tales" in the eighth volume (1911) of his *Collected Works*.

It was only when Bierce joined the *San Francisco Examiner* in 1887 as William Randolph Hearst's star editorial writer that both his political satires and his short fiction began appearing in great numbers.

During his first five years with the *Examiner*, Bierce published the bulk of the stories he included in his two landmark collections, *Tales of Soldiers and Civilians* (1891) and *Can Such Things Be?* (1893). The former (later retitled *In the Midst of Life*) contained Civil War tales as well as tales of what is now termed "psychological horror," whereas the latter consisted chiefly of stories of the supernatural. During this time a third body of fiction began to emerge—his political satires.

One week after he published the brief but amusing "For the Ahkoond" in the *Examiner* for 18 March 1888, the major satire "The Fall of the Republic: An Article from a 'Court Journal' of the Thirty-first Century" appeared, occupying four columns of that Sunday's "feature" section of the *Examiner*. Its appearance at that time was probably no accident. In January, Edward Bellamy's *Looking Backward: 2000–1887* was published, quickly reaching bestseller status and becoming one of the most widely discussed books of the later nineteenth century. This utopian novel, which proposed a radical redistribution of wealth to achieve social and economic equality, embodied political principles very different from those held by Bierce; and "The Fall of the Republic" may be among the earliest of the many responses to and imitations of Bellamy's novel that appeared over the next several decades.

Only a few weeks later, Bierce published a lengthy sketch, "The Kingdom of Tortirra." It was the first of eleven pieces published between 1888 and 1907 that Bierce weaved together into the Swiftian satire "The Land Beyond the Blow," which at 21,000 words constitutes his longest work of fiction. The first four pieces appeared in 1888-89. After a hiatus of a full decade, three more appeared in 1898-99, and the remaining four were published sporadically in 1903-07. The result is somewhat of a hodgepodge, featuring a mixture of political satire, philosophical ruminations, and send-ups of current events such as the Spanish-American War. Nevertheless, as Bierce's most imaginative flight of fancy it deserves wider recognition.

The Future Historian began appearing with frequency as a narrator of Bierce's satires (along with such other characters as the Timorous

Reporter, the Curmudgeon Philosopher, the Sentimental Bachelor, and the Bald Campaigner) in short pieces written shortly after Bierce moved to Washington, D.C., for health reasons in late 1899. At this time his work was being syndicated nearly simultaneously in Hearst's *New York Journal* (later *American*) and the *Examiner;* in some cases, his contributions appeared in only one paper or the other. Several of the Future Historian sketches were merely nested within such recurring columns of editorial commentary as "Prattle," "The Passing Show," or "The Views of One"; others were published as self-standing articles. Bierce gathered only three of these pieces—those that had appeared in Hearst's magazine *Cosmopolitan* in 1908-09—under the heading "The Future Historian" in the twelfth volume (1912) of his *Collected Works.*

As early as 1895, Bierce had assembled a collection of his political satires under the title *The Fall of the Republic and Other Satires.* For more than a decade he tirelessly shopped the book around to various publishers, but to no avail. The first we hear of the enterprise is in early January 1896,[1] when Bierce prods the Chicago publisher Stone & Kimball to make a decision on the book; the tone of his remarks suggests that the publisher had retained the manuscript for some time. In the absence of any specifications by Bierce, it is difficult to ascertain what items could have been included in this volume. "The Fall of the Republic" itself, in its original version, is only 6250 words, while the first four segments of what later became "The Land Beyond the Blow" would only have added another 13,500 words. If "John Smith," "For the Ahkoond," and another brief futuristic story, "The Strike of 1899" (1895), were included, the total wordage of the book would come to about 25,000 words. Such a small volume would not have been unheard of at the time: Stone & Kimball had in fact just published a very slim collection of the renowned architect Ralph Adam's Cram's ghost stories, *Black Spirits and White* (1895), comprising only 27,000 words.

In any event, Stone & Kimball rejected the book, for at the end of

---

1. AB to Stone & Kimball, 12 January 1896 (ms., Univ. of Pennsylvania).

1897 Bierce had submitted his "satires—of the Lucian-Swift sort"[2] to another Chicago firm, Way & Williams. He states that the publisher actually accepted the book along with *Fantastic Fables*, although he received no contract; but by May 1898 the two books were "coolly returned."[3] The book of fables appeared in 1899 from Putnam's, but the book of satires remained without a publisher.

We hear of no more attempts by Bierce to market his collection until early 1905. At this time we learn that the revised version of "The Fall of the Republic," "Ashes of the Beacon," having appeared in both the *Examiner* and the *New York American* in February, had been submitted the previous August or September to Robert Mackay, the editor of *Success* magazine and a sporadic correspondent of Bierce. Mackay had found the story "unsuitable" for his magazine,[4] but Bierce responded to the story's rejection with the following proposition:

> Now, I have a whole book of satires in the manner of "The Ashes of the Beacon". I've always thought *that* could be made to go, but have long despaired of making anybody else think so. If you'd care to look at it you may. I could finish compiling it in a few days. Some of "The Ashes" would fit into the leading satire (entitled "The Downfall of the Republic") for it is written along the same line of thought.

This suggests a number of interesting things. Firstly, it appears that "The Fall of the Republic" still existed as a viable work, and had not been replaced by "Ashes of the Beacon." Secondly, the contemplated collection was now in a state of flux, since Bierce suggests reworking it somehow by incorporating portions of "Ashes of the Beacon" into "The Fall of the Republic." Possibly he had further augmented the volume with the several additional episodes of "The Land Beyond the Blow" that had been written by this time.

Mackay did attempt to market the book for Bierce, but by Septem-

---

2. AB to Myles Walsh, 23 December 1897 (ms., Univ. of Cincinnati).
3. AB to Myles Walsh, 19 May 1989 (ms., Univ. of Cincinnati).
4. AB to Robert Mackay, 1 March 1905 (ms., Yale University).

ber 1905 Bierce was asking for the return of the manuscript, since Mackay was manifestly unsuccessful. Bierce vowed "to make a try at all the firms in the country with it,"[5] but the degree to which he followed through on this ambitious plan is not clear. By June 1906 another literary colleague, John O'Hara Cosgrave (editor of *Everybody's Magazine*)—who had been instrumental in persuading Doubleday, Page & Co. to issue Bierce's *Devil's Dictionary*, published later that year[6]— tried his hand at peddling *The Fall of the Republic*. But Cosgrave had as little success as Mackay and Bierce himself, and by November Bierce is again asking for the return of the manuscript.[7]

Bierce then thought of employing an agent to market the book, something he had rarely done on previous occasions. The agent in question was one Daniel Murphy. By August 1907 Murphy had collected four rejections of the book; Bierce acknowledges Murphy's industry by the wry comment: "That is lively work on his part."[8] Shortly thereafter Bierce's disciple Herman Scheffauer offered to market the book in London, as he was going on a tour of England and the Continent. Bierce stated, "I'd rather that it would come out there than here, but don't think it will find favor in either country."[9] But Scheffauer had no luck, and by April 1908 the manuscript was back from England.[10]

By this time, Bierce's young friend friend Walter Neale had proposed the publication of Bierce's *Collected Works* in ten volumes (later expanded to twelve) with his fledgling firm, the Neale Publishing Company. By early June Bierce announced that he had finished com-

---

5. AB to Robert Mackay, 28 September 1905 (ms., New York Public Library).

6. AB to Robert H. Davis, 20 June 1906 (ms., NP). The book was published as *The Cynic's Word Book*.

7. AB to John O'Hara Cosgrave, 8 November 1906 (ms., Univ. of Virginia).

8. AB to Herman Scheffauer, 17 August 1907 (ms., Bancroft Library, Univ. of California).

9. AB to Herman Scheffauer, 30 September 1907 (ms., Bancroft Library).

10. AB to Walter Neale, 17 April 1908 (ms., Huntington Library).

piling the first volume, which included "Ashes of the Beacon," "The Land Beyond the Blow," "For the Ahkoond," and "John Smith" (now titled "John Smith, Liberator"), but not "The Fall of the Republic."[11] The rapidity with which Bierce assembled the volume suggests that much of the material had been assembled beforehand.[12] Indeed, it seems likely that the book marketed from 1905 onward by Mackay, Cosgrave, Murphy, and Scheffauer consisted of these four stories or some approximation of them, as they fill about 40,000 words. Two segments of "The Land Beyond the Blow"–"The Conflagration in Ghargaroo" (*Cosmopolitan*, February 1906) and "An Execution in Batrugia" (*Cosmopolitan*, May 1907)–had not yet been published, but all the others had, and it is likely that Bierce had assembled much of "The Land Beyond the Blow" well before 1905. "Ashes of the Beacon" was expanded by absorbing two articles published in *Cosmopolitan*, "The Jury in Ancient America" (August 1905) and "Insurance in Ancient America" (September 1906), so that it now stood at 14,000 words, thereby becoming Bierce's second-longest work of fiction.

The fact that Bierce included four political satires in the first volume of his *Collected Works* is of significance: it attested not only to his high regard for those works but also, perhaps, to a desire to lure readers with the prospect of material that had not been previously gathered in book form. (Half of the volume consists of the satires, the other half contains his stirring memoirs of the Civil War, "Bits of Autobiography." None of these items had previously appeared in Bierce's published books.) About a year after the publication of the volume, Bierce unqualifiedly deemed "Ashes of the Beacon" (although still referring to it under its old title, "The Fall of the Republic") his "most notable work."[13] The

---

11. AB to Walter Neale, 3 June 1908 (ms., Huntington Library).

12. The typesetting copy of this volume does exist at the Huntington Library, but it is difficult to conjecture from it what the putative *Fall of the Republic* might have been. All that is evident is that at one time the order of "Ashes of the Beacon" and "The Land Beyond the Blow" was reversed.

13. AB to Walter Neale, 2 December 1910 (ms., Huntington Library).

book of satires that he had marketed for so long had finally achieved print; and because he had complete editorial control over the contents, it presumably appeared much as he wished it.

The question of the literary influences that may have affected Bierce's political satires is not easily answered, since Bierce himself is virtually silent on the matter in both his letters and his published writings. One of the few hints we have on the matter is the fact that Bierce read Swift and Voltaire in 1868 at the instigation of James T. Watkins, departing editor of the *News Letter.* It is therefore not surprising that Bierce's earliest excursions into political satire date from this period (McWilliams 84). It is worth noting that the parenthetical remark included below the title of "The Land Beyond the Blow"—"(After the method of Swift, who followed Lucian, and was himself followed by Voltaire and many others.)"—was added to the text only after the rest of the manuscript had been submitted to Neale for typesetting. Bierce explained: "My reason is that if I do not myself point out that the method (not the style) is as old as literature the contemporary critics will surely 'jump on' the stuff as 'plagiarism' from Swift. Of Lucian and Voltaire they know not."[14]

Bierce refers to the fact that Swift's *Gulliver's Travels*—of which "The Land Beyond the Blow" is quite obviously an imitation—itself had a dim predecessor in Lucian's *True Story* (*Alethōn diegēmatōn*; sometimes translated as *True History*). In fact, there is little similarity between the two works, as Lucian's whimsical skit—a deliberately absurd account of a man who boards a vessel that travels to various fantastic realms, including the moon, the interior of a giant whale, and the Isles of the Blest—is a conscious parody of the "poets, historians and philosophers of old, who have written much that smacks of miracles and fables" (*Lucian* 1.251). There is no political or social satire directed at the lands or people encountered by the narrator, as there is in Swift, Voltaire, and Bierce.

---

14. AB to Walter Neale, 20 November 1908 (ms., Huntington Library).

It may be of some interest to ascertain what edition of Lucian Bierce may have read. Not fluent in Greek, he was reliant on English translations, and there were few translations of Lucian in his day. Unless he read a four-volume collected edition published in 1864, it is likely that Bierce had at some point read *Trips to the Moon*, translated by Thomas Francklin (New York: Cassell, 1886). This volume contains only *A True Story*, *How to Write History* (*Pōs dei historian syngraphein*), and *Icaromenippus*. Bierce shows his familiarity with the second work when he advises a correspondent to read Lucian "on the writing of history,"[15] but does not exhibit knowledge of any other works by Lucian aside from the *True Story*.

The reference to Voltaire is similarly a bit of a stretch. It is true that Voltaire's *Micromégas* (1752) was itself inspired by *Gulliver*, but this account of the voyage to Earth by a native of the star Sirius, accompanied by a native of the planet Saturn, is chiefly a philosophical, not a political, satire. Perhaps to that degree it may have inspired the one segment of "The Land Beyond the Blow" ("An Interview with Gnarmag-Zote") that is purely philosophical, but the connexions between the two works are not strong. Bierce may also have been thinking of such a work as Voltaire's *L'Ingénu* (1767), in which a Frenchman raised by the Huron tribe of Canada comes to France and makes observations on French society and religion; but this work is more in the tradition of Montesquieu's *Persian Letters* (1721)—the tradition of a foreigner, unaware of the patterns of European society, making *faux-naïf* comments that hint at a society's absurdities and artificialities unperceived by its own members. Both Swift and Bierce reverse the surface form of these works—a member of our own society travels to other realms and takes note of their customs, differing or similar as the case may be—although in the end the thrust of the satire is analogous.

"The Land Beyond the Blow" is no "plagiarism from Swift," but it

---

15. AB to Blanche Partington, 17 August 1892 (ms., Bancroft Library).

does indeed owe a significant debt to *Gulliver*. Bierce borrowed or adapted many small particulars of Swift's satire for his own. One of the most striking of these is the use by both authors of a highly eccentric array of terms designating the languages of the various mythical regions entered by both narrators. (Bierce had initiated this practice as early as the "Letters from a Hdkhoite.") Like Swift (see *Gulliver's Travels* 129), Bierce devises novel terms to denote measurements of height, distance, and the like. Bierce's use, in "The Tamtonians," of reversed words (e.g., *cilbuper* for "republic") may be a subtle imitation of the passage in *Gulliver* in which Swift invents the regions Tribnia and Langden (*Gulliver's Travels* 227)—anagrams for Britain and England. The effect of these linguistic inventions in both Swift and Bierce is to render an impression of distance between the known world and his imaginary realms in the eyes of an unbiased observer, while still knowingly implying that many similarities nevertheless exist between the two.

One of the most amusing facets of Bierce's narrative is the bland depiction of the bizarre social customs pertaining to his mythical realms ("the King . . . look[ed] over my head to signify that the interview was at an end; and I retired from the Presence on hands and feet, as is the etiquette in that country"). Swift does not make as much of this in *Gulliver*, but in one instance he does so:

> A messenger was dispatched half a day's journey before us, to give the King notice of my approach, and to desire that his Majesty would please to appoint a day and hour, when it would be his gracious pleasure that I might have the honour to *lick the dust before his footstool*. That is the court style, and I found it to be more than matter of form. . . . Nay, sometimes the floor is strewed with dust on purpose, when the person to be admitted happens to have powerful enemies at court. . . . There is indeed another custom, which I cannot altogether approve of. When the King hath a mind to put any of his nobles to death in a gentle indulgent manner, he commands to have the floor strowed with a certain brown powder, of a deadly composition, which being licked up infallibly kills him in twenty-four hours. (*Gulliver's Travels* 243)

Aside from glancing parallels of this sort, it is only in *Gulliver* that we find exhaustive discussions of the political, social, economic, legal, and cultural tendencies of the various regions visited by Gulliver, and these discussions—in both broad and minor particulars—are duplicated in "The Land Beyond the Blow."

Of course, differences between *Gulliver* and "The Land Beyond the Blow" abound. Swift is unusually precise in supplying the dates of Gulliver's various expeditions, and scarcely less precise in specifying the locations of his imaginary realms, complete with maps. Bierce provided dates in the original newspaper appearances of some stories but later removed them; and he never gave the remotest hint as to the locations of his invented regions. In the century and a half that had passed between Swift's and Bierce's heydays, the "unknown" parts of the world had largely been charted, so that Bierce could not plausibly follow Swift in topographical specificity—setting the floating island of Laputa off the coast of Japan, for example. Also, Bierce makes no attempt to suggest the genuineness of his narrator's voyage by the accumulation of realistic detail. Swift, however, is manifestly interested in effecting a kind of hoax with *Gulliver*, since his novel imitates the travellers' narratives of the period and was published as if Gulliver himself, not Swift, were the author.

In a more general sense, however, Bierce's narrator clearly echoes Lemuel Gulliver's own hope that his account will lead to extensive moral, political, and aesthetic reformation:

> I desired you would let me know by a letter, when party and faction were extinguished; judges learned and upright; pleaders honest and modest, with some tincture of common sense; and Smithfield blazing with pyramids of law-books; the young nobility's education entirely changed; the physicians banished; the female Yahoos abounding in virtue, honour, truth and good sense; courts and levees of great ministers thoroughly weeded and swept; wit, merit and learning rewarded; all disgracers of the press in prose and verse condemned to eat nothing but their own cotton, and quench their thirst with their own ink. (*Gulliver's Travels* 4–5)

Bierce makes no such explicit statement of purpose in "The Land Beyond the Blow," but he hardly need have done so: the above passage encapsulates in a remarkably complete way the overall moral thrust of Bierce's tale and, perhaps, of his entire career as a satirist. As Lawrence I. Berkove has emphasised, Bierce's satire is almost always driven by moral concerns. Although he himself habitually disclaimed any inclination toward the moral reformation of his contemporaries, his work can be read not as a misanthrope's indiscriminate abuse but as a pungent revelation of moral and intellectual failings; by implication, Bierce was recommending the exact opposite of the modes of behaviour he was lampooning.

I have already remarked on the possibility that Bellamy's *Looking Backward: 2000–1887* may have been the immediate impetus for the writing of "The Fall of the Republic," published only two months after the appearance of Bellamy's work. In no sense can Bellamy be said to have been any real influence, literary or political, since Bierce had written several previous "future histories" long before he ever read Bellamy. It is true that an "Author's Preface" at the beginning of *Looking Backward* is purportedly written by an anonymous professor at the "Historical Section, Shawmut College, Boston, 26 December 2000," but otherwise Bellamy's novel is not a "future history" in the sense that Bierce's tales are, since most of the work consists merely of political discussions between Julian West—a man who had lapsed into an hypnotic trance in the year 1887—and the characters he finds upon waking in the year 2000. The political views of the two writers differ so radically that one might be inclined to think that Bierce published his work when he did as a direct response to Bellamy. The first known mention of Bellamy in Bierce's journalism appears in a passing, and rather derisive, mention in a "Prattle" column (*San Francisco Examiner*, 27 May 1888). Two years later he directed a particularly tart fable, "The Bellamy and the Members," at the author of *Looking Backward*:

> The Members of a body of Socialists rose in insurrection against their Bellamy.

"Why," said they, "should we be all the time tucking you out with food when you do nothing to tuck us out?"

So, resolving to take no further action, they went away and looking backward had the satisfaction to see the Bellamy compelled to sell his own book. (*Collected Fables* 159-60; first published in the *Oakland Tribune* [26 July 1890].)

Similarly, William Dean Howells's *A Traveler from Altruria* (1894) cannot be thought of as an influence upon Bierce, although some similarities exist between the two works, at least in regard to the social and political issues they treat. In contrast to Bierce's "The Land Beyond the Blow," Howells's Altrurian (whose countrymen seek to follow literally the original teachings of Christ by devoting themselves to altruism) spends much of the novel criticising American social and political institutions, devoting particular attention to such issues as the conflict between labour and capital, class hatred, and suppression of women's political rights. Only toward the end does the Altrurian speak at length of the moral and political circumstances of his own land. Bierce lost little time in heaping abuse, not so much upon Howells's work itself (although no doubt he thought its precepts utterly unrealistic in light of the actual facts of human nature), as upon the array of "Altrurian colonies" that sprung up as a result. The following is only one instance among several: "Of the amiable asses who have founded the 'Altrurian' colony at Mark West it ought to be sufficient to explain that their scheme is based upon the intellectual diversions of such humorists as Plato, More, Fourier, Bellamy and Howells. That assures the ludicrous fizzle of the enterprise."[16] And yet, the fact that Howells's sequel to his novel, *Through the Eye of the Needle*, appeared in 1907, at the very time when Bierce was making renewed attempts to market his own book of satires, may be of significance. In a letter Howells remarked: "There is

---

16. "Prattle," *San Francisco Examiner* (21 October 1894): 6. Lawrence I. Berkove addresses this issue in detail in "Two Impossible Dreams: Ambrose Bierce on Utopia and America," *Huntington Library Quarterly* 44 (1981): 283-92. Berkove's perspicacious article is one of the few devoted to Bierce's political satires.

now a revival of interest in such speculations, and the publishers think the book, with an interesting sequel, giving an account of life in Altruria, will succeed" (cited in *Altrurian Romances* xxx). Possibly the appearance of Howells's sequel—and the belief that such accounts might prove popular with readers—had some slight influence in Bierce's decision to include his future histories in the first volume of his *Collected Works*, published two years later.

A purely literary evaluation of these satires, without regard to their political content, may be difficult, but the attempt is worth making: surely these works can be gauged in regard to their literary values whether or not they echo our own political and social predilections. Bierce was not primarily a political philosopher, but a satirist and wit; and he would have wished us to appreciate his tales on a literary level even if we disagreed with the political message he was conveying.

Each group of works—the future histories and the fantastic voyages—presents certain features not found in the other. The former tales gain some of their greatest piquancy from their suggestion that the facts of history may have been transmitted in a dim, fragmented way, resulting in comical errors, and that our own understanding of history may be similarly distorted. One wonders whether Bierce hints that there has been an actual collapse of our existing civilisation and a period of primitivism or barbarism before the emergence of a new age: such is indeed the implication in "For the Ahkoond" (1888), where we learn that the entirety of the North American continent east of the Rockies has not merely been depopulated, but reinhabited by the beasts of prehistory, such as pterodactyls and mastodons. Similarly, in "John Smith, Liberator" the future era has suffered a collapse of technological knowledge (the telegraph, the steam locomotive, and printing are lost arts) and knowledge of pure science (the Copernican theory is regarded as false). Bierce's repeated suggestion that the people of the future will not understand our mode of reckoning time—specifically the use of the terms "A.D." or "Christian era"—suggests that the Christian religion, like the myths of classical antiquity, will have no practical significance in the future.

A variant of this device tempers the criticism of the "ancient Americans" as found in "Ashes of the Beacon." The Future Historian's condemnation of such hallowed American principles as republican government and the rule of the majority might appear intolerably smug and high-handed if the historian himself did not reveal, not merely his severely erroneous grasp of the facts of "ancient" history, but his bland disbelief that his own "gracious Sovereign" could "by any possibility [be] wrong." Remarks of this kind do not necessarily subvert the historian's criticism of our own time, but qualify it by a covert suggestion that his own period is, in spite of his protestations, flawed in many particulars.

"Ashes of the Beacon" is far and away the finest of Bierce's future histories, and "For the Ahkoond" perhaps the most amusing. His later contributions of this kind seem to reveal somewhat of a falling off, largely because he was content to produce very short squibs—possibly written for a newspaper deadline—that did not allow his satirical skills their full play. Many of these were inspired by relatively transient events, ranging from serious but short-lived political crises (the Boxer Rebellion, disputes over the Panama Canal) to mere sporting events (Sir Thomas Lipton's attempt to win a yacht race). "The Maid of Podunk" (1901), a tart send-up of temperance advocate Carry Nation, is a meritorious exception; and several late sketches skewering Theodore Roosevelt's boasted prowess as a soldier and hunter are among the most delightful of the future histories.

Of the fantastic voyages, "The Land Beyond the Blow" is clearly the chief specimen. The nearly twenty-year gestation period and the seeming randomness of its assemblage compromise its unity, and in several particulars it is open to the charge of repetition: the criticism of Americans' fondness for accumulating wealth is elaborated upon in both "Sons of the Fair Star" and "A Conflagration in Ghargaroo," while "The Tamtonians" and "The Kingdom of Tortirra" partially duplicate each other in their suggestions of flaws in the American political system. "An Interview with Gnarmag-Zote," a purely philosophical discourse, seems out of place, and "The Dog in Ganegwag" is simply a flippant exhibition (one of many throughout Bierce's work) of his detestation of dogs. Despite its weaknesses, "The Land Beyond the Blow" remains compellingly readable on many counts: its imaginative scope in envisioning the anomalous customs and physical particulars of the imaginary realms; the exceptionally sharp satire directed at American politics (culminating, perhaps, in "The Tamtonians," where the presidential and vice-presidential nominees consist of an idiot and a corpse); and, overall, a crispness of prose that propels the narrative dynamically and pungently.

An analysis of the full range of Bierce's political and social views is beyond the scope of this introduction, but those aspects bearing on his political satires must necessarily be discussed. In so doing, care must be taken on several fronts. Firstly, we must guard against the tacit assumption that Bierce should be criticised for not reflecting our own opinions on the subjects in question; secondly, we should try to duplicate his own practice of ruthlessly cutting through the political rhetoric both of his day and of ours, so as to discern the fundamental issues at the core of the debate; and thirdly, we must be aware that the opinions expressed in his satires are exaggerated, distorted, or in other ways twisted for comic purposes, so that such remarks must be interpreted in the light of Bierce's actual views (so far as they can now be ascertained).

Bierce's boldness in criticising the fundamentals of the American political and social system is, for the most part, praiseworthy. Few American writers have had the courage to question such hallowed dogmas as the very principle of republican government and the efficacy of democracy, universal suffrage, and the legal system. On the whole, Bierce maintained a firm independence of thought, refusing to adhere to a party line and always seeking to probe to what he felt was the heart of a given issue. But to what degree can we accept his criticism of democracy? To what extent is a democracy merely a tyranny of the majority? If (as stated in "Ashes of the Beacon") selfishness is the "dominant characteristic and fundamental motive of human nature and human action respectively," and if the majority is "ignorant, restless and reckless," then people as a mass cannot possibly "govern themselves." Bierce's most compact expression of his skepticism of democracy occurs in a single sentence of "Ashes of the Beacon": "An inherent weakness in republican government was that it assumed the honesty and intelligence of the majority, 'the masses,' who were neither honest nor intelligent." In such a scenario, politicians can only be demagogues, and people will be swayed not by the soundest views but by the sweetest tongue. A generation later the writer H. P. Lovecraft came to very much the same conclusion:

> Democracy—as distinguished from universal opportunity and good treatment—is today a fallacy and impossibility so great that any serious attempt to apply it cannot be considered other than a mockery and a jest. ... Government "by popular vote" means merely the nomination of doubtfully qualified men by doubtfully authorised and seldom competent cliques of professional politicians representing hidden interests, followed by a sardonic farce of emotional persuasion in which the orators with the glibbest tongues and flashiest catch-words herd on their side a numerical majority of blindly impressionable dolts and gulls who have for the most part no idea of what the whole circus is about. (Letter to Robert E. Howard, 7 November 1932; *Selected Letters* 4.106-7)

An honest analysis of the last several presidential campaigns may convince us of the sad truth of this assertion.

What alternative did Bierce suggest? Did he have an alternative in mind? In his role as satirist Bierce repeatedly mocked the notion that he was merely "tearing down" without putting something in its place—that he was criticising existing institutions without offering a viable replacement. Bierce was vehement in denouncing this attitude, as in the following (in the context of a critique of religion): "I fatigue and fall ill of this hoary, decrepit, and doddering protest of brainless imbecility;

it is the first, last, intermediate and only argument of mental vacuity. . . . Truth is better than anything or all things; the next best thing to truth is absence of error. When you are in the dark, stand still; when you do not know what to do, do nothing."[17] On the issue in question, it does not seem likely that Bierce is seriously suggesting a return to monarchy: although in *The Devil's Dictionary* he defines "Monarchical Government" with the single word, "Government" (suggesting that monarchy is the only system that is, for good or ill, a government in a meaningful sense), and although a good many of his future histories clearly state that the world will indeed become monarchical again, it seems highly unlikely that Bierce ever conceived the United States as readopting this form of government. Nevertheless, it is evident that he wished for some kind of higher political authority: if "self-government" is a paradox in that the people are incapable of governing themselves, then the only alternative would appear to be an aristocracy or an actual dictatorship. Bierce was not shy about embracing the latter; in remarking, as early as 1879, on some "rigorous measures" taken by the Czar of Russia and Chancellor Bismarck in suppressing Nihilists and Socialists, he noted:

> In the Czar of Russia and the Chancellor of the German Empire lie the hopes of civilization, for they are in all Christendom the only strong men—the one by virtue of great governmental powers which his predecessors had not the folly to fritter away, the other through similar, those lesser, powers and colossal brains. I firmly believe that if the despotic energies wielded by these two men fail of the purpose to which they are set the days of our civilization are numbered, and in the near future the continents of Europe and America will be devastated by barbarians from the Asian steppes, or infested with cut-throat savages sprung from our loins and wearing the skins of animals about their own. ("Prattle," *Argonaut* [24 May 1879]; rpt. in *Sole Survivor* 150–51)

In the same column Bierce went on to say: "If government has any meaning or function it means the restraint of the many by the few—the subordination of numbers to brains. It means the determined denial to

---

17. "Prattle," *Argonaut* (21 December 1878): 17.

the masses of the right to cut their own throats." What this suggests is an aristocracy of "brains" in a paternalistic government that would, by the restriction of civil liberties (Bierce explicitly mentions "a vigilant censorship of the press, a firm hand upon the church," and other measures), protect the people from harming themselves. No doubt Bierce had a low view of both the intelligence and the morality of the masses; but he seems to have fallen into the fallacy that high intelligence must necessarily engender high moral standards. Indeed, he frequently repeated the view (extending back to Plato) that sin and crime are merely aspects of folly: "The criminal is merely a fool considered under another aspect—an idiot with an opportunity."[18]

It is manifest that many of Bierce's concerns on this issue were engendered by his scorn of anarchy and anarchists. The outrageous statement in "Ashes of the Beacon" that socialism and even reform are merely watered-down versions of anarchy is echoed in many of his newspaper columns. No doubt Bierce would have violently disagreed with the principles of philosophical anarchism—which stressed the elimination of all state authority and the organisation of society purely on the basis of voluntary cooperation—but it is not likely that he even knew these principles, as expounded by such leading philosophical anarchists as Pierre Joseph Proudhon or, in the United States, Benjamin R. Tucker. Instead, Bierce looked only to the violence and death produced by anarchists following the theories of Mikhail Bakunin, who indeed advocated force in the overthrow of existing governments. The widespread public fear of anarchist violence in the last two decades of the nineteenth century is perhaps mirrored today by our fears of terrorists. Bierce's concerns may have reached their apex when President William McKinley was assassinated in 1901 by a professed anarchist, but his worries had emerged long before that. The Haymarket riots of 1886 (the subject of his editorial "Prevention vs. No

---

18. "The Passing Show," *New York Journal* (5 August 1900): 26; *San Francisco Examiner* (5 August 1900): 24.

Cure") were blamed upon anarchists, and (as we shall see presently) also fed Bierce's concerns about the dangers of labour unions.

Bierce's bland recommendation, in "Ashes of the Beacon," that suspected anarchists should simply be locked up and prevented from speaking or publishing is echoed by similar comments in his columns; but it does not appear that Bierce quite realises the implications of his remarks. Who, exactly, are the "bad men" and "malcontents" who should be thus restrained? It may not be so easy to decide; and in some cases, or under certain regimes, comments such as those made by Bierce himself might be interdicted. He repeatedly stated that Americans have an excessive reverence for "freedom of speech" as a sacred principle; but the United States has always had laws against explicit advocacy of violence or of the overthrow of the government. Perhaps Bierce was thinking of England, whose constitution, lacking an analogue to our First Amendment, makes it far easier for the government to suppress what it perceives to be "seditious" speech.

Bierce's observations on legal and judicial matters are similarly thought-provoking. Once again he seems to put his finger on a number of troublesome issues, but what recommendations for improvement he has to offer are unclear or even paradoxical. With Bierce's low view of the intelligence of the "masses," it is hardly surprising that he would scorn the mere possibility that a jury trial could produce a fair verdict; as he states in a "Prattle" column: "Every human institution is a failure, but the jury system as a means of justice is the most lamentable failure of all. There is no way to get together twelve men of sufficient intelligence, honesty and skill in analysis of evidence to determine the simplest question of fact when the lawyers have done with it."[19] Analogously, Bierce was incensed over the fact that lawyers are in some instances compelled to defend clients they know to be guilty, and to act in court as if they were innocent. The problem is a real one, and Bierce may well be right in declaring that the practice causes a serious corrup-

---

19. "Prattle," *San Francisco Examiner* (19 September 1897): 18.

tion of some lawyers' moral standards. But again, what is the alternative? Does Bierce think guilty defendants should not receive legal defence?

Bierce similarly speaks frequently about the overturning of certain verdicts in criminal or civil cases, or even of statutes passed by the government, on appeal. He is right to point out the iniquity of confining a defendant in jail while his or her appeal is being decided: if the defendant is ultimately found innocent, then he or she will have served prison time unjustly. But the issue of the overturning of statutes is perhaps not so clear. Following Bierce's argument to its ultimate logical conclusion, we would be compelled to assume that all laws passed at any time in our history are and will be eternally valid. This posits a highly inelastic conception of history and would prevent different historical eras from determining their own legal and judicial fate. It would suggest, for instance, that such a decision as the Supreme Court's sanctioning of the "separate but equal" principle in race relations (*Plessy v. Ferguson,* 1896) could not, and should not, have been overturned by *Brown v. Board of Education* in 1954. Bierce's complaint seems to have been directed at what he perceived to be judges' overturning of statutes on whim or caprice, but his solution would appear to be worse than the problem.

One aspect of jurisprudence on which Bierce remained unwavering throughout his life was the issue of capital punishment. To be sure, as a vigorous proponent of it he could entertain himself cheaply by poking fun at the poor arguments advocated against it by theosophists,[20] but his fundamental argument that capital punishment is indeed a deterrent—an argument broached frequently by its proponents today—is not supported by any clear-cut evidence, then or now. Other of Bierce's arguments are scarcely worth addressing: his contention that the death penalty is a form of societal "self-defence" is pure sophistry; his opposition to the plea of innocence by reason of insanity, on the

---

20. See "Blithering Blavatskians," *San Francisco Examiner* (28 November 1897): 18.

ground that the lunatic is better off dead anyway, is vicious and contemptible; and his assertion that it doesn't matter if an innocent man ("particularly the kind of innocent man that is likely to be accused and convicted of murder") is killed now and then might have been moderated if he himself had been one of those innocent men.

Where Bierce does put his finger directly on an issue of great sensitivity even today is the question of executing female criminals. He is certainly correct in affirming that if a society is to have capital punishment at all, punishment should be exacted upon males and females alike. Bierce was resolutely facing an issue that many members of his society were squeamish to address; the residual chivalry, patronisation, and chauvinism that held women to a higher moral standard, or perhaps tacitly regarded them as weak and therefore the objects of pity, continue to deprecate the execution of women—solely or largely because they are women—found guilty of crime, as the cases of Ethel Rosenberg in 1953 and Karla Faye Tucker in 1998 attest. Bierce's comments on this issue may have been inspired by two notorious instances. One of them, the so-called Nan Patterson case, involved a young actress in New York who was accused of killing a bookmaker, a married man named "Caesar" Young, while they were riding in a hansom cab on 4 May 1904. After two separate trials ended in hung juries, Patterson was freed in May 1905. Evidently Bierce regarded her as manifestly guilty, and her release outraged him.[21] At about this very time a second case was reaching its culmination, as Mary Mabel Rogers, clearly guilty of conspiring to kill her husband in 1902, was executed in December 1905 in Vermont, over the protests of many individuals across the country. It is the subject of Bierce's essay "Some Thoughts on the Hanging."

On the general question of women's rights—an issue that fuses

---

21. See the Little Johnny sketch "The Nan Patterson Case," *New York American* (21 May 1905): 22; *San Francisco Examiner* (28 May 1905): 48; and "Views of One," *New York American* (14 June 1905): 14; *San Francisco Examiner* (21 June 1905): 16.

political, economic, and social concerns—Bierce mercifully does not spend a great deal of space in his satires. Throughout his career he relentlessly opposed woman suffrage, expansion of economic opportunities for women, and virtually every other facet of women's liberation (see the extracts cited in *Sole Survivor* 96-97, 227-39). It appears that Bierce had an excessively narrow view of the "proper" sphere of woman's activity, and he regarded it as self-evident that women were physically, intellectually, and morally inferior to men. Although he counted numerous women among his acquaintances and correspondents, they were invariably the sort who accepted their limited social and political roles; the moment any of them sought to expand her horizons (such as the novelist Gertrude Atherton, who developed feminist tendencies from the 1890s onward) Bierce at once ceased association with her. It is typical that, in "Ashes of the Beacon," his historian points out that the incursion of women into the work force brought them no significant "material advantage": the historian (whose opinions here manifestly reflect Bierce's own, as found frequently in his journalism) cannot envision any other kind of advantage, such as the increase in self-esteem and self-sufficiency accruing from securing gainful employment and being free of economic subservience to men. And Bierce's simplistic argument that the entry of women into the work force would displace men and produce widespread unemployment has proven fallacious: the world economy has shown itself to be sufficiently flexible to accommodate this increase in the work force by the creation of new industries and services.

In other aspects of economics, Bierce similarly sought order and efficiency, even at the expense of individual rights and liberties. On an issue that exercised the attention of a great many politicians, economists, and businessmen of the period—"protection" vs. free trade—Bierce declared himself emphatically in the latter camp. In contrast to today's political alignments, protective tariffs were vigorously urged by the Republicans of Bierce's day (perhaps in an effort to curry favour with the wealthy businessmen throughout the country who would stand to gain by tariffs on foreign goods), whereas the Democrats were advocates of free trade. In a rare instance of an explicit avowal of his political faith, Bierce affirmed that he himself had been a Mugwump (a Republican who had deserted his party in 1884 by refusing to vote for the party's presidential nominee, James G. Blaine) and had become a Democrat over the issue of free trade ("Prattle," *San Francisco Examiner* [8 July 1888]; in *Sole Survivor* 219). Bierce's remarks on the matter—exemplified in such editorials as "'Protection' vs. Fair Trade" (1887) and "Commercial Retaliation" (1898)—are cogent and perspicacious.

Where Bierce radically parted from his Democratic colleagues was over the complex issue of the dispute between labour and capital, summed up in the catchphrase of the period, "industrial discontent." Bierce was by no means alone in regarding the emergence of labour unions from the 1860s onward with alarm: hostility was directed toward them as potentially violent and anarchistic from many quarters in the business and political world. It should be remembered that such unions actually were outlawed in many European countries for centuries: England legalised trade unions only in 1871; France had done so in the 1860s, but the unions' radicalism caused a rapid shift of public opinion against them. Bierce had, as early as his *News Letter* period (1868-72), expressed opposition to such things as the campaign for an eight-hour working day, and his justifiable contempt for the Workingmen's party in California—led by the racist rabble-rouser Dennis Kearney—was of long standing. As mentioned, the Haymarket riots not only brought bad publicity to anarchists, but to labour unions as well: the Knights of Labor were held responsible for inciting the riots, although that group in fact had no involvement in them. From this point on, Bierce's opposition to unions was unremitting. It seems incredible that he could genuinely believe that the violence resulting from union strikes were solely the responsibility of the unions, but such indeed seems to have been his position. His harsh words in regard to the Homestead strike of 1892—in which hundreds of Pinkerton detectives hired by management attacked striking workers' pickets, killing ten of them—

sums up his views: "At Homestead and Wardner the laborers committed robbery, pillage and murder, as striking workmen invariably do when they dare, and as coward newspapers and scoundrel politicians encourage them in doing. But what would you have? They conceive it to be to their interest to do these things." And he goes on to dismiss the arguments that the capitalists were doing violence of their own with the flippant remark: "This is the baldest nonsense."[22] Perhaps Bierce was merely seeking to counteract what he felt was the biased reporting of papers like his own union-supporting *Examiner*; but he rarely expressed the view that a strike is justified or that labour has any valid complaints against capitalist owners.

What Bierce refused to recognise is that unionisation was the direct product of the "trusts" and monopolies that were dominating an increasing number of businesses. In "Ashes of the Beacon" the historian actually asserts that "combinations of labor entailed combinations of capital," when in fact the matter was exactly reversed. Bierce's bland assumption that a given worker, if unsatisfied with his pay or working conditions, should merely quit his job and seek better work elsewhere seems more suitable for the artisan worker phase of capitalism of a century earlier than the circumstances of his own day.

In some senses, however, his attitude toward trusts is ingenious: he asserts that it is in their own interest to sell products as cheaply as possible, so that society would benefit if all industries were in the hands of trusts. What he overlooks—except in the editorial "A Backslider" (1892)—is that, once a trust or monopoly has cornered the market on any given product or service, it can then raise the cost of that product or service at will; and, especially in big businesses such as oil, steel, or railroads, it would be difficult for other businesses to step in and begin competitive marketing of their own products or services, because of the immense expense involved in initiating such enterprises. One would think that someone who had spent the better part of his journalistic

---

22. "Prattle," *San Francisco Examiner* (24 July 1892): 6.

career fulminating against the monopolistic practices of the railroads would have known better. In "The Jumjum of Gokeetle-guk" Bierce startlingly suggests that the trusts should be rigidly supervised by the government—an anomalous instance of "socialism" from this diehard free trader. In "Concerning Trusts" (1899) he goes so far as to say: "Governmental ownership and Governmental control [of trusts] are what we are coming to by leaps and bounds"—a claim that would have floored even some of the more radical proponents of the New Deal two generations later.

And yet, Bierce's assertion in a letter of 1902 that "I am something of a Socialist myself"[23] is no better exemplified than by his repeatedly expressed belief that all able-bodied persons who wish to work should be provided work—by the government, if necessary. In some senses his advocacy of this measure was part of his solution to rid the country of "tramps," but in the essay "Concerning Legislation 'To Solve the Tramp Problem'" (1900) he makes it abundantly clear that the "right to labor" is really a matter of human dignity.

On a broader economic issue—the attainment of wealth—Bierce similarly reveals certain quasi-socialistic beliefs. One of the most striking passages in "Ashes of the Beacon" is his condemnation of Americans' furious and single-minded quest for the acquisition of money. The "prosperity" of the country was purchased at a high price:

> By the neglect of all education except that crude, elementary sort which fits men for the coarse delights of business and affairs but confers no capacity of rational enjoyment; by exalting the worth of wealth and making it the test and touchstone of merit; by ignoring art, scorning literature and despising science, except as these might contribute to the glutting of the purse; by setting up and maintaining an artificial standard of morals which condoned all offenses against the property and peace of every one but the condoner; by pitilessly crushing out of their natures every sentiment and aspiration unconnected with accumulation of property, these civilized savages and commercial barbarians attained their sordid end.

---

23. Letter to George Sterling, 15 March 1902; *Much Misunderstood Man* 83.

Whether the essay "The Road Wealth Is Open to All—Get Wealthy Ye Who Can" (1902) qualifies this searing condemnation is debatable: there Bierce merely asserts that opportunities for accumulating wealth are, in his day, abundant, and that it only takes brains and gumption to secure as much money as anyone wants.

One final aspect of Bierce's thought may be addressed here—his unremitting hostility to insurance. In some senses this may seem merely to be one of his crotchets, as with his dislike of dogs; but his attitude may seem less unusual if we realise the relative recency of the whole phenomenon of insurance. Although insurance of some sort can be traced as far back as ancient Babylonia, in reality it was chiefly a product of the later eighteenth and nineteenth centuries. In the United States, the first casualty policy was offered in 1832, while the Prudential Insurance Company, the pioneer of life insurance in America, was founded as recently as 1875. As such, insurance seemed to Bierce merely a new and alarming con game; in short, a form of gambling in which one could never beat "the man who kept the table." Bierce errs in some of his views—such as his assumption that the premiums paid on property over a lifetime would exceed the value of that property—but in other areas he seems on target. He shrewdly points out that insurers' boasts of the extent of their assets are an unwitting admission that they take in far more than they pay out. For Bierce, insurance was simply one more instance of the follies, hypocrisies, and inefficiencies infecting American society.

Ambrose Bierce never enunciated the entire range of his political, social, aesthetic, or philosophical opinions in a systematic way, and so his views must be collated or inferred by consultation of a vast aggregate of journalism. Perhaps he was better at pointing out what was wrong with the American political, legal, economic, and social system than at recommending viable solutions, but he saw this criticism as a legitimate exercise of his satirical, journalistic, and polemical talents. He also perceived that to couch his criticisms in the form of fiction, rather than essays or treatises, might be a far more potent and penetrating way of influencing his contemporaries.

What place do Bierce's satires occupy in his own work? Is he correct in thinking "Ashes of the Beacon" his most "notable" work? To be sure, such tales as "An Occurrence at Owl Creek Bridge," "Chickamauga," and "The Death of Halpin Frayser" allow the critic more latitude for analysis, in regard to character development, dramatic irony, and the mingling of horror, pathos, and satire. But as flights of imagination, and certainly as fictionalised expressions of many facets of Bierce's political, social, and aesthetic thought, the satires rank supreme. Perhaps a comparison between the satires and his other tales is futile, given their radical difference in form, content, even style and tone; and perhaps it is best merely to appreciate both bodies of work for their own distinct virtues.

II. Bierce as Fabulist

Bierce wrote nearly 850 fables in a literary and journalistic career that spanned more than forty years. Less than half of these fables have, until recently, been reprinted from their original appearances in newspapers and magazines of a century or more ago, and Bierce himself reprinted scarcely more than a third of them in the two editions of his *Fantastic Fables* (1899, 1911). His fables are unique of their kind, and yet they reveal a thorough familiarity with the long history of the fable as a literary form; indeed, much of their merit resides in their adaptation and expansion of that form.

What sets Bierce's fables apart from others of their kind—aside from their sheer quantity and their consistent brilliance—is their pungently satirical "morals," their skewering of a wide array of political, social, and even literary foibles, and their exemplification of his sharp scepticism in regard to human character and endeavour. The man who urged a budding writer to remember that "this is a world of fools and rogues, blind with superstition, tormented with envy, consumed with vanity, selfish, false, cruel, cursed with illusions—frothing mad!" ("To

Train a Writer" [1899]; *Sole Survivor* 248) spent a lifetime enunciating that view in his fables.

The tradition of the fable in English—especially in America—cannot be said to be notably distinguished. Certainly, if we look at the rich history of the poem, the drama, the novel, and the short story, we find the fable presenting only intermittent instances of brilliance and long periods of mediocrity or neglect.

Matters are not helped by the fact that the precise nature and characteristics of the fable are difficult to specify. The canonical definition by the Greek rhetorician Theon—"a fictitious story picturing a truth" (Perry xx)—could be applied to virtually all literary forms that make some claim to presenting "truth" within the context of fiction. Nor, as we shall see presently, is compactness a requisite of the fable, although most of those in the Aesopic tradition are preeminent instances of literary concision. Similarly, the utterance of an explicit "moral," whether at the beginning (*promythium*) or at the end (*epimythium*), was considered optional even in antiquity. The use of animals as interlocutors is predominant but not exclusive in the ancient fable, whose characters can consist of ordinary human beings, gods, and even on rare occasions inanimate objects.

What is not in doubt is that the fable as a literary form is as old as literature itself. The two dominant traditions are the Aesopic fable and the "Eastern" fable arising out of India or the Middle East. The former is far more familiar to English-speaking readers, although the latter may predate it by more than a millennium.

Whether there ever was a writer named Aesop is open to doubt. If he did exist (and his most diligent scholar, Ben Edwin Perry, believes he did), then he "came originally from Thrace, not from Phrygia; . . . he was at one time a slave on the island of Samos in the service of a man named Iadmon; who later freed him; . . . [and] he was a contemporary of the poetess Sappho in the early sixth century B.C." (Perry xxxv). It was, however, not until the fourth century B.C.E. that the Aesopic fables (in prose) were collected by Demetrius of Phalerum.

At that time the fable was not conceived by the Greeks as a literary form, but rather as a means for rhetorical ornament in oratory. It only became a literary form when the Latin poet Phaedrus (first half of the first century C.E.) and the Greek poet Babrius (second half of the first century C.E.) adapted many of the Aesopic fables into verse. It is from the work of these two poets that the bulk of the fables that we call "Aesop's" are known.

The Eastern fable derives from an entirely different tradition, although at a later period it may have been influenced by the Aesopic tradition. Fables or fable-like material can be found as early as 1800 B.C.E. in wisdom books, but the two chief volumes of Eastern fables are the *Fables of Bidpai* (or *The Book of Kalilah and Dimnah*, also known as the *Panchatantra*) and *The Tales of Marzuban* by Sa'd al-Warawini. The former originated in India as part of Buddhist literature; it was brought to Persia no later than 570 C.E. The latter was originally composed in Old Persian in the early thirteenth century C.E. The Eastern fable is significantly different from the Aesopic form in being considerably longer (some fables are tantamount to short stories or even novellas) and more discursive, so that the "moral" is not as easily discernible as in the compressed Aesopic version. Bidpai (or Pilpay) was translated into English as early as 1570 by Thomas North, with other translations appearing in 1747 (anonymous), 1818 (by John Milford), and 1819 (by Wyndham Knatchbull). But the Eastern fable has had minimal influence upon English and American literature.

William Caxton translated Aesop's fables from the French in 1484, but it was Roger L'Estrange's translation (1692–99) that made Aesop a familiar name to English readers. It was followed by Samuel Croxall's translation of 1722, which continued to be reprinted far into the nineteenth century. Translations by Thomas James (1848) and George Fyler Townsend (1867) were also widely read, as was Christopher Smart's 1765 verse translation of Phaedrus.

It was, indeed, in poetic form that the fable became popular; but in the process it withdrew further and further from the Aesopic original.

The fables of Jean de la Fontaine (1621–1695), published in twelve books between 1668 and 1693, are largely versified renditions of Aesop, but some of La Fontaine's later fables are original. Dryden's *Fables Ancient and Modern* (1700) are merely retellings of stories out of Homer, Ovid, Boccaccio, and Chaucer; his long introduction—certainly a masterwork of criticism in its own right—never mentions Aesop. John Gay's *Fables* (fifty of them published in 1727, sixteen more in 1738) are a perfect delight, for once matching the compactness of the Aesopic original and adding a refined elegance that only Georgian poetry can achieve. But whether we should even regard such book-length "fables" as Bernard Mandeville's *Fable of the Bees* (1714) or such modern works as George Orwell's *Animal Farm* as fables at all is an open question; certainly they have departed from the Aesopic original in form, and perhaps even in substance. The mere use of animals as characters in place of human beings to point a moral may not be sufficient to classify a work as a fable, for modern fantasy literature is full of such instances.

We do not know what edition of Aesop was read by Ambrose Bierce; but that he had read Aesop at a relatively early stage of his literary career is evident, as adaptations of the Greek fabulist appear in his earliest fables. He had read La Fontaine at some point as well: he quotes the adage "An empty stomach has no ears" in one of his early fables (48)[24] and also in a late article, although in the latter he attributes it to Rabelais ("Concerning Wit and Humor"). Another fable (419) adapts a fable found only in La Fontaine. That Bierce, however, must have been at least casually familiar with the Eastern fable is clear from his earliest fables, "The Fables of Zambri, the Parsee." These appeared in two series in the British humour magazine *Fun* in 1872–73 and were reprinted with some revisions and reorganisations in Bierce's *Cobwebs from an Empty Skull* (1874). And yet, the Zambri fables have little connexion with the Eastern fable aside from random elements of

---

24. The numbers I use for fables is taken from my edition of *The Collected Fables of Ambrose Bierce.*

setting and nomenclature; they are direct and compact rather than lengthy and discursive, and several of them manifestly adapt well-known fables of the Aesopic tradition.

What led Bierce to write these fables, which precede nearly the whole of his output of short fiction? A better question might be why Bierce did not write more of them; for in the fable he seemed to find an ideal means to convey his pungent opinions on life, literature, and society, and his mastery of the fable is only symptomatic of his mastery of many of the shortest and most condensed literary forms in English. This is hardly the place for a detailed study of Bierce's life, let alone his thought, or even his views on satire; but some notes on these subjects may help to place his fables in their proper context.

After growing up as a poor farm boy in Ohio and Indiana and participating in some of the most horrific battles of the Civil War, Bierce eventually settled down in San Francisco. His earliest literary work was journalism for the *San Francisco News Letter and California Advertiser* (1868-72); but in the three and a half years of his tenure on this weekly paper he was no cub reporter, but rather the imposing "Town Crier" who wrote a column of random opinion on any subject that entered his mind. The columns may each have been up to 2500 words in length, but they comprised dozens of discrete paragraphs, some no more than a sentence or two in length. This was a practice Bierce maintained for nearly the whole of his literary and journalistic career.

His first "fable" may perhaps date to this period, if the following item—from the "Town Crier" column of 16 September 1871 and reprinted under the title "The Pridies" in an early collection, *Nuggets and Dust* (1873)—counts am a fable:

> Mr. Pridy and his female returned home, drawn by a pair of horses. (Mr. P. and his f. had been driving for their health.) Straightway appeared upon the scene ten white-headed Pridies, of assorted sizes, screaming like infuriated fiends, leaping like maniacs, and gesticulating like a tempest of windmills. A nice way to welcome these staid and respectable parties! The horses turned aside in disgust, sprang deliberately off a bank, sank breathless through the yielding air, stopped when they got to the bottom,

and Madame Pridy was a melancholy remain.
MORAL: If people will have children— Bah! of course they will. (33)

Mildly amusing as this is, it does not greatly resemble the fables even of his early period, let alone the great fables of *Fantastic Fables*.

Bierce's transplantation to England in 1872 was in all likelihood meant to be permanent, but in the event it lasted only three years. Almost immediately upon his arrival he began writing the Zambri fables for the weekly comic journal *Fun*, edited by Thomas Hood the Younger, with whom Bierce rapidly formed a close friendship. Sometimes as many as eight fables would appear in one issue, at other times as few as two. They were published under the pseudonym he used for the bulk of his English period, Dod Grile; and the first series of fifty-seven fables proved popular enough that a second series of seventy-eight began publication after a two-month hiatus. In light of Bierce's later work in the fable form, the Zambri fables appear loose and a little verbose; they perhaps strain a little too hard to be funny. Like much of his writing at this time, they are apprentice work by a young man who knows perhaps too well that he is clever and gifted; but, like the best apprentice work, they are a harbinger of better things to come.

When his wife, Mollie, already burdened with two small children and with a third on the way, tired of London literary life and returned to San Francisco in the spring of 1875, Bierce felt he had no recourse but to follow her a few months later. After two years of literary quiescence he joined the staff of the newly formed weekly paper, the *Argonaut*. Bierce reprinted a good many of the Zambri fables in the paper but wrote no new fables; the bulk of his creative work went into his controversial column "Prattle," which consisted as before of discrete paragraphs of commentary. It was at this time that he began writing a series of "Fables and Anecdotes" in the voice of an imaginary backwoods boy, Little Johnny, a character that had evidently proved popular with British readers of *Fun*, where Johnny had made his debut; but these "fables"—written in an almost impenetrable patois of deliberate solecisms and misspellings—are radically different from Bierce's later work in the fable form. They are so voluminous that they would require a volume—perhaps several volumes—all to themselves.

After a bootless effort in 1880-81 to mine gold in the Black Hills of the Dakota Territory, Bierce returned to San Francisco. Denied his old job at the *Argonaut*, he quickly gained employment as associate editor of another weekly paper, the *Wasp*, where his tart wit found a ready haven. For five and a half years he ground out weekly "Prattle" columns (only 1500 words each, however) for the *Wasp*, along with a wide range of poetry, fiction, humorous sketches, memoirs, and essays.

But what of fables? In December 1883 a column of fables entitled "Anecdotes of Animals" appeared; and in September and October of 1884 five columns of fables, headed either "Fables without Political Morals" or "Fables without Political Meaning," were published. All are unsigned. Are they by Bierce? There is clearly a great deal of unsigned material by Bierce in the *Wasp*; and he had used or would use two of the three titles of these fables in other work ("Anecdotes of Animals" had appeared in the *Argonaut* for some Little Johnny material; "Fables without Morals" was a long-running if sporadic column in the *San Francisco Examiner*). Given this, and given the thoroughly Biercian style and content of these fables, I believe their attribution to Bierce is sound.

It was in the *Wasp*, of course, that Bierce began his *Devil's Dictionary*: it first appeared in serial form beginning in 1881. This work is his greatest triumph of concision: he can pack more venom in a single sentence, sometimes in a single word, than any writer in literature. On occasion he would elaborate his definitions with little stories that are manifestly fables.

By the fall of 1886 Bierce was out of a job again, and it was only in the spring of the next year that—as he relates with his typically understated wit ("A Thumb-Nail Sketch," in *Sole Survivor* 201-5)—the twenty-three-year-old William Randolph Hearst came to his house in Oakland and asked him to be the star editorial writer for the *San Francisco Examiner*. For the next twenty years Bierce was allowed unprecedented space and editorial freedom to expound on whatever topics he wished.

Although the majority of his creative work went into the writing of "Prattle," which attained epic proportions in bulk, sizzling satire, and notoriety, Bierce also produced the greater proportion of his short fiction—both the Civil War stories that went into *Tales of Soldiers and Civilians* (1891) and the supernatural tales that fill *Can Such Things Be?* (1893)—along with poems, essays, and, of course, fables. More than six hundred fables were written in the twenty years Bierce worked for the *Examiner* and, later, Hearst's *Cosmopolitan*, and it was here that he came into his own as a fabulist.

The opportunity to collect Bierce's fables into a book did not, however, emerge until 1899.[25] The previous year Putnam's had reissued his first story collection—now titled (after the 1892 London edition) *In the Midst of Life*, and shortly thereafter agreed to publish a volume of fables. *Fantastic Fables* appeared in early 1899 and contained only 245 fables. I say "only" because Bierce had by this time written twice as many fables for the *Examiner* alone, not counting his earlier fables for *Fun* (which, as with nearly all his English writing, he seemed intent on forgetting) and (assuming they are his) the *Wasp. Fantastic Fables* itself consists almost entirely of fables published in the *Examiner* between 1887 and 1893—which, indeed, represents the bulk of Bierce's output in this form. In this volume appear forty-seven fables in the section "Æsopus Emendatus," originally published in the *Oakland Tribune* for 1890, at a time when Bierce—probably at the urging of his friend Edward F. Cahill, editor of the *Tribune*—was contributing to this small rival of the *Examiner* across the bay.[26] It is in these fables that Bierce

25. In an undated letter to Carroll Carrington (envelope postmarked 28 February 1898), Bierce takes note of the fact that Carrington has seen an advertisement for *Fantastic Fables* from the publisher Way & Williams, but Bierce writes: "They have as yet not even sent me a contract to sign, nor has there been any correspondence about terms; so I think it odd that they should announce something that they have not really bought" (ms., University of Virginia). Shortly thereafter Bierce came to terms with Putnam's for the book.

26. The "Æsopus Emendatus" columns derive from four of the five columns published in the *Tribune* between 12 July and 9 August 1890. Oddly, no fables from

reveals most thoroughly his knowledge of Aesop, for here we find piquant revisions of the moral thrust of many familiar Aesopic fables—revisions that signal Bierce's impatience with the conventional morality found in Aesop, and which exhibit facets of his hardheaded perception of human folly and duplicity.

From this point on, Bierce's production of fables becomes sporadic. It had, perhaps, always been so: even during the heyday of his work for the *Examiner* (1887–99), months or even a year or two would pass between the publication of fables. There are no fables for the whole of 1888, and none between an unprecedentedly long period between September 1893 and November 1896, although some of this latter period (February to May 1896) was occupied with Bierce's lobbying against a funding bill advocated by railroad baron Collis P. Huntington; the bill's defeat in Congress was Bierce's greatest journalistic triumph.[27] In late 1899 he was forced to move to Washington, D.C., for health reasons (the fogs in San Francisco were playing havoc with his steadily worsening asthma), and for the next decade he would have repeated disputes with Hearst and his editors over their tampering with the work he submitted. His columns and other matter were now first appearing in the *New York Journal* (later *American*), to be reprinted a week or two later in the *Examiner*; some material appeared only in the *Journal.* Perhaps Bierce's creative energies were also flagging; his columns grew shorter and less pungent, and both his stories and his fables appeared more intermittently.

Nevertheless, Bierce had a large supply of fables ready for any contemplated reprint of *Fantastic Fables*; but when that dream turned into a reality—as part of the sixth volume of his *Collected Works* (1909–12)—he chose to include only fifty-nine new fables, while at the same

---

the column of 19 July were reprinted; perhaps Bierce somehow did not have access to this column when compiling *Fantastic Fables.*

27. Two unsigned columns of fables appeared in the *Examiner* at this time, "Aesop's Fables Up to Date" (20 March 1896) and "Aesop Up to Date" (23 April 1896); but they are manifestly not by Bierce.

time dropping ten fables from the first edition of *Fantastic Fables*. Eight of these new fables are "Fables in Rhyme," originally published between 1897 and 1902. Curiously, Bierce inserted, before the "Æsopus Emendatus" section, a series of fifteen "Fables from *Fun*," which are extensively revised versions of some Zambri fables. These are significantly altered from their original appearances. Bierce manifestly gave considerable thought to the arrangement and content of the fables he chose to collect in book form. His revisions were almost always for the better, although in some cases he truncated fables so that they would be even more pointed than before.

The reasons for Bierce's failure to include more than half of his fabular output in book form are intimately connected with the nature and purpose of the fable as he apparently conceived it. (We have no writing by Bierce on the fable as a literary form, not even any prefaces to his books of fables, so that his views on the fable must be inferred by random comments in letters or newspaper columns and by the character of the fables themselves.) His fables undergo a striking development in both form and content, so that his greatest fables—those of the 1890s—underscore many facets of his personal philosophy more powerfully, pungently, and piquantly than anything he wrote, with the exception of *The Devil's Dictionary*.

But what is that philosophy? Bierce of course was not a philosopher, and one should not expect any systematic exposition of his views. A series of comments made as early as 1872, in the persona of the departing "Town Crier," may be as succinct an expression his worldview as we will find:

> The only talents that he has are a knack at hating hypocrisy, cant, and all sham, and a trick of expressing his hatred. . . . Be as decent as you can. Don't believe without evidence. Treat things divine with marked respect—don't have anything to do with them. Do not trust humanity without collateral security; it will play you some scurvy trick. Remember that it hurts no one to be treated as an enemy entitled to respect until he shall prove himself a friend worthy of affection. Cultivate a taste for distasteful truths.

And, finally, most important of all, endeavor to see things as they are, not as they ought to be. ("Town Crier" 9)

What we find here are a series of assertions stressing the following points: scepticism, specifically of politics and religion; distrust of the sincerity of many human motives; and, overarchingly, an unflinching quest to see through the layers of "hypocrisy, cant, and . . . sham" that mask so much human behaviour. It is, indeed, no accident that that final remark anticipates his later definition of "Cynic" in *The Devil's Dictionary*: "A blackguard whose faulty vision sees things as they are, not as they ought to be." Bierce strove, both in his personal comportment and in his public utterances, to adhere to the bulk of these assertions throughout his life.

"The Fables of Zambri, the Parsee" only broach some of these issues, and do so in a way that rarely departs radically from the Aesopic fabular form that Bierce is imitating. The cynicism encapsulated in the remark that human beings are "every way inferior to snakes—except in malice" (59) is found only rarely in these fables, and many of the moral failings they chastise are commonplace: making a virtue of necessity (7, 34), using trickery to gain an advantage or to escape punishment (2, 16, 108), self-preservation overcoming family feeling (31). Perhaps somewhat more specifically Biercian are those fables that satirically display pure and unadulterated viciousness within the family circle (33, 90): Bierce, in his "Town Crier" period, claimed to take delight in reporting accounts of the suicide of a beleaguered husband or wife, a parent's murder of his or her children, and the like. To be sure, much of this malevolent glee was designed merely for shock value and cannot be said to echo any personal sentiment on Bierce's part; but its underlying purpose—to show to his Victorian readers that the sanctity and placidity of family life is a "sham" worth exposing—is clear.

Several fables touch upon religious credulity (15, 32, 95) and again echo many comments found in the "Town Crier" columns. But nineteenth-century religion's great foe, science, is not exempt from ridicule (102)—although perhaps here the satire is directed more specifically at the folly of individual scientists. Bierce also found the pomposity, impracticality, and credulity of philosophers a target too good to pass up (62, 69).

Bierce's most radical departure from the fabular tradition was the use of fables for purposes of political satire, but we find only the slightest hints of this in the Zambri fables. Fable 38 may be his first political fable, although its theme (a king wishes to avoid the usurpation of his throne during his absence) is very general. On the other hand, fable 44, in its attack on Fabian socialism, is too specific to have any broader political message.

As it is, the greatest significance of the Zambri fables may be in their gradual departure from the standard Aesopic form. While almost all the fables utilise animals as interlocutors, one delightful fable (50) plays upon this very usage: a man is terrified when he comes upon a succession of animals who speak to him. Many of the fables lack explicit morals altogether; others present "morals" that are really no morals at all (see 86), or morals that are deliberately self-deflating by reason of their literalness or triviality; still others end up being merely the excuses for puns (13, 113) or other self-parodic jokes.

It is evident that, in the ten-year interval between the Zambri fables and the series of fifty fables found in the *Wasp* (1883–84), Bierce's conception of the fable underwent a considerable change. These fables, although perhaps not of the high quality we find in *Fantastic Fables* and others written during his *Examiner* period, nevertheless approach those fables in form and substance far more than do the Zambri fables. That five out of the six groups of *Wasp* fables have the word "political" in the title is sufficient to indicate the shift of focus. Several of these fables (481, 495) directly address the presidential election of 1884, when those Republicans who deserted their party's chosen candidate, James G. Blaine, gained the sobriquet "Mugwumps." (Bierce later confessed that he was one of them.)[28] Here we have not only few animals as char-

---

28. "Prattle," *San Francisco Examiner* (8 July 1888); *Sole Survivor* 219.

acters but such eccentric interlocutors as a "Record Without a Blot," a "Grasping Monopoly," a "Brilliant Peroration," and so on.

It is difficult to characterise the nearly six hundred fables Bierce wrote for the *Examiner*, but we can start by noting that he has by now almost entirely given up the traditional fabular practice of using animals as interlocutors. In one of the few instances in which he does so, the intent is to make a joke on the physical resemblance of animals to certain human beings who are the targets of his satire: in 198, a zebra is likened to a man in a penitentiary, while a kangaroo with a full pouch brings to mind a thieving legislator. (The fable is perhaps an adaptation of one of the Zambri fables [65], where a somewhat similar idea is found.)

It is also instructive to examine which fables Bierce chose to reprint in *Fantastic Fables* and which he did not. It is certainly the case that the overwhelming bulk of the fables collected in the volume deal with political, legal, or social topics; and Bierce appears intent on presenting only those fables that might be capable of conveying some broader moral or political point. Indeed, the rapidity with which Bierce digested some incident in local, national, or international politics and extracted its quintessence in a fable is remarkable. Accordingly, he either rewrote some fables (usually by replacing a specific name with a generalised description) when reprinting his fables in book form, or chose not to reprint some of his best fables at all, in the apparent belief that some topical fables (especially on local events) would be too recondite to a general readership or had lost their punch after the incidents themselves had passed from public consciousness.

If this is indeed Bierce's motivation, then it seems at least partly contradictory to his normal practice. The overwhelming bulk of his literary and journalistic work—even his fiction—is satirical; and from the beginning of his career Bierce had allied himself with the tart, mordant satire of Juvenal as opposed to the mild, genial satire of Horace. Moreover, throughout the course of his life Bierce justified his attacks on specific individuals –many of whom would now have achieved merited oblivion had they not been embalmed in his own work—as being typical of all satiric practice:

> In satirizing real persons I follow the example of *all* satirists who succeed. It does not at all matter how obscure, or how anything-else, the persons satirized may be; the merit is *in the satire*. Do you suppose that the merit of Heine's, of Pope's, or Byron's attacks on *persons*—has any relation to the personality . . . of the objects of it. The merit is *intrinsic*. Nobody cares who was hit—nobody reads, for example, the explanatory notes to "The Dunciad" or the "English Bards and Scotch Reviewers", which fool publishers think it necessary to insert. These things of mine would have the same literary value (and I'm bound to assume that they have *some*) if they bore any other names than the ones they do bear. Would it add anything to the interest of a personal satire to entitle it "Atticus" instead of "Arthur McEwen"? I'm not running a guessing game: I prefer human names as Byron did.[29]

But perhaps, in his fables, he considered not only the persons but some of the issues (such as a controversy over the location of the Post Office site in San Francisco, or the building of the City Hall tower) so remote from his readers' present interests that even the satire had lost much of its sting.

In *Fantastic Fables*, then, are any number of general attacks on "hypocrisy, cant, and . . . sham." The repeated satires on the venality of lawyers (160, 226), politicians (172, 205, 248, 258, 265), and courts (195, 220, 235, 270) are what one might expect from a "cynic" determined to "see things as they are," and parallels to many of these views can readily be found in his journalism.

More to the point, perhaps, are Bierce's censures on the stupidity of the electorate (271), which provides frequent opportunity for dema-goguery (255, 263, 354); for it is here that we approach the essence of his own political philosophy. Bierce refused to ally himself with either political party of the day, feeling that there was an abundance of rascali-ty on both sides; if in his journalism he finds more to attack in Republi-cans than in Democrats, that may only be because the former were in power for a large portion of the later nineteenth century. But his attacks

---

29. Bierce to Herman Scheffauer, [c. September 1902] (ms., Bancroft Library).

go far beyond mere abuses of the democratic system; he condemns the very foundations of that system (see 294, 842).

Given Bierce's long tenure in California, it is not surprising that, even in *Fantastic Fables,* a book intended for a broader audience, he presented fables attacking the leniency of California courts (182, 201): Bierce constantly lamented the ease with which defendants whom he believed clearly guilty were acquitted, and the reluctance of jurors and judges to impose the death penalty. Related to this complaint is his scorn and contempt for anarchists (see 310, 345). It is difficult in our age to realise the widespread alarm that the anarchist movement caused throughout Europe and America, and Bierce is not alone in thinking that even philosophical anarchists secretly sought the violent overthrow of all government. Such concerns were bolstered by the suspicion (erroneous in many cases) that anarchists were behind the assassination of several world leaders, including President William McKinley in 1901.[30]

Some of Bierce's later fables in *Fantastic Fables* do attack specific individuals in the McKinley and Roosevelt administrations; indeed, in one case (339) the subject of attack is not mentioned by name, as Bierce presumably felt that he was sufficiently notorious that his audience would readily grasp the allusion. The writer and political theorist Edward Bellamy is also a target (403). Such personal satires, however, are rare. In most cases where Bierce's fables are not general, he jeers at institutions or phenomena that had long earned his wrath. The attack on state militias (158) may seem puzzling to those who have not read Bierce's relentless criticisms of such bodies as being mere play soldiers who are useless in cases of actual conflict. In his later fables the army itself does not escape scrutiny (324, 330, 331), and his fable (346) on the military's careless waste of money would seem very timely today.

---

30. There is a further irony here, as far as Bierce was concerned. Some years later the political enemies of William Randolph Hearst claimed that McKinley's assassin had been led to his crime by reading the Hearst papers, and specifically a poetic squib by Bierce himself in which he appeared to predict or even to encourage the assassination. See "A Thumb-Nail Sketch," *A Sole Survivor* 202–3.

A number of fables poking fun at women poets (174), reporters (218), and writers in general (262, 274) echo long-standing complaints on Bierce's part. He had an exceptionally narrow view of woman's proper place in society, so that it is by no means surprising that he opposed woman suffrage and ridiculed women politicians (344).

In *Fantastic Fables* Bierce is not shy in ridiculing religion (or, perhaps more specifically, religious people) on a variety of grounds: venality (159), intolerance (197, 207, 301), illiteracy (299), cynicism (317), and the like. Bierce himself was manifestly an agnostic, perhaps an atheist; and he well knew that hypocrisy, cant, and sham had as wide a field of play in religion as in politics.

It would of course be too limiting to state that Bierce's later fables are solely on political, religious, or social topics. One piquant phase of his fabular output is a series of fables on literary subjects, especially literary criticism. As a writer whose patience had been tried on numerous occasions by careless or inept critics, Bierce was not slow to poke fun at them (150, 318). Bad poets (350) were also a sore trial to Bierce, if the frequency of their skewering in his journalism is any indication.

As noted, Bierce's uncollected fables were probably consigned by their author to apparent oblivion because he felt that they did not allow for generalisation. It is in these uncollected pieces that we find fables on political and other events of the 1890s that had already faded out of public consciousness by the turn of the century: the threat of a war with Chile in 1891 (677), the World's Fair of 1893 (707), the Cuban crisis of 1896 (766). It is perhaps a little surprising that, in 1911, Bierce decided to reprint none of his several fables about the Spanish-American War or the war in the Philippines; but perhaps some of the issues he dealt with—for instance, the controversy over naval manoeuvres at the Battle of Santiago (see 802)—seemed to him too recondite or insignificant to evoke a responsive chord in his audience. At any rate, it is in these uncollected fables that we see most clearly Bierce's absorption of the political events of the day and his deftness in moulding their elements of absurdity, hypocrisy, or grotesqueness for purposes of pungent satire.

Can Bierce be considered America's greatest prose fabulist? Very few names can be put forth as his equals, let alone his superiors. The Uncle Remus stories of Joel Chandler Harris (1848-1908) are remarkable specimens of their kind, an affecting distillation of African American folklore; but they are more of the nature of short stories or vignettes than fables, at least in terms of length (the shortest of them is at least 750 words, the longest up to 2500 words). They first appeared in the *Atlanta Constitution* in 1879–after Bierce had written his Zambri fables but well before he began his later work in the fable form–and were collected in *Uncle Remus, His Songs and His Sayings* (1880) and many other volumes. Bierce, however, showered abuse on Harris for his use of dialect, a literary practice he abominated.

Then there is George Ade (1866-1944), who achieved spectacular if transient fame with *Fables in Slang* (1900), first published in the *Chicago Record* for 1897. Ade's fables–collected in more than a dozen volumes– are considerably longer than Bierce's, and to my taste reveal an arch sophistication and preciousness that seriously disfigure them as literary works; and their colloquialism dates them far more than Bierce's austere classicism. Some advocates may find Ade's "amiable cynicism" (Coyle 43) appealing, but my feeling is that the majority of literate readers will prefer Bierce's deliberately unamiable cynicism. The mere fact that Bierce used the title "Fables without Slang" for several columns in 1901 and 1902 suggests that he did not look upon Ade's work with favour; and a passage in his "Small Contributions" column in *Cosmopolitan* for July 1907, subtitled "Some Sober Words on Slang," clinches the matter:

> Among large classes of our countrymen, [slang] is held in so high esteem that whole books of it are put upon the market with profit to author and publisher. One of the most successful of these, reprinted from many of our leading newspapers, is called, I think, 'Fables in Slang'–containing, by the way, nothing that resembles a fable. This unspeakable stuff made its author rich, and naturally he 'syndicated' a second series of the same. (335)

In spite of the advocacy of H. L. Mencken, Ade's work seems to have lapsed into obscurity.

As for the *Fables for Our Time* (1940) and *Further Fables for Our Time* (1956) by James Thurber (1894–1961), they are as inimitable as any of Thurber's other works. His fables too tend to be somewhat milder than Bierce's, although tarter than Ade's. One should not allow mere quantity to determine aesthetic worth, but certainly the sheer number of fables by Bierce contained in this volume dwarf the few dozen by Thurber, and not many would deny that the best of Bierce's can easily hold their own with the best of Thurber's. Both Ade and Thurber affix explicit, if wry, morals at the end of their fables, creating a certain mechanical effect that Bierce avoids by allowing tenders to deduce the morals for themselves.

Comparisons are inevitably odious, so it is perhaps fruitless to dwell on the issue of America's greatest fabulist. Suffice it to say that both the quantity and consistently high quality of Ambrose Bierce's fables should guarantee them a place in the canon of American literature. Whether we regard them as the ultimate American homage to Aesop, or as the outpourings of a writer never inclined to suffer fools gladly, or even as a contribution to the literature of fantasy, Bierce's fables engage our admiration by their wit, their concision, and preeminently by their exposure of the follies, hypocrisies, and absurdities of our human species.

III. What Happens in "The Death of Halpin Frayser"

In the entire range of supernatural literature it would be difficult to find a parallel to Ambrose Bierce's "The Death of Halpin Frayser" (1891)—a tale that is uniformly praised as a masterwork of the supernatural but whose very plot has been the subject of debate by decades of critics and scholars. Bierce himself must share some responsibility for this state of affairs, for the peculiarly fractured nature of his narration of this tale has baffled readers and critics alike; but in large part, it is those critics whose careless reading of the tale—and, more particularly, failure to read and absorb some of the key passages in the tale—that has led to widely varying opinions as to what actually happens in it.

Let me then begin by outlining what I believe is the essence of the plot of "The Death of Halpin Frayser." I will then seek to justify this interpretation and then discuss other critics' views of the matter.

Halpin Frayser, whose mother, Catherine, has an unnatural affection for him, leaves for California. Some years later, Catherine, now widowed, follows him. She and Frayser marry, *living under the name Larue*. Frayser then murders his mother, but, overwrought by his actions, loses his memory of these events. In accordance with the epigraph (a passage from the prophet Hali), Catherine rises from the dead, a soulless lich, and murders Frayser over her own grave in a California cemetery. Bierce leaves sufficient clues for the piecing together of this scenario; the comment by one of the two detectives tracking Frayser down—"There is some rascally mystery here" (815)—does not indicate that the story is inexplicable, but rather that something supernatural (and therefore not amenable to "solution" by ordinary methods of detection) has occurred.

The number of misconceptions this story has spawned must set some kind of record. And yet, one of Bierce's earliest critics—one who wrote a largely favourable account of his work, and especially of this story, while Bierce was still alive—came tantalisingly close to the essence of the tale. In his chapter on Bierce in *Some American Story Tellers* (1911), Frederic Taber Cooper wrote as follows:

> . . . it remains to single out one typical example [of Bierce's supernatural work] in which perhaps he reached the very pinnacle of his strange fantastic genius, "The Death of Halpin Frayser." The theme of the story is this: it is sufficiently horrible to be confronted with a disembodied spirit, but there is one degree of horror beyond this, namely, to have to face the reanimated body of some one long dead from whom the soul has departed—because, so Mr. Bierce tells us, with the departure of the soul all natural affection, all kindliness has departed also, leaving only the base instincts of brutality and revenge. Now in the case of Halpin Frayser, it happens that the body which he is fated to encounter under these hideously unnatural

conditions is that of his own mother; and in a setting as curiously and po-
etically unreal as any part of "Kubla Khan" he is forced to realize that his
mother whom he had in life worshiped and she worshiped him is now, in
spite of her undiminished beauty, a foul and bestial thing intent only upon taking his life. In all imaginative literature it would be difficult to find
a parallel for this story in sheer, unadulterated horror. (352)

Well, evidently there is "one degree of horror" even beyond this—that
this beloved mother had in fact been living with her son as husband
and wife, and that Frayser himself had killed her, only to be killed by
her in turn. What other conclusion can we draw? The two policemen
who are hunting Frayser—the deputy sheriff Holker and the detective
Jaralson—make no bones about this: "'You remember Branscom [i.e.,
Frayser]?' said Jaralson . . . 'The chap who cut his wife's throat?' [replies
Holker]" (811). Later, when coming upon both the dead body of
Frayser (lying atop Catherine Larue's grave) and seeing the tombstone
marker, Holker exclaims, "Larue, Larue! . . . Why, that is the real name
of Branscom—not Pardee. And—bless my soul! How it all comes to me—
the murdered woman's name had been Frayser!" (815). (How exactly
Holker had come to know all this is never clarified—but evidently the
sheriff had done his share of investigation of the case.)

But if this is the case, why does Frayser, at the outset of the story,
"waking from a dreamless sleep," say the words "Catherine Larue"?—
whereupon the third-person narrator remarks, "He said nothing more;
no reason *was known to him* why he should have said so much" (804; my
emphasis). This is an enormously clever stroke on Bierce's part: we are
led to believe that the name Catherine Larue is meaningless to Frayser,
and that therefore he cannot have anything to do with her subsequent
murder; but the words I have emphasised are meant to point to a later
passage, during Frayser's vivid dream of wandering through a blood-
drenched forest; at one point, in the dream, he reflects: "It seemed to
him that it was all in expiation of some crime which, though conscious
of his guilt, he could not rightly remember" (805). This may be the
most important sentence in the story—one that most other critics have
either ignored or whose full significance they have failed to grasp.

What it suggests is that Frayser has not only forgotten that he had married his own mother, but that he had then killed her. The narrator later refers to Frayser's attempt "to reproduce the moment of his sin" (806)–referring both to the unnatural marriage and to his murder–and then remarks that Frayser "felt as one who has murdered in the dark, not knowing whom nor why" (806).

Part II of the story, telling of Frayser's youth and upbringing, makes no secret of the unnatural attraction of Frayser and his mother–an attraction, perhaps, more on the mother's side than on Frayser's. It is noted that he had "from early childhood" (808) called his mother Katy, and the narrator proceeds to remark pregnantly:

> In these two romantic natures was manifest in a signal way that neglected phenomenon, the dominance of the sexual element in all the relations of life, strengthening, softening, and beautifying even those of consanguinity. The two were nearly inseparable, and by strangers observing their manner were not infrequently mistaken for lovers. (808)

Bierce has nearly given the show away. Indeed, he may wish us to think that Frayser's decision to leave his native Tennessee and move to California was a means of escaping from his unwholesome attraction to his mother–or his mother's unwholesome attraction to him. She wonders wistfully, after having a purportedly prophetic dream, "Perhaps it does not mean that you will go to California. Or maybe you will take me with you?" (808). Frayser does indeed go to California, although once there is is shanghaied "aboard a gallant, gallant ship, and sailed for a far countree" (809), not returning for six years. In my judgment, this was done merely to provide a suitable length of time for Catherine (Katy) Frayser to become a widow, thereby freeing her up to marry again. Holker remarks: "The woman whose throat he [Frayser] had the bad taste to cut was a widow when he met her. She had come to California to look up some relatives" (812)–i.e., Frayser himself.

In spite of Bierce's repeated parrotings of Poe's ideas on the "unity of effect" in short story writing, some elements of the story fit only tangentially into the overall plot as I have outlined it. The long poem that is found in Frayser's pocketbook next to his dead body is one of these. Both Holker and Jaralson read it, and the latter remarks that it sounds uncannily like the work of Myron Bayne, the colonial poet who was an ancestor of the Fraysers. Jaralson remarks that Bayne "wrote mighty dismal stuff; I have his collected works. That poem is not among them, but it must have been omitted by mistake" (814). This comment betrays a surprising knowledge of an obscure poet; indeed, it is exactly this remark—as well as the earlier statement that "while a Frayser who was not the proud possessor of a sumptuous copy of the ancestral 'poetical works' (printed at the family expense, and long ago withdrawn from an inhospitable market) was a rare Frayser indeed" (807)—that led Robert C. Maclean to make one of the most ingenious (and bizarre) interpretations of the plot of the story. In his view, the story is not supernatural at all; rather, the murderer of Halpin Frayser is his own father, disguised as the private detective Jaralson. This interpretation is too involved to examine here; suffice it to say that there is, in my judgment, insufficient evidence to support it, and that my own interpretation accounts for the details of the story better than Maclean's. In any case, to say that few or no Fraysers owned a copy of Bayne's poetical works does not imply that *only* Fraysers owned it. And although the narrator remarks, of Frayser himself, that "Not only had he never been known to court the muse, but in truth he could not have written correctly a line of verse to save himself from the Killer of the Wise" (807), leading one to doubt whether the poem in Frayser's notebook was actually written by Frayser, the narrator goes on to note significantly: "Still, there was no knowing when the dormant faculty might wake and smite the lyre" (807). I think the suggestion is that Frayser, under the extraordinary circumstances of his dream of being killed by his mother, awoke his "dormant faculty" to write the poem in question—which, indeed, is nothing but a poetical description of his dream. The fact that it breaks off in mid-stanza is meant to suggest the exact time when he, in his dream (and, presumably, in actuality), is throttled by his mother. (Just as Frayser's dream is a reworking of one of Bierce's own dreams as chronicled in the essay "Visions of the Night," so is Frayser's poem an extensive reworking of a poem that Bierce had published in his "Prattle" column in the *San Francisco Examiner* for 12 June 1887.)

The dominant interpretation of the story—that the plot of the story cannot be coherently reconstructed, and that the tale is therefore a deliberate tease to readers and critics—has been propounded by Cathy N. Davidson in *The Experimental Fictions of Ambrose Bierce* (1984). But her own account is, I fear, occasionally devoid of sense and coherence. She begins by casting doubt upon the validity of the epigraph from Hali, whom she labels a "bogus mystic" (104). But in what sense is he "bogus"? Clearly, he is fictitious—there was, in fact, no such person, mystic or otherwise, as Hali—but his epigraph seems both entirely real and entirely sound. What is more, Davidson overlooks the plain fact that, in the several other Bierce stories that feature epigraphs, every one of these is an accurate predicter of the story's outward plot and basic theme. "An Inhabitant of Carcosa" contains another epigraph from Hali that precisely outlines the events of the tale. "The Man and the Snake" has an epigraph from Morryster's *Marvells of Science* that tells of the "magnetick propertie" of a serpent's eye, just as in the story itself a man is paralysed with terror by the shiny eyes of a toy snake.

Davidson goes on to quote what I have noted as the central fact of the story, and one that explains many of its seemingly perplexing features—the fact that Frayser has lost memory of his marriage to his mother and his murder of her—and actually uses it to declare the story itself inexplicable: "If this passage symbolizes anything, it indicates the futility of looking for a moral justification for Halpin's fate. He seeks his crime in his memories for the same reason and with the same success that various critics seek it in his dream. In short, what the symbology gives with one hand it takes away with the other" (106). I am not at all clear what Davidson is saying here. The mere fact that *Frayser* cannot recollect what he has done does not mean that we, as readers, are unable to ascertain it. Bierce, I maintain, has provided ample clues so that Frayser's confusion need not be our own.

Davidson actually concludes, on no evidence that I can see, that Catherine Frayser/Larue is "murdered by a second husband" (109) rather than by Frayser himself. But who can this second husband be but Frayser? Davidson compounds her error in thinking that Larue is a separate person—"the man who cut his wife's throat [and] later kills his former stepson too" (112). But there is no such person, and nothing in the text warrants our assumption of his existence. Davidson's error was probably derived from M. E. Grenander's still more erroneous interpretation of the events of the story, whereby she states that Catherine Frayser/Larue "had been widowed, remarried, and murdered by her second husband since the last time Halpin Frayser saw her, although he does not know any of these facts" (109). Both critics have evidently been misled by Jaralson's bland comment, upon seeing the corpse of Halpin Frayser, that it was "the work of a maniac . . . It was done by Branscom—Pardee" (815). But this is merely Jaralson's initial attempt to frame the matter as a case of simple murder; he cannot yet bring himself to believe that anything supernatural has occurred. It is true that all critics of the story have failed to grasp that the second husband of Catherine Frayser is in fact Halpin Frayser; and it is true that nowhere in the story is this identification explicitly made; but this is exactly the point that Bierce wants readers to understand for themselves, and he has laid out an abundance of clues pointing to this exact interpretation. The mere fact that the two detectives have good reason for looking in the cemetery for Catherine Larue/Frayser's husband/killer, and that they end up finding Halpin Frayser there, is really all the evidence we need.

It is worth noting that Grenander compounds her error by assuming that this phantom second husband of Catherine killed Frayser, and that he is the one whose "low, deliberate, soulless laugh" (815) is heard at the end by Jaralson and Holker, when it is plain that this laugh is produced by the soulless "lich" (804) that Catherine Frayser has become, as exactly indicated by the epigraph from Hali. Grenander is inclined to this interpretation because she does not want the story to be merely about "zombies and the supernatural" (114), which she evidently regards as somehow subliterary.

When she comes to the concluding segment of the story, involving Holker and Jaralson, Davidson uses Jaralson's comment—"There is some rascally mystery here"—to imply that the tale itself is incoherent: the comment "suggests that we might be skeptical of the ways in which these two would make the mystery disappear" (110). Davidson is, however, correct in believing that the appearance of these "Keystone Cops" (110) detectives is tonally jarring: "What has hitherto been a tragic tale of the supernatural suddenly becomes a comic detective yarn" (111). But I maintain that this flaw—if it is such—is a flaw attributable to the author, not an additional piece of evidence that the story is not designed to make sense on the level of plot. Bierce was so addicted to satire that, even in a weighty and "tragic" story of this kind, he could ill resist the temptation to make fun of his characters in a way that emphasised their buffoonery and his own intellectual superiority. My feeling is that this last segment of the story goes on too long and does diminish the atmospheric potency of the story; but it was necessary to provide the final pieces of the puzzle that allow the reader to understand what has actually happened.

In the end, Davidson can only conclude: "The largest point, then, is that the reader cannot apprehend the death of Halpin Frayser on any logical level" (112). But it is her own misreading of the plot that creates the confusion. Bierce has created a supernatural jigsaw puzzle that requires an astute reader to assemble; but the fact is that such an assembly is indeed possible to illuminate this most daring and appalling of his horror tales.

Works Cited

Berkove, Lawrence I. "Ambrose Bierce's Concern with Mind and Man." Ph.D. diss.: University of Pennsylvania, 1962.

Bierce, Ambrose. *The Collected Fables of Ambrose Bierce*. Ed. S. T. Joshi. Columbus: Ohio State University Press, 2000.

————. "Concerning Wit and Humor." *San Francisco Examiner* (23 March 1903): 12.

Bierce, Ambrose. "The Death of Halpin Frayser." In *The Fiction of Ambrose Bierce: A Comprehensive Edition.* Ed. S. T. Joshi, Lawrence I. Berkove, and David E. Schultz. Knoxville: University of Tennessee Press, 2006. 804–17 (Volume 2).

————. *A Much Misunderstood Man: Selected Letters of Ambrose Bierce.* Ed. S. T. Joshi and David E. Schultz. Columbus: Ohio State University Press, 2003.

————. *Nuggets and Dust Panned out of California.* London: Chatto & Windus, 1873.

————. "Small Contributions." *Cosmopolitan* 43, No. 5 (July 1907): 335–37.

————. *A Sole Survivor: Bits of Autobiography.* Ed. S. T. Joshi and David E. Schultz. Knoxville: University of Tennessee Press, 1998.

————. "The Town Crier." *San Francisco News Letter* (9 March 1872): 9.

Cooper, Frederic Taber. "Ambrose Bierce." In *Some American Story Tellers.* New York: Henry Holt, 1911. 331–53.

Coyle, Lee. *George Ade.* New York: Twayne, 1964.

Davidson, Cathy N. *The Experimental Fictions of Ambrose Bierce.* Lincoln: University of Nebraska Press, 1984.

Grenander, M. E. *Ambrose Bierce.* New York: Twayne, 1971.

Howells, William Dean. *The Altrurian Romances.* Ed. Clara and Rudolf Kirk. Bloomington: Indiana University Press, 1968.

Lovecraft, H. P. *Selected Letters.* Ed. August Derleth, Donald Wandrei, and James Turner. Sauk City, WI: Arkham House, 1965–76. 5 vols.

Lucian of Samosata. *Lucian.* With an English translation by A. M. Harmon. Cambridge, MA: Harvard University Press, 1913f. 8 vols.

————. *Lucian's Works.* With Life by Ferrand Spence. London, 1864.

Maclean, Robert C. "The Deaths in Ambrose Bierce's 'Halpin Frayser.'" *Papers on Language and Literature* 10 (Fall 1974): 394–402.

McWilliams, Carey. *Ambrose Bierce: A Biography.* New York: A. & C. Boni, 1929.

Mencken, H. L. "George Ade." In *Prejudices: First Series.* New York: Knopf, 1919. 113–22.

Perry, Ben Edwin. "Introduction." In *Babrus and Phaedrus*. Tr. Ben Edwin
    Perry. Cambridge, MA: Harvard University Press; London: William
    Heinemann (Loeb Classical Library), 1965. xi–cii.

Swift, Jonathan. *Gulliver's Travels*. 1726. In *Gulliver's Travels, A Tale of a
    Tub, The Battle of the Books, etc.* Ed. William Alfred Eddy. New York:
    Oxford University Press, 1933.

Stein, William Bysshe. "Bierce's 'The Death of Halpin Frayser': The Po-
    etics of Gothic Consciousness." *ESQ* 18 (2nd Quarter 1972): 115-22.

A Triumvirate of Fantastic Poets: Ambrose Bierce, George Sterling, and Clark Ashton Smith

The literary and personal relationship of Ambrose Bierce (1842–1914?), George Sterling (1869–1926), and Clark Ashton Smith (1893–1961) forms a distinctive chapter both in the history of American (and, specifically, Californian) literature and in the development of fantastic poetry. Although only Smith can be said to have specialised in weird verse, the elements of horror, fantasy, and cosmicism enter distinctively into each writer's poetic work; and their multitudinous involvements with one another—with Bierce serving as mentor to the young Sterling, while the older Sterling fulfilled that same function in regard to the young Smith—allow us to read their fantastic poetry in a provocative new light.

Ambrose Bierce not merely disavowed the role of weird poet, but the role of poet altogether:

> I don't think of myself as a poet, but as a satirist; so I'm entitled to credit for what little gold there may be in the mud I throw. But if I professed gold-throwing the mud which I should surely mix with the missiles would count against me. Besides, I've a preference for being the first man in a village, rather than the second man in Rome. Poetry is a ladder on which there is now no room at the top . . . When old Homer, Shakespeare and that crowd—building better than Ozymandias—say: "Look on my works, ye mighty, and despair!" I, considering myself specially addressed, despair. (Bierce to Sterling, 21 October 1903)[1]

Bierce may have been excessively humble, but his point is well ta-

---

1. All letters between Bierce and Sterling quoted here are derived from manuscripts at the Henry W. and Albert A. Berg Collection, New York Public Library.

ken. In a forty-year career as a journalist for a variety of newspapers and magazines in San Francisco, London, and New York, Bierce developed the reputation as a satirist of commanding and fearsome presence. His best work was done for William Randolph Hearst's *San Francisco Examiner*, for which he wrote for nearly twenty years (1887–1906). In today's parlance he would probably be called a columnist or op-ed writer; certainly, opinion was the keynote of all his journalistic work. But his columns—the most famous of which was called "Prattle," running first in the *Argonaut* (1877–79), then in the *Wasp* (1881–86), then in the *Examiner*—ordinarily dwelt not on a single subject but on a great many; a typical column would have twenty or thirty discrete paragraphs on a wide range of topics, from local figures to events of national and international significance. Inserted in no particular order or arrangement within these columns were self-standing poems, usually without title. Titles were affixed only when Bierce gathered his poems in book form, first in *Black Beetles in Amber* (1892), then in *Shapes of Clay* (1903), then in the revised and augmented versions of those two books in the fourth and fifth volumes of his *Collected Works* (1909–12).

Bierce was correct in believing that he had few peers as a satirist and wit, at least in his time and country. He may today remain America's finest satirist (only H. L. Mencken, Nathanael West, and Gore Vidal can contest him), and poetry was a forceful weapon in lambasting his contemporaries. Even those poems that exercise his broader flights of imagination often end—startlingly and bitingly—with abuse of some hapless politician, journalist, or other individual who had the misfortune of earning Bierce's wrath. Hence, "Finis Æternitatis" begins with a spectacular vista of the end of civilisation, even the end of time itself—but then concludes with a satire on the railroad baron Charles Crocker. "A Vision of Resurrection" is similar, ending with a literary dagger-thrust at one of Bierce's perennial foes, the journalist George K. Fitch. Probably the most amusing example of this technique is the poem first published without title in "Prattle" (12 June 1887), which concludes with a pungent satire on a local politician. But Bierce must have recognised the effectiveness of this brooding, atmospheric poem, for he incorporated it in revised form—and without its final stanza, specifically addressed to the politician—into one of his finest tales of horror, "The Death of Halpin Frayser."

Other poems are purer in form, maintaining their imaginative power without any admixture of satire. The transience of human civilisation is the focus of "The Passing Show"; a bird's-eye view of humanity is presented in "A Morning Fancy"; "Geotheos" underscores the throbbing vitality of Nature. Still other poems bring us closer to the Bierce we know from his masterful tales of horror and the supernatural: "Subterranean Phantasies" and "A Guest" are succulent examples of the graveyard humour for which he has become notorious. A few poems fuse fantasy and satire in a seamless fashion: "Land of the Pilgrims' Pride" displays, by means of a fantastic dream, Bierce's frequently expressed disdain of democratic institutions; "A Vision of Doom," perhaps his finest poem, employs cosmicism to condemn the social, political, and moral failings of his countrymen; and in the pensive "My Day of Life," one of his last poems, a cosmic perspective is brought to bear on Bierce's own life and achievements. "To Maude" may be of some significance in its fusion of love and cosmicism, something that we will find extensively in the work of Sterling and Smith.

Aside from being a daunting satirist and wit, Bierce also acted as a kind of unofficial literary adjudicator for the West Coast. Few Californian writers of any consequence failed to come under his influence at some time or other, while a variety of pretenders to literary eminence were condemned to the oblivion they deserved and are now known only by Bierce's embalming of them in the amber of his verse and prose. W. C. Morrow (who actually preceded Bierce in the writing of weird tales and may have influenced his great contemporary more than he was influenced by him), Emma Frances Dawson, Gertrude Atherton, Herman George Scheffauer, John Vance Cheney, and a host of lesser-known writers benefited from Bierce's tutelage. Perhaps the greatest of his pupils was George Sterling.

Born in Sag Harbor, Long Island, and educated there and in Maryland, Sterling decided to head to California both to pursue a career—his wealthy uncle, F. C. Havens, was a prosperous businessman in the Bay Area—and to develop his literary gifts. He quickly became acquainted with Bierce's older brother Albert and Albert's son, Carleton, and also with Joaquin Miller, the flamboyant poet who had gained celebrity in England with the publication of *Songs of the Sierras* (1871). It was not long before Sterling came under Bierce's spell. His first letters to the satirist date to 1897, and it was about this time that Sterling began to send Bierce his early poems. Bierce was impressed to the degree of quoting them in full in some of his newspaper columns of 1899, and in 1901 he arranged for the publication of Sterling's "Memorial Day" in the *Washington Post*.

In early 1902 Sterling began work on the poem that would bring him his first taste of fame. *The Testimony of the Suns*—Sterling's "star poem"—elicited immediate enthusiasm from Bierce:

> Where are you going to stop?—I mean at what stage of development? . . . This last beats any and all that went before—or I am bewitched and befuddled. I dare not trust myself to say what I think of it. In manner it is great, but the greatness of the theme!—that is beyond anything.
>
> It is a new field, the broadest yet discovered. . . . The tremendous phenomena of Astronomy have never had adequate poetic treatment, their meaning adequate expression. You must make it your domain. You shall be the poet of the skies, the prophet of the suns. (Bierce to Sterling, 15 March 1902)

The poem was completed in May. In many ways it is Sterling's greatest poem. This vibrant depiction of cosmic conflict, although occasionally obscure in sense and diction, is a triumph of the imagination; but Sterling knew that it was not without human significance: "I hope that it will be clear enough to the intellectual reader that my invocation to the stars is only an allegory of man's search of the universe for the secret of life" (Sterling to Bierce, 3 June 1902).

The poem was far too long to be published in a magazine, even if Sterling had had a poetic reputation by that time; so he arranged for its inclusion in his first book, *The Testimony of the Suns and Other Poems* (1903), published by a San Francisco businessman, W. E. Wood. Shortly thereafter, in 1904, it was reprinted by A. M. Robertson, the bookseller and publisher who would issue the majority of Sterling's books. Many copies of that second edition were destroyed in the San Francisco earthquake and fire of 1906, so Robertson reprinted it in 1907. Sterling and Scheffauer also arranged for the publication, with Wood, of Bierce's *Shapes of Clay*, which had been circulating among publishers for at least a decade. Sterling largely financed the venture.

Meanwhile Sterling continued to send his poems to Bierce for approval and comment. He quoted bits of "A Wine of Wizardry"—which he referred to as "a poem of 'pure imagination'"—in a letter of 2 January 1904; at that time it already included two of its most striking lines:

> The blue-eyed vampire, sated at her feast,
> Smiles bloodily against the leprous moon.

Bierce was not slow to respond, noting that the above lines "give me the shivers. Gee! they're awful!" (Bierce to Sterling, 8 January 1904). By the end of the month the poem was finished. Its "plot," if such it can be called, is simple: the poet drinks wine and awakens his "Fancy," who ventures on a variety of fantastic voyages, alternately lovely and horrific. (This is what led Upton Sinclair, a fervent teetotaler, to supply a wry retitling of the work—"The Wizardry of Wine.") On occasion the poem descends to mere catalogues of jewelled words and phrases, but on the whole it is a powerful exercise of imagination—a more earthly imagination, certainly, than *The Testimony of the Suns*, but one in which horror and fantasy are interweaved in an inextricable union.

What occurred now was a several-year saga in which Bierce strove to secure the magazine publication of "A Wine of Wizardry." Although not as long as *The Testimony of the Suns*, it was still a long poem (210 lines), hence not easily saleable; and its exoticism made it doubly difficult to market at a time when an attenuated Victorianism still required poets to speak in a reserved and conventional manner. Bierce sanguinely predicted that "It is impossible to imagine a magazine editor rejecting that poem" (Bierce to Sterling, 11 May 1904), but that is exactly what happened. *Scribner's, Harper's,* the *Atlantic Monthly, Munsey's,* the *Metropolitan,* the *Bookman,* even Bierce's own magazine, *Cosmopolitan* (for which he had begun writing in 1905) all turned the poem down. Bierce showered abuse down on the heads of the editors of all these magazines, but perhaps a bit unjustly: the poem's length, its horrific imagery, and the fact that Sterling was by no means a well-known literary figure all militated against its ready acceptance.

Bierce then sent the poem to Herman Scheffauer (an earlier poetic pupil of Bierce's who, much to his own irritation, quickly took second rank as a disciple once Sterling emerged) to market in England, but with no success. Sterling himself offered it to *Sunset,* a West Coast magazine that had run some of his earlier verse, but it too rejected the poem. For a time it looked as if Walter Neale (the young publisher who in 1909 began issuing Bierce's *Collected Works*) might include it in a magazine he was contemplating, but the magazine was never begun. A. M. Robertson thought of bringing out the poem as a pamphlet in a 500-copy edition on Japanese vellum, but Bierce expressed disapproval of this kind of "limited edition," correctly believing that it would restrict the poem's audience to collectors. Finally, a new editor, Sam Chamberlain, took over at *Cosmopolitan* in the summer of 1907, and expressed a wish to run the poem. Bierce had by this time written an effusive article, "A Poet and His Poem," which would run concurrently with "A Wine of Wizardry." The article and poem appeared in the September 1907 issue; Sterling received $100 for it.

A firestorm of controversy emerged. Some readers and critics, perhaps offended by Bierce's high praise of the poem, misconstrued his essay and maintained that Bierce believed the poem to be the greatest ever written in America. In fact, much of the incredulity and scoffing to which "A Wine of Wizardry" was subject was a result of two passages in Bierce's essay, the first about *The Testimony of the Suns* ("Of that work I have the temerity to think that in both subject and art it nicks the rock as high as anything of the generation of Tennyson, and a good deal higher than anything of the generation of Kipling") and the second about Sterling in general:

> I steadfastly believe and hardily affirm that George Sterling is a very great poet—incomparably the greatest that we have on this side of the Atlantic. And of this particular poem I hold that not in a lifetime has our literature had any new thing of equal length containing so much poetry and so little else. (*Collected Works* 10.181)

Note carefully what Bierce actually says here: Sterling is the greatest *living* American poet, and "A Wine of Wizardry" has more quintessential poetry than any other poem written within Bierce's lifetime. Neither of these statements is, as we can now see, as controversial as his contemporaries believed. It is a brute fact that American poetry, from the death of Longfellow in 1882 to the emergence of Edwin Arlington Robinson and Robert Frost in the 1920s, was at a particularly low ebb, so that to affirm in 1907 that George Sterling was America's finest living poet was to speak what could very well be the truth. Bierce's second comment is perhaps a bit of an exaggeration, as it seems to give short shrift to Swinburne (a clear influence on Sterling, at least in regard to diction) and the Pre-Raphaelites; but Bierce was not fond of these poets and genuinely believed Sterling to be their superior. Other parts of Bierce's essay—especially when he likens some portions of "A Wine of Wizardry" (notably the "blue-eyed vampire" lines) to celebrated passages in Coleridge and Keats—do indeed make one question whether his fondness for Sterling had gotten the better of his critical judgment.

But the furore over the poem was, as Bierce correctly saw, a product of two quite different elements: first, the fact that very few individuals of his day (and, sadly, of ours) had any true grasp of the essence of poetry, hence could not recognise it when they saw it; and, second, the fact that several of Bierce's enemies were waiting for an opportunity to pay him back in recompense for the abuse they had themselves received. Accordingly, a variety of hostile, jeering, or supercilious remarks about both Bierce and Sterling began appearing in the Hearst newspapers (notably the *San Francisco Examiner* and the *New York American*) and elsewhere. Bierce himself relished the fray: he recognised that his later journalistic work lacked the fire of his *Examiner* columns of the 1880s and 1890s, and he welcomed the chance to practise his polemical gifts again. The December 1907 *Cosmopolitan* published a fiery broadside, "An Insurrection of the Peasantry," in which Bierce took to task all the critics of Sterling and himself, in particular those (such as George Harvey, then editor of *Harper's Weekly*) who had written that "A Wine of Wizardry" had a kind of superfluity of poetic imagination—as if a poem could ever have too much!

Two years later, Sterling's *A Wine of Wizardry and Other Poems* appeared from A. M. Robertson. It contains many other fine works aside from its title poem, notably "Three Sonnets on Oblivion," with its emphasis on human transience, and poems on Edgar Allan Poe and Bierce himself, the latter of which was reprinted as a broadside by Walter Neale. *The House of Orchids* (1911) and *Beyond the Breakers* (1914) also have superb work: "The Black Vulture," one of Sterling's most reprinted poems and a grim portrayal of the all-destroying power of Death; "The Thirst of Satan," whose cosmic imagery is reminiscent of *The Testimony of the Suns*; and "The Ashes in the Sea," a delicate elegy on Nora May French (1881-1907), the young poet who committed suicide in November 1907 while staying at Sterling's cabin in Carmel.

Bierce—who had left San Francisco in late 1899 and moved to Washington, D.C., because of his health—returned to California for lengthy visits in 1910 and 1912, going with Sterling and some others to Yosemite and to the Grand Canyon (the latter trip inspiring Sterling's "To the Grand Cañon"); in the summer of 1911 he visited Sterling at Sag Harbor. But the two men were growing apart, and a final split occurred in early 1913. The causes for the end of their friendship are a matter of conjecture, since neither Bierce nor Sterling ever discussed them in any detail. We have only suggestive hints: Sterling's continued adherence to socialism (as well as his friendship with the fervent socialist Jack London, whom Bierce disdained) did not sit well with the increasingly conservative satirist; Sterling's involvements with married women (especially one Vera Connolly, about whom Sterling's wife Carrie wrote some poignant letters to Bierce in late 1911) were highly offensive to Bierce's strict sexual morality; and some of Sterling's later poems displayed sexual freedoms that Bierce did not feel worthy of inclusion in verse. Bierce, in any event, had apparently been systematically banishing a good many of his close colleagues from his attention as he made his plans to visit Mexico (ostensibly to witness the Mexican Civil War) in late 1913, so perhaps it is not surprising that the greatest of his poetic disciples would also be shown the door.

It was, however, in early 1911 that Sterling himself gained the opportunity to become a mentor of a young poetic disciple of his own; for it was then that Clark Ashton Smith, having just celebrated his eighteenth birthday, wrote his first letter to Sterling. Sterling had by this time largely taken over Bierce's function as literary leader of the West Coast, and—especially upon his moving to Carmel in 1905 as the vanguard of a literary colony there—had gathered a group of like-minded colleagues of his own: Jack London, Mary Austin, Harry Leon Wilson, Upton Sinclair, Nora May French, James Hopper, even (briefly) the young Sinclair Lewis. It was, then, natural that Smith—then living in Auburn in the Sierra foothills—should write to Sterling, although no doubt Smith had found much inspiration in Sterling's early "cosmic" verse. (Auburn, incidentally, is the subject of Bierce's tart satire, "The Perverted Village"—a product of Bierce's own habitation there for a brief time in 1884–85.)

Smith was not, however, entirely an unknown quantity. He had already published a few poems in 1910 in the *Overland Monthly*, a flagship publication on the West Coast, founded in 1868 by Bret Harte. Sterling remarked that the poems Smith sent to him were considerably "above the average of what comes to me from stranger and friend" and that "a bright future awaits you" (Sterling to Smith, 31 January 1911; *SU* 19). Only a few months later, Sterling took the "unwarranted liberty" (Sterling to Smith, 13 April 1911; *SU* 22) of quoting the entirety of

Smith's sonnet "The Last Night" in an interview he gave to the San Francisco weekly, *Town Talk*. Sterling, perhaps the finest sonneteer in American literature, could hardly fail to be struck by Smith's sudden mastery of this form.

Just a month later, however, Smith made this interesting comment:

> I've been trying my hand at some cosmic verse lately, and a month's work, and a lot of spoiled paper have led me to the conclusion that your "Testimony of the Suns" is about the last word in that line, and that the subject is too big for me to handle, anyway. I'd better stick to butterflies and roses, etc. . . . instead of trying to wipe out half the constellations (on paper) and put the rest askew. (Smith to Sterling, 21 May 1911; *SU* 25)

Smith was, of course, guilty of excessive humility, for one of the specimens he wrote at this time was "Ode to the Abyss." When Smith sent this poem to Sterling a month or two later, the latter responded ecstatically:

> I don't believe you're 18 years old! You're 35, and have been stuffing yourself for eight years on Hyperion, Prometheus Unbound, Paradise Lost and (I say it as shouldn't) The Testimony of the Suns. Your splendid "Ode to the Abyss" is fitted to rank, so far as quality goes, with the first three, and is better than the last. . . .
>
> Well, perhaps you are eighteen. Genius *happens*, as Whistler wrote. . . . I must, am forced to, against my own sense of literary caution, consider that this amazing ode of yours is the most remarkable example of youthful . . . genius in the history of literature. Pope and Keats are nowhere in comparison. (Sterling to Smith, 13 July 1911; *SU* 27)

Again, note carefully what Sterling is saying: he is not saying that Smith's poem is *better* than anything by Pope or Keats, but merely that the poem is a greater instance of *youthful* genius than anything in Pope or Keats. Sterling couldn't resist sending the poem to Bierce, who remarked a bit less enthusiastically but nevertheless with considerable approbation:

> Kindly convey to young Smith of Auburn my felicitations on his admirable "Ode to the Abyss"—a large theme, treated with dignity and power. It has many striking passages—such, for example, as "The Romes of ruined spheres." I'm conscious of my sin against the rhetoricians in liking that, for it jolts the reader out of the Abyss and back to earth. Moreover it is a

metaphor which belittles, instead of dignifying. But I like it. (Bierce to Sterling, 7 August 1911)

Sterling tried to get the poem published in a magazine, but evidently failed in the attempt.

Smith continued to send an array of his early poems to Sterling, all of which met with the latter's approval. Then, in November, on one of his few trips to San Francisco, Smith met A. M. Robertson, who invited him to submit some of his poems for possible book publication (see Smith to Sterling, 12 December 1911; *SU* 33). This is of some interest; for although Sterling would later work closely with Smith throughout 1912 in the preparation of *The Star-Treader and Other Poems*, the initial impetus came from Robertson without, evidently, any direct intervention by Sterling.

By the spring of 1912 proofs were being generated by Robertson, both Sterling and Smith going over them. Sterling paid tribute to the young poet by writing "The Coming Singer," which he explicitly stated was "suggested by *you*" (Sterling to Smith, 22 March 1912; *SU* 38). (Amusingly enough, Sterling later included this as one of the 100 sonnets he wrote to his lover, Mary Craig Kimbrough; they were published posthumously as *Sonnets to Craig* [1928].) Sterling even offered to pay Smith's fare to come to San Francisco (in part to meet Bierce), but for some reason Smith was unable to go, as he later admitted that he had never met Bierce.[2]

Then, in August 1912, several months before the appearance of *The Star-Treader*, another literary firestorm—somewhat reminiscent of the contretemps over "A Wine of Wizardry"—broke out. Articles on Smith appeared nearly simultaneously in several San Francisco newspapers, all proclaiming him a poetic child prodigy. One Boutwell Dunlap claimed credit for the discovery, but both Sterling and Smith were quick to point out that Dunlap only first heard of Smith by way of the Sterling

---

2. Smith to R. H. Barlow, 19 September 1933 (ms., John Hay Library, Brown University).

interview in *Town Talk* in April 1911. It was at this point that Bierce got into the act. He had been widely quoted as expressing extravagant praise of Smith, and he set the record straight in a letter to *Town Talk* dated 6 August 1912:

> Editor Town Talk, Sir:
>
> In a single day of last week all the daily newspapers of San Francisco published long eulogistic articles on the genius and work of young Clark Ashton Smith, the poet of Auburn. Some of them have repeated their raptures with further quotations from Mr. Smith's verses to justify the transports. That all these writers should be persuaded to see the light at once is obviously more than a coincidence, yet I think it does not imply the interested activity of a "press agent"—only the zeal of some fool friend more concerned for the glory of a discoverer than for the good of the discoveree. I call this "team work" and its instigation pretty "raw," and having myself a good opinion of Mr. Smith, his verses and his possibilities, am sorry to see him thrown to the lions of reaction from so many hands—one might almost say from several sides of the arena at once.
>
> In nearly all these eulogies I find myself credited with praises that I never uttered. One paper has me affirming Mr. Smith's "extraordinary genius," another "declaring" that his poems are "no way inferior to those of Keats," and so forth. These falsehoods have doubtless a common origin in the mind of the fool friend herein before mentioned but to me unknown.
>
> Several weeks ago I had from a correspondent a manuscript copy of Mr. Smith's "Ode to the Abyss." It seemed to me uncommonly good work and a promise of better work to come. So I commended it—in just what words I do not recollect, but if I said any of the things recently attributed to me I beg my correspondent to cover me with shame and confusion by quoting them from my letter—and filing the letter in proof.
>
> My correspondent is Mr. George Sterling.
> > Sincerely yours,
> > —Ambrose Bierce.[3]

On reading this letter, Smith concluded: "The old boy treated me pretty well, under the circumstances" (Smith to Sterling, 18 August 1912; *SU* 57).

The Star-Treader was widely reviewed upon its publication—even in

---

3. Letter to the Editor, *Town Talk* No. 1042 (10 August 1912): 10–11; rpt. in *SU* 288–89.

the august *New York Times Book Review*. On the whole the reviews were favourable, although several expressed impatience with the dominance of the "cosmic" motif Smith actually predicted this outcome: "The amount of work in my book descriptive of the death of suns and worlds, is, I confidently expect, the chief thing the critics are going to slam me for. . . . I'll get the reputation of being a sort of cosmic deca-dent—a sidereal Baudelaire" (Smith to Sterling, 11 September 1912; *SU* 62). Several years later—although by this time Smith's poetical palette had broadened considerably—Sterling issued the warning: "I'm hoping you'll turn to other themes before long. The Abyss obsesses you over-much" (Sterling to Smith, 6 March 1915; *SU* 119). Sterling had already noted, as early as 1912, that he himself would write no more such verse ("I have to say that I fear anything of any length I might write would be too much of an anticlimax to 'The Testimony of the Suns'" [Sterling to Smith, 11 February 1912; *SU* 36]), so his warning was understandable. But Smith responded with vigour:

> Why shouldn't the Abyss be the dominant theme of my work? Other poets have made their main work a series of expatiations on some central sub-ject, and no one has risen up to rebuke them for monotony or self-repetition. . . . However, it may be well to vary the images and symbols a bit, and I shall write less about the gulf for awhile. (Smith to Sterling, 11 March 1915; *SU* 120)

As early as 1913 Sterling also advised Smith "to 'go slow' on 'horror' poems, and see your best energies along the lines of sheer beauty" (Sterling to Smith, 19 August 1913; *SU* 94)—as if horror and beauty are somehow mutually exclusive in poetry!

Sterling kept after Smith for years to write a poem on Nora May French, but Smith continually refused because he did not feel comfortable writing "personal" poems of that sort. Finally, in the spring of 1916, he began the work, although it was not completed until the summer of 1920. Of course, Smith was not personally acquainted with French, but only knew of her from her work—the posthumously published *Poems* (1910)—and from Sterling's discussions of her; but the resultant poem is a remarkable distillation of her life and work, and Sterling reacted with emphatic approval.

By this time Smith had published a second volume—the slim *Odes and Sonnets* (1918), issued by the prestigious Book Club of California—and was working on a third, which he resolved to call *Ebony and Crystal.* He had also written a poem that easily eclipsed "A Wine of Wizardry" and even *The Testimony of the Suns* as an excursion into poetic fantasy—*The Hashish-Eater; or, The Apocalypse of Evil,* apparently begun in early 1920 (300 lines had been written by the end of January) and completed in March. Sterling responded with enthusiasm, but with some interesting caveats:

> "The Hashish-Eater" is indeed an amazing production. My friends will have none of it, claiming it reads like an extension of "A Wine of Wizardry." But I think there are many differences, and at any rate, it has more imagination in it than in any other poem I know of. Like the "Wine," it fails on the esthetic side, a thing that seems of small consequence in a poem of that nature. (Sterling to Smith, 10 June 1920; *SU* 183)

The perceptions of Sterling's unnamed "friends" seem to suggest a certain deficiency in critical acumen, at least where fantastic poetry is concerned, since the two poems have little in common aside from a plethora of bizarre imagery. And Sterling never explains that final remark as to why the poem is an aesthetic failure. Smith responded tactfully to Sterling's comments:

> I'm sorry that people think "The H. Eater" a mere extension of "A Wine of Wizardry". That's no mean compliment, however—"The Wine of Wizardry" has always seemed the ideal poem to me, as it did to Bierce. But the ground-plan of "The H. E." is really quite different. It owes nearly as much to "The Temptation of Saint Anthony" as to your poem. But few American critics will prove sufficiently well-read and perspicacious to notice the former debt. (Smith to Sterling, 10 July 1920; *SU* 184)

Sterling himself, of course, had not been idle in his own poetic work. *The Caged Eagle* (1916), *Thirty-five Sonnets* (1917), and *Sails and Mirage* (1921) had solidified his reputation, at least on the West Coast. He later regretted issuing a collection of war poems, *The Binding of the*

Beast (1917), but there are some worthy items even there. And, of course, there are his two scintillating poetic dramas, *Lilith* (1919) and *Rosamund* (1920), the former perhaps his greatest single work. Later poems show Sterling abandoning some of the stiff and archaic diction that had caused much of his early work to seem both antiquated and inauthentic to readers of the 1920s; such things as "To Life" (in which fantastic imagery underscores the horror and bitterness of existence), the superb atheistic sonnet "To Science," and "The Meteor," with its modified resurrection of cosmic motifs, show that Sterling's poetic vigour was undiminished. Although Henry Holt issued his *Selected Poems* in 1923 and Macmillan published a new edition of *Lilith* in 1926, with a preface by Theodore Dreiser, Sterling's poetic star was inevitably falling: his work was simply not in conformity with the imagistic, free-verse poetry of the Modernists, and he became increasingly embittered by his failure to gain national renown. Life for him had become an endless sequence of alcohol and women, as testified in a letter to H. L. Mencken: "I did more screwing and less drinking in 1925 than in 1924. Even at that I had over a thousand drinks" (6 January 1926; *From Baltimore to Bohemia* 224). It is scarcely a surprise that, when he found the effects of alcohol too onerous for his physique to bear, he took his own life in late 1926 by swallowing the vial of cyanide he always kept about him for that purpose.

Smith was devastated:

> I am desolate and heart-broken over the terrible news. George was easily the first of living American poets, and there is no one left now to carry on the classic tradition. His work, I feel sure, will outlive most of the verse that has been written in English since the beginning of this present century. Sooner or later, there is bound to be a reaction in favour of pure poetry.[4]

Smith went on in this letter to say that "I hope to write an elegy that will not be too unworthy of him," and he did just that the very next

---

4. Smith to James D. Phelan, 19 November 1926 (ms., Bancroft Library).

month in "George Sterling: A Valediction," one of several poems written to his mentor over the course of his life.

In a sense, though, Smith and Sterling had been growing apart in a manner somewhat similar to that of Sterling and Bierce. To be sure, there was no abrupt surcease of correspondence, which remained cordial to the end; but Sterling and Smith were, aesthetically, clearly proceeding in divergent directions. Sterling had little regard for Smith's artwork, believing it crude and a waste of his time. In 1923, in response to a love poem by Smith, Sterling remarked: "I'm glad to see you leaving behind the demonic, which you have done more justice to than any other poet, and turning to more important things, which include love" (Sterling to Smith, 20 August 1923; *SU* 235). Smith did not respond to this salvo, but things were very different when Sterling disparaged Smith's burgeoning efforts at prose fiction. In late 1925 Smith's "The Abominations of Yondo" exacted this response:

> All highbrows think the "Yondo" material outworn and childish. The daemoniac is done for, for the present, so far as our contemporaries go, and imagination must seek other fields. You have squeezed every drop from the weird (and what drops!) and should touch on it only infrequently, as I on the stars. (Sterling to Smith, 28 November 1925; *SU* 263)

Smith's response was forceful:

> I can't agree with the high-brows that the "weird" is dead—either in poetry or anywhere else. They're all suffering from mechanized imaginations. But I, for one, refuse to submit to the arid, earth-bound spirit of the time; and I think there is sure to be a romantic revival sooner or later—a revolt against mechanization and over-socialization, etc. If there isn't—then I hope to hell my next incarnation will be in some happier and freer planet. Neither the ethics or the aesthetics of the ant-hill have any attraction for me. (Smith to Sterling, 1 December 1925; *SU* 264)

Since 1922, Smith had been in touch with H. P. Lovecraft, and their mutual encouragement would result in fruitful work in prose fantasy for both writers. When Lovecraft himself died in 1937, Smith was inspired to write "To Howard Phillips Lovecraft," certainly the finest elegy Lovecraft ever received and one of the finest elegies in all literature.

After Sterling's death, however, Smith's devotion to poetry was only intermittent. He spent much time, sporadically, in translating Baudelaire's *Les Fleurs du mal*, but verse production fell off drastically during the 1930s, when most of his energies were directed toward the writing of more than a hundred short stories of fantasy and horror. *Ebony and Crystal* (1922) and *Sandalwood* (1925) had both been published at Smith's own expense (the latter funded by his own new disciple, Donald Wandrei) by his local paper, the *Auburn Journal*, and later volumes emerged only from specialty presses: *Nero and Other Poems* (1937) from the Futile Press; *The Dark Chateau* (1951) and *Spells and Philtres* (1958) from Arkham House; *The Hill of Dionysus* (1962) from Roy A. Squires. The enormous *Selected Poems*, prepared by Smith between 1944 and 1949, appeared from Arkham House only in 1971. Smith's poetry has never been issued by a major publisher, and as a result he has never been accorded the place he deserves as a major poet in twentieth-century American literature. And yet, his poetry, like his prose fiction, refuses to die, and its repeated reissuance even by small presses serves to keep it before the public eye.

The weird verse of Bierce, Sterling, and Smith seems to be receiving a modicum of renewed attention, at least in the small press. As long ago as 1980, Donald Sidney-Fryer edited an exemplary volume of Bierce's fantastic poetry, *A Vision of Doom*; more recently, I have assisted in the publication of the complete poetry of both Smith and Sterling. These multi-volume editions are perhaps difficult for the uninitiated to pore through, and a judicious selection might be helpful. When so much other poetry of the twentieth century—by turns blandly prosaic or tortuously obscure—has fallen into merited oblivion, perhaps the poetic work of Ambrose Bierce, George Sterling, and Clark Ashton Smith will emerge as a rare tonic for the sensitive view.

Works Cited

Bierce, Ambrose. *Collected Works.* Washington, DC: Neale, 1909–12. 12 vols.

———. *A Vision of Doom.* Ed. Donald Sidney-Fryer. West Kingston, RI: Donald M. Grant, 1980.

Mencken, H. L., and George Sterling. *From Baltimore to Bohemia: The Letters of H. L. Mencken and George Sterling.* Ed. S. T. Joshi. Rutherford, NJ: Fairleigh Dickinson University Press, 2001.

Smith, Clark Ashton. *Complete Poetry and Translations.* Ed. S. T. Joshi and David E. Schultz. New York: Hippocampus Press, 2007–08. 3 vols.

Sterling, George. *Complete Poetry.* Ed. S. T. Joshi and David E. Schultz. New York: Hippocampus Press, 2012. 3 vols.

Sterling, George, and Clark Ashton Smith. *The Shadow of the Unattained: The Letters of George Sterling and Clark Ashton Smith.* Ed. David E. Schultz and S. T. Joshi. New York: Hippocampus Press, 2005.

Gertrude Atherton: Death and Women

The long life of Gertrude Atherton (1857–1948) spans a significant portion of this country's history. Born four years before the onset of the Civil War and dying three years after the end of World War II, Atherton saw—and, in at least a modest way, helped to effect—the radical social, political, and cultural changes that transformed the United States from a raw, new nation of limited ambitions to a superpower whose influence spanned the globe. Although she was chiefly concerned, in her life and in her work, with changes in society and culture, she could not help but be affected by the multifarious developments that affected every aspect of American life.

Gertrude Horn was born on 30 October 1857, in San Francisco, the daughter of Thomas and Gertrude (Franklin) Horn. Thomas Horn was a well-to-do tobacco merchant, deemed a fitting husband for the daughter of Stephen Franklin, a domineering and wealthy farmer and landowner who had come to California in 1849 and summoned his family to join him two years later. Gertrude Horn's marriage, however, was an unhappy one, and she created a scandal by divorcing her husband in 1860. The young Gertrude and her mother went to live with grandfather Stephen in a ranch near San Jose. Much to young Gertrude's displeasure, her mother remarried in 1865, becoming the wife of a broker, John Frederick Uhlhorn. The child was raised largely by a nurse, Rose Stoddard, as her mother devoted much of her time to personal adornment and attending fashionable parties in San Francisco. Young Gertrude was an enthusiastic reader, absorbing all kinds of literature from *Jane Eyre* to the popular romantic novels of the day. Her formal education was conducted at various day schools and academies around San Francisco.

John Uhlhorn's business was not progressing well, and in 1870, after he was suspected in crooked business dealings, Stephen Franklin demanded that he leave the household, taking over the care of his daughter and granddaughter himself. Young Gertrude was put to the task of reading to him, thereby gaining a love for literary classics. In 1875, Franklin invited a young business associate, the twenty-four-year-old George Atherton, to court his daughter, even though she was fourteen years his senior. Atherton's family, however, as Catholics disapproved of any marriage he might conduct with a divorcée, but he solved the problem by becoming attracted to Franklin's eighteen-year-old granddaughter. George and Gertrude were married on 15 February 1876. That November, Gertrude's first child, George Goñi Atherton, was born, but he died of diphtheria in 1882. Gertrude, who professed an entire absence of the maternal instinct, had allowed the boy to be raised largely by his Chilean mother-in-law, Dominga. On 14 July 1878, Gertrude's second child, Muriel, was born.

The death of her son appears to have stimulated Atherton to a wholesale revaluation of her life. Exactly what is it that she wished to do with herself? She found the answer in an article in a San Francisco newspaper about a family tragedy. She immediately began fictionalising the article, producing her first novel, *The Randolphs of Redwoods*, in three months. The novel was serialised in a leading San Francisco weekly paper, the *Argonaut*, in 1883, but was never published in book form. A sensational family chronicle set in California, it was published anonymously, but her authorship quickly leaked out. A second novel was rejected by Houghton Mifflin, and later the manuscript was destroyed by rats as it lay in the attic. Atherton, already exhibiting the strength of character she would display her whole life, felt that she needed to move to San Francisco to be closer to social and literary contacts; her husband reluctantly followed. Some years later, George, at loose ends, decided to join the crew of the *Pilcomayo*, a ship that was sailing to Valparaiso, Chile. While on board he died of a kidney stone on 21 March 1887; his body was brought back to San Francisco in a barrel of rum.

Atherton was by this time relieved to be rid of a husband: the physical side of marriage never appealed to her, and she was not one to submit to the canons of wifely meekness accepted in the Victorian era. Her work reflected her social radicalism: *Hermia Suydam* (1889) created a scandal in its depiction of a woman who has an extramarital affair. Atherton was by this time writing prolifically, although her work was not meeting with uniform approval in the centres of American culture on the East Coast. She was, however, becoming well-travelled, visiting London in 1889 and making frequent trips to New York and other locales on the Atlantic seaboard. Although she professed an occasional boredom with California, she nonetheless produced an effective series of stories about early California life, published as *Before the Gringo Came* (1894). Some of the stories in her chief collection of weird tales, *The Bell in the Fog and Other Stories* (1905), were inspired by trips she took to fashionable watering-holes on the East Coast, as Joseph Pulitzer had commissioned her to write articles on high society for the *New York World*. Throughout the 1890s she travelled widely—to the Chicago World's Fair in 1893, the north of England (where she visited Brontë sites in Yorkshire), Brittany and other locales in France, and the like. And yet, perhaps the best novel she ever wrote was an evocation of her native land, *The Californians* (1898).

During her visits to England she had met William Sharp and other literary figures, including Henry James. She received permission from James to dedicate *The Bell in the Fog* to him, and his influence is also manifest in the novel *American Wives and English Husbands* (1898). Returning to the United States in 1899, she wrote a fiery political novel, *Senator North* (1900), the product of much time spent in Washington, D.C. She went to Cuba (then a U.S. protectorate) to research another book, but it was never written. By this time she had become fascinated with the figure of Alexander Hamilton, who embodied her ideal of a strong, determined, Nietzschean superman; her historical novel focusing on him, *The Conqueror* (1902), was an immense bestseller and remained in print for decades.

Atherton was living in San Francisco at the time of the earthquake and fire of April 1906, and she wrote several poignant accounts of the destruction of her native city. But she still spent much time overseas—chiefly in Munich and London—although she now began to write somewhat less frenetically. Throughout her career she was criticised for writing too much and too hastily, and although her books frequently outsold the work of other such women writers as Edith Wharton and Willa Cather, she expressed resentment at being considered their literary inferior.

In 1910 she went to London to do research on a feminist play about woman suffrage, designed for the actress Minnie Maddern Fiske. She met the radical suffragettes Emmeline Pankhurst and her daughters Christabel and Sylvia, who were using violent means to advocate the cause of woman suffrage. The play that she subsequently wrote, *Julia France,* was a disaster (it had only one performance in Toronto before closing down), and the text of the play was lost and never published; but the novel that she produced shortly thereafter, *Julia France and Her Times* (1912), marked Atherton as a leading feminist. She would later write many articles on the subject, some of them evoking tremendous controversy; some were collected in a late volume, *Can Women Be Gentlemen?* (1938).

Like many Americans, Atherton was not notably concerned with the outbreak of World War I, but the sinking of the *Lusitania* in 1915 caused her to embrace the cause of the Allies and turn violently anti-German. In 1916 she covered aspects of the war in France for the *Delineator* and the *New York Times*; she would later write a war novel, *The White Morning* (1918), combining her loathing of Germany with feminism. She did valiant work in raising money for French hospitals, for which she eventually received the Legion of Honour from the French government.

After the war, she was invited by producer Samuel Goldwyn to write for the movies, but in her two-year stint in Hollywood she wrote only one screenplay. By this time Atherton, well past sixty, was feeling sluggish and mentally enervated. She then read of a radical rejuvenation technique being advocated by Dr. Eugen Steinach. Atherton went to New York to see Steinach's colleague, Dr. Harry Benjamin. The technique involved directing low-level X-rays at a woman's ovaries to stimulate hormone production, and Atherton underwent the treatment. She later claimed that it gave her an entirely new lease on life, both mentally and physically, although the Steinach treatment was later discredited. In short order Atherton produced a novel, *Black Oxen* (1923), that lightly fictionalised this entire series of events, portraying a woman who leaves the United States and comes back years later disguised as her own daughter. *Black Oxen* was a bestseller, but in interviews Atherton denied that she was the model for the central character.

In the later 1920s, as a result of discussions with an occultist, Cora Potter, Atherton appears to have become half convinced that she was the reincarnation of Aspasia, the strong-willed Greek woman who was the consort of Pericles in the Athens of the fifth century B.C.E. Under this influence she wrote several historical novels of ancient Greece, including *The Immortal Marriage* (1927), about Pericles and Aspasia. By this time Atherton's globe-trotting days were largely over, and she had settled in San Francisco, her daughter Muriel taking care of her. She did manage to get to Paris in 1925, where she met another strong-willed woman writer, Gertrude Stein. Each despised the other's writings, but they found each other pleasing companions. Later, in 1935, when Stein was giving a lecture tour in America, she asked Atherton to arrange many of the details of her speaking engagements in California.

Atherton remained vigorous to the end. Her autobiography, *Adventures of a Novelist* (1932), was praised for its affecting portraits of such associates as Ambrose Bierce (whom she had first met in 1891), James D. Phelan (mayor of San Francisco and later senator from California, whom she had met in 1902 and whose death in 1930 was a great blow to her), and others. She produced a final collection of short stories, *The Foghorn* (1934), consisting of three shorter tales and one novella. In her later years she was the recipient of many honours, including honorary degrees from the University of California and Mills College and election to the National Institute of Arts and Letters. Her last book, published when she was almost ninety, was *My San Francisco: A Wayward Biography* (1946). Gertrude Atherton died on 14 June 1948.

Atherton's prodigious literary output—thirty-eight novels, three short story collections, an autobiography, and several other works of nonfiction—has now been largely forgotten, but unjustly so. To be sure, she wrote too much and not always with scrupulous care, and to some extent she followed popular fashion and sought to capitalise on deliberately controversial topics and points of view. But as the most popular American woman novelist of her period she deserves at least some consideration by literary historians; her role in advancing the cause of feminism has yet to be adequately chronicled; and her novels and tales about California make her a regional writer of significance. And yet, her relatively small output of weird fiction may in some senses represent one of the leading justifications for her continuing regard, as its invariably fine craftsmanship and emotive power has the potential to endure long after her lengthy novels on the passing trends of the day have lapsed into oblivion. It is these tales, inspired in part by her association with such masters of the form as Ambrose Bierce and Henry James, that we will now consider in greater detail.

In a scant nine stories, Gertrude Atherton has effectively displayed mastery in several of the significant subdivisions of the weird tale: the fantastic allegory or parable ("The Caves of Death," "When the Devil Was Well"), the psychological horror tale ("A Tragedy," "The Greatest Good of the Greatest Number"), the orthodox ghost story ("Miss Markham's Wedding Night"), the tale of supernatural realism ("The Striding Place"), the ambiguous horror tale ("Death and the Woman," perhaps "The Bell in the Fog"), or sundry combinations of these. Her apparently casual tossing off of these stories in the course of a career devoted to very different concerns points to the truth of her own comment in "The Bell in the Fog": "Possibly there are few imaginative writers who have not a leaning, secret or avowed, to the occult."[1]

One of the central concerns in Atherton's weird work is the awesome threshold of death. At least three of the stories utilise this topos in varying ways. The conception may have had an autobiographical significance. The death of her grandmother, Eliza Franklin, in 1865, when Atherton was eight years old, apparently traumatised her. Her biographer Emily Wortis Leider tells of her reactions, quoting from her autobiography, *Adventures of a Novelist*:

> Little Gertrude not only attended the funeral but was forced to kiss her dead grandmother in her coffin. "The faint smell of corruption mingled with tube roses" (*Adventures*, p. 13) lingered in her nostrils, tormenting her; she felt it would never leave, and she never lost her horror of dead bodies. As an adult she managed to be absent from the funerals of most of the important people in her life. (Leider 26)

Much later, she read Ambrose Bierce's story "A Watcher by the Dead" (first published in the *San Francisco Examiner* for 29 December 1889, and gathered in Bierce's landmark story collection *Tales of Soldiers and Civilians* [1891]), which is nothing more than an account of a man, Jarette, who, on a dare from a Dr. Helberson, is locked in a morgue with a recently deceased corpse and goes mad when the corpse appears to come to life (in fact, the "corpse" was a friend of Dr. Helberson who

---

1. H. P. Lovecraft echoes this point in his treatise "Supernatural Horror in Literature" (1927): ". . . no one need wonder at the existence of a literature of cosmic fear. It has always existed, and always will exist; and no better evidence of its tenacious vigour can be cited than the impulse which now and then drives writers of totally opposite leanings to try their hands at it in isolated tales, as if to discharge from their minds certain phantasmal shapes which would otherwise haunt them." *The Annotated Supernatural Horror in Literature*, ed. S. T. Joshi (New York: Hippocampus Press, 2nd ed. 2012), 27. That last comment is surely meant in whimsy.

hoped to give Jarette a scare). Atherton, who apparently read the story in the *Examiner*, wrote to Bierce: "That is the one thing I hate you for. It kept me awake for a week, and I have been afraid to sleep alone ever since. This is not intended as a subtle and skillful compliment, but as an honest and feminine appeal" (Leider 115). One hesitates, in delicacy, to bring up the fact that her own husband's body was brought back in a barrel of rum, although there is no suggestion that she was similarly traumatised by the sight of it.

"The Caves of Death" (first published in the *San Francisco News Letter* for 25 December 1886, and a previously unknown and unreprinted work by Atherton)[2] is a manifest allegory of the afterlife. It should be emphasised that the tale does not necessarily affirm Atherton's belief in an afterlife: firstly, the story suggests that the narrator's vision of the afterlife is a dream (even though the opening sentence states that the narrator has woken suddenly from sleep), and secondly, Atherton herself frequently expressed beliefs ranging from agnosticism to actual atheism. In this tale she has used the dream or vision of an afterlife as a means for the expression of a number of cynical reflections on human foibles, for it is evident that those who have gone to the Great Beyond are afflicted with the same follies, hypocrisies, and vanities that they carried in life.

The other allegory in Atherton's work, "When the Devil Was Well," was included as the final story in her volume of California tales, *Before the Gringo Came* (1894). It too is highly cynical in its suggestion that the Devil will find in California a ready haven for his machinations. Whether there is an anti-Catholic bias in this account of a priest who yields readily to the temptations of the flesh is difficult to determine: Atherton did express occasional impatience with the fervent religiosity of her Catholic mother-in-law, Dominga, but she appears to

---

2. The work is not listed in Leider nor in Charlotte S. McClure's bibliography. I reprinted it in my anthology, *Great Tales of Terror* (Mineola, NY: Dover, 2002).

be making a broader point that all human beings are subject to moral weakness, whatever their outward tokens of uprightness.

"Death and the Woman" (first published in the London *Vanity Fair,* 14 January 1893) presents a straightforward expression of the fear of death, embodied here both by the dying man and the apparent presence of the actual figure of Death at the end. Is this latter merely a metaphor? Does the wife, increasingly agitated by the trickling away of life from her husband, merely hallucinate the presence of Death coming up the stairs and into the death-chamber? Atherton wisely leaves the matter unresolved, rendering this an ambiguous horror tale, where it cannot be decided whether the supernatural has come into play or not. Henry James was a master of this form: Atherton had very likely read several of his ghost stories—stretching back to his earliest specimens, dating to 1868—and learned from them.

"The Greatest Good of the Greatest Number" (first published in *The Bell in the Fog*), the third of Atherton's stories focusing specifically on death, is a very different proposition. The very title speaks of its philosophical underpinnings, pointing to the central principle of the utilitarian moral philosophy as outlined by Jeremy Bentham and John Stuart Mill. Of course, these philosophers would by no means have advocated the withholding of medical attention from the sick, as Atherton's physician does here: his ultimate decision that the death of the ailing woman will benefit several others in her circle, whereas her continued existence will only create a continuation or augmentation of misery, is in some senses a reflection of a Social Darwinist mentality that Atherton had adopted early in life and retained to the end. For Atherton, only those who are "fit" to live deserve to live; and clearly the morphine-riddled woman at the centre of the tale is not one of these. As Atherton wrote in her late collection of essays, *Can Women Be Gentlemen?* (1938):

> Immense numbers of the human race, blind victims of indifferent Na-
> ture, are far less intelligent than dogs and cats; they are of no use in the
> world, add nothing, give nothing, and those who are of use work their

brains dry or until their fingers ossify, and then die prematurely of heart disease, in order that the superfluous may live. (107)

The physician in "The Greatest Good of the Greatest Number" is not about to let one of these "superfluous" people live on; although momentarily weakened by thoughts of his invalid mother, he soon regains his resolve and crushes the needle that would have saved the addict's life.

The power of this tale rests not in its display of the supernatural— for there is no supernatural phenomenon—but in its careful dissection of psychological states, both that of the physician and that of the dying woman. Atherton's masterpiece in this regard is a previously unknown and uncollected story, "A Tragedy," first published in the London *Vanity Fair* for 11 February 1893. This extraordinary account of a woman who is, at the outset, ignorant of the fact that she has been housed in an insane asylum for decades was later rewritten—not necessarily with greater effectiveness—in the long story "The Foghorn" (first published in *Good Housekeeping*, November 1933), the opening tale of Atherton's late collection, *The Foghorn* (1934). The secret of the tale's effectiveness is the gradual manner in which the woman—and, accordingly, the reader—comes to be aware that she has woken not merely from a single night's sleep, but from decades of amnesia or madness. And because she "was a woman who revelled in her beauty, worshipped it" (as Atherton's own mother and, perhaps, Atherton herself did), the revelation of her true state is manifested largely by physical tokens: the fact that her hair has been cut ("That glorious mane, of which she had been so proud!"), the fact that her once-beautiful hands had become "large-veined [and] skinny"; and so forth. It is particularly ironic, given her own physical repulsiveness, that the man "who had sent her here" (presumably by jilting her) was himself "a wonderfully preserved man; sixty, probably, but looking more than forty." To some degree Atherton may be guilty of an antifeminist concentration on physical beauty and its decay; but in reality the tale underscores the "tragedy" of a wasted life in which twenty years have passed as if in a single night.

Skilful as several of these tales are, Atherton's signature piece of weird fiction remains "The Striding Place"; it has appeared in more than a half-dozen anthologies of supernatural tales and is the tale by which she is chiefly recognised by devotees of the genre. The story had been rejected by the *Yellow Book* as too gruesome (Leider 156) and was published in the *Speaker* for 20 June 1896, under the title "The Twins." As a tale of purely physical horror, in which the grisly climax is suddenly revealed in the final line, it is difficult to surpass. It underscores the peculiarly philosophical nature of the weird tale in that it is exemplifies the "truth" of a casual utterance made by Gifford ("I cherish the theory . . . that the soul sometimes lingers in the body after death"), who little knows that he himself will verify that utterance at the end. One of the chief distinguishing features of supernatural, as opposed to mimetic, fiction is its ability to refashion the universe in accordance with the philosophical views of the author: in a tale purporting to be realistic, a comment like Gifford's would carry little significance; but in a weird tale that utterance can be made "real" in the most emphatic way.

Considerably more conventional is "Miss Markham's Wedding Night," another uncollected and previously undiscovered story that appeared in the London *Vanity Fair* for 28 November 1895. A relatively straightforward ghost story, it begins as a light-hearted social comedy but quickly turns darker. The concluding dialogue between Miss Markham and Carter Lee, a Southerner who had attracted her but who died suddenly, again reveals Atherton's Social Darwinist tendencies: Lee himself states that his death constitutes "a waste of good material," and he urges Miss Markham to carry on his work in his name. The title thereby becomes something of an irony, for the "wedding" that Miss Markham has experienced is her decision, at Lee's urging, not to marry anyone else for the whole of her life but instead to retain both intellectual and emotional devotion to a ghost.

"The Dead and the Countess" (first published in the *Smart Set* for August 1902) appears, at the outset, rather quaintly allegorical, as we are led to believe that the dead spirits in a cemetery in Brittany find their re-pose disturbed by the rumbling of a new train line—a charming conceit expressing protest at the ruin of a pristine natural landscape by techno-logical development. But although the train itself ("a brute of iron and live coals and foul smoke") in some senses suggests the fires of hell, the tale resolves into an uneasy mix of allegory and supernatural realism.

"The Bell in the Fog" (first published in *The Bell in the Fog*) could qualify as an ambiguous horror tale: we can never be quite certain that the little girl at the centre of the narrative is or is not a reincarnation of the girl depicted in the painting found in the portrait gallery at Chillingsworth. But the chief focus of the tale is on the psychology of Ralph Orth, who is manifestly a Henry James stand-in: he is an American who left the United States "soon after his first successes," who focuses on portrayals of European society, and who remains single and unattached. Atherton's passing comment about "his own famous ghost stories" makes one realise that she has read them with care.

This story in particular reflects the degree to which Atherton was affected by her physical surroundings. The England of "The Striding Place" and "The Bell in the Fog," the Brittany of "The Dead and the Countess," and the California of "When the Devil Was Well" are depicted with the crisp realism of first-hand experience, as Atherton put her far-flung travels to good use. We have seen that the stories in *The Bell in the Fog* were a byproduct of her reporting of fashionable sites on the Eastern Seaboard, and her portrayal of high society rings true in "Miss Markham's Wedding Night." Much of Atherton's work is an intimate outgrowth of her life as a globe-trotting woman writer at the turn of the twentieth century, and her horror tales, for all their departures from mundane realism, echo her travels and experiences no less than her mainstream fiction.

One other story by Atherton should be addressed, if only because of its title. *A Christmas Witch*, a nearly novel-length work of about 40,000 words published in *Godey's Magazine* for January 1893, suggests the supernatural in a number of features, but resolves itself into a non-supernatural *Bildungsroman* of an unruly and headstrong girl (clearly based on Atherton herself as she remembered her own childhood and upbringing), the daughter of a French count who has come to California to seek his fortune. At one point she and her father return to their chateau in France, and the girl, Heloise, becomes fascinated with an ancestor, a girl named Noël, who killed all the members of her family one night. Although the tale is full of hints of werewolves, ghosts, and the like (and even a suggestion that Heloise is the reincarnation of Noël), nothing genuinely supernatural occurs. Perhaps its most memorable feature is a delightful portrait of Ambrose Bierce, disguised as a curmudgeonly recluse whom Heloise comes upon in the California foothills. Another story, "The Eternal Now," included in *The Foghorn*, is a curious tale apparently involving a man who, fascinated with fourteenth-century France, somehow goes back in time to that era, but with faint recollections of his life in the twentieth century.

Atherton's weird work has been largely ignored even by critics and biographers favourable to her other work. Charlotte S. McClure, in her critical study *Gertrude Atherton* (1979), merely takes note of "The Bell in the Fog" and its portrayal of Henry James, remarking dismissively of her two early short story collections, *Before the Gringo Came* and *The Bell in the Fog*: "Neither collection added to her development as a writer" (*Gertrude Atherton* 77). In a much more sensitive, albeit very brief, analysis of Atherton's ghostly work, Jack G. Voller, noting that Atherton's weird work has been largely neglected, observes: "What is most striking about such neglect is that Atherton is clearly working quite adeptly in the psychological strain of the supernaturalist tale" (21). In sum, it can be stated unequivocally that Atherton's relatively small corpus of weird fiction, influenced only in part by Bierce and James, stands as a substantial contribution to both the supernatural and the psychological horror literature of its time. But whatever their value in literary history, the greatest virtues of these stories—forceful conceptions worked out with meticulous craftsmanship, a prose of impressive suppleness, strength, and grace, an attention to fine nuances of character, and an almost Poe-like focus on abnormal or disturbed psychological states—render them pleasurable on first reading and rewarding on multiple rereadings. The great majority of Atherton's literary work, like that of all but the most eminent of her contemporaries, has been largely forgotten, but her weird tales have the potential to survive by both the power of their ideas and the subtlety of their execution.

Works Cited

Atherton, Gertrude. *Can Women Be Gentlemen?* Boston: Houghton Mifflin, 1938.

Leider, Emily Wortis. *California's Daughter: Gertrude Atherton and Her Times.* Stanford: Stanford University Press, 1991.

McClure, Charlotte S. "A Checklist of the Writings of and about Gertrude Atherton." *American Literary Realism* 9 (Spring 1976): 102–41.

———. *Gertrude Atherton.* New York: Twayne, 1979.

Voller, Jack G. "Gertrude Atherton." In *Gothic Writers*, ed. Douglass H. Thomson, Jack G. Voller, and Frederick S. Frank. Westport, CT: Greenwood Press, 2002. 20–23.

Bram Stoker: *Dracula* and Others

Bram Stoker would have been astounded that his novel *Dracula* would become the prototype of the vampire myth and the source for more adaptations—in film, theatre, television, and other media—than almost any other work in literary history. For much of his life, Stoker did not even consider himself primarily a literary man; instead, he snatched the time to write his dozen novels and a handful of short stories in the midst of a career of a very different sort.

Abraham Stoker was born on 8 November 1847, in Clontarf, a coastal town near Dublin, the third of seven children of Abraham and Charlotte Stoker, a well-connected Protestant Irish family. An unspecified childhood illness prevented him from walking unassisted until the age of seven, but thereafter he became known for his strength and vigour. Entering Trinity College, Dublin, in 1863, he excelled at a variety of sports and also developed a taste for the theatre. This latter interest impelled him, upon his graduation from Trinity with a bachelor's and master's degree in 1871, to accept an unpaid position as drama critic for the Dublin *Daily Mail*. He had followed his father's footsteps by obtaining a civil service job in the Irish government, but it was his role as drama critic that would transform his life irrevocably. He had first seen the celebrated stage actor Henry Irving as early as 1867, but when he saw him again in a performance of *Hamlet* in Dublin in December 1876, Stoker was captivated anew. Invited to dinner with Irving, Stoker fell entirely under his sway. The friendship ripened, and in November 1878 Stoker agreed to become Irving's business manager and personal secretary; over the next thirty-five years he would write half a million letters on Irving's behalf.

Changes were in the offing in Stoker's personal life also. On 4 December 1878, Stoker married Florence Balcombe, a young Irishwoman eleven years his junior, and whose chief claim to fame was to have inspired a long-term infatuation by Oscar Wilde. On the last day of 1879 their only child, Noel, was born. But Stoker's wife and child took a decided back seat to the affairs of the Lyceum, the London theatre where Irving and his company performed. Their widely publicised after-theatre dinners in what came to be called the Beefsteak Room attracted the cream of the British intellectual and political elite, from Wilde to W. S. Gilbert to William Ewart Gladstone to Hall Caine, a popular novelist of the day who became a close friend of Stoker and, under the nickname "Hommy-Beg," received the dedication of *Dracula*.

Although Stoker had published a few short stories in the early 1870s, his work for Irving monopolised a substantial proportion of his time; and there is some evidence that Irving did not fully return the devotion and trust that Stoker bestowed upon his idol. The Lyceum company toured the United States for four seasons during the years 1883–88, during which time Stoker met another of his idols, the ageing Walt Whitman. His first novel, *The Snake's Pass*, a romantic tale about Ireland, was published in 1890, the very year he conceived and began work on *Dracula*. Whereas most of his other works were written with some rapidity, in the fleeting moments when work for Irving could be put aside, Stoker spent a full six or seven years crafting his most famous novel.

But *Dracula* was not a commercial success. Although receiving generally positive reviews, it sold poorly, and, surprisingly, there was no American edition to match the British edition published by Constable. In a few years the book had fallen out of print and would not be reissued until 1901. Although Stoker himself prepared a hasty dramatic version, chiefly to protect his copyright for such an adaptation, no actual drama of *Dracula* appeared until after his death. Stoker had every reason to believe that his years-long effort in researching and writing the novel had been wasted.

Dracula has spawned not only countless adaptations but a cottage industry tracing its sources and influences. By all accounts it is his most autobiographical novel; as his most recent biographer, Barbara Belford, has noted, "He dumped the signposts of his life into a supernatural cauldron and called it *Dracula*" (256). Something so trivial as the name of the hapless solicitor Jonathan Harker has been traced to one Joseph Harker, a scene painter at the Lyceum. In Harker's wife, Mina, the prototype of the pure, virginal, deferential woman whom Stoker manifestly saw as the ideal for the female sex, we perhaps see some features of the personality of the famous actress Ellen Terry, who frequently shared the stage with Henry Irving and became one of Stoker's closest friends. In the more disturbing character of Lucy Westenra, who appears willing to bestow her feminine charms upon a succession of willing suitors, we may perhaps see a dim echo of Stoker's vision of his own wife, Florence, who had dallied with Oscar Wilde before agreeing to link her fate with another Irishman. The American adventurer Quincey Morris no doubt derives from the numerous colourful figures Stoker met during his American tours of the 1880s—perhaps he was thinking specifically of Buffalo Bill Cody, with whom he shared a stage in 1886. As for Abraham Van Helsing, the valiant Dutch psychic detective who finally defeats the vampire, his first name echoes that of Stoker's own father, as is fitting for this benevolent father-figure. And in Dracula himself it is difficult not to see the figure of Henry Irving, whose roles as Hamlet and Macbeth showed him a master of the forbidding hero-villain.

Literary and historical sources for *Dracula* also seem to abound. The pioneering research of Radu Florescu and Raymond McNally has identified the historical Dracula as Vlad Tepes, the fifteenth-century Hungarian tyrant whose ruthless campaigns against the Turks caused him to be known as Vlad the Impaler. Vlad, of course, was not a vampire, nor was even rumoured to be a vampire, but he became one significant component of a manifestly composite picture. Stoker found the name Dracula in William Wilkinson's *An Account of the Principalities of Wallachia and Moldavia*: "Dracula in the Wallachian language means Devil. Wallachians were accustomed to give it as a surname to any person who rendered himself conspicuous by courage, cruel actions or cunning" (cited in Belford 222). A book by Stoker's brother George, *With the Unspeakables; or, Two Years' Campaigning in European and Asiatic Turkey*, provided the background for the Transylvanian setting of *Dracula*'s opening chapters. The numerous parallels between *Dracula* and Shakespeare's *Macbeth* (staged at the Lyceum in 1888-89) are noteworthy, chief among them the three female vampires in Dracula's Transylvania castle, echoing the three "weird sisters" in Shakespeare. Count Dracula's frequent use of hypnotism may owe something to the celebrated character Svengali in George du Maurier's novel *Trilby* (1894). As for previous vampire literature itself, Stoker took at least a few hints from a number of his predecessors, whether it be such potboilers as James Malcolm Rymer's *Varney the Vampire; or, The Feast of Blood* (1847) or more artistic works such as John William Polidori's *The Vampyre* (1819) or Joseph Sheridan Le Fanu's novella "Carmilla" (1872), a distinctive treatment of a female vampire, with strong suggestions of lesbianism. Indeed, it is believed that Stoker omitted an early chapter of *Dracula* out of respect for Le Fanu; titled "Dracula's Guest," it later served as the lead story in the posthumous collection *Dracula's Guest and Other Weird Stories* (1914).

But *Dracula* is far more than the sum of its sources and influences. From the opening pages in Transylvania to its conclusion at Dracula's British abode, Carfax, the chilling figure of the seemingly omnipotent vampire hovers over the entire novel, even though he is offstage for much of it. Stoker's chief accomplishment was in codifying what Les Daniels, in *Living in Fear: A History of Horror in the Mass Media* (1975), piquantly referred to as the "care and feeding of vampires." Daniels proceeds to outline Dracula's characteristics:

> Unlike most of the vampires described in the purportedly factual manuscripts of olden days, Dracula can transform himself into a mist, a wolf, or a bat. He has a marked aversion for symbols of Christianity and a chauvinistic fondness for female victims. Other debatable points include Stok-

er's declaration that this cursed condition is contagious and that the proper cure is a wooden stake through the monster's heart (vampires were most
commonly burned by those who believed in them). At any rate, Stoker's
deviations from tradition were dramatically sound, and they helped ensure
his book's success. (63)

The most controverted point concerns Dracula's ability to walk about
in daylight. Van Helsing, in his lecture on vampires in chapter 18 of
the novel, states ambiguously that "His power ceases, as does that of all
evil things, at the coming of the day" (264)—a remark that may perhaps
express more of a hope than a reality. (In *The Lady of the Shroud* a
character notes that "the Vampire is, according to the theory, free to
move at will" [89] only at night.) In fact, Dracula is seen toward the end
of the novel in broad daylight, and it was only the film *Nosferatu* (1922)
that definitively depicted the vampire as shunning the sun.

In hindsight, the sexual overtones of *Dracula* seem to us
unmistakable; and yet, contemporary readers and reviewers—who only a
few years earlier had expressed outrage at the seeming sexual perversion
hinted at in Arthur Machen's *The Great God Pan* (1894)—appear to
have overlooked it. Stoker's horror of unconventional sexuality
manifests itself on several levels: the perceived threat of sexually
aggressive women is seen in the attempt of the three female vampires to
seduce Jonathan Harker in the depths of Dracula's castle, and also in
the fate of Lucy Westenra, who is punished for her suggestions of
sexual dalliance by becoming a vampire herself and suffering a hideous
perversion of a bride's deflowering when she is staked through the
heart by her fiancée, Lord Godalming. Perhaps the most dramatic
scene in *Dracula*, from this perspective, is Dracula's seduction of Mina
at the very time she is sharing a bed with her new husband, Jonathan,
as he forces her to suck blood from his own breast—a transparent
metaphor both for oral sex and for the Victorian male's ever-present
fear of female infidelity.

But it would be unfair to see *Dracula* as the only novel of Stoker's
that merits our attention. Although he followed it up with a mediocre

romance, *Miss Betty* (1898), he then produced the able witchcraft novel *The Mystery of the Sea* (1902) and the even more impressive tale of Egyptian horror, *The Jewel of Seven Stars* (1903). *The Mystery of the Sea*, set in Cruden Bay and lovingly described in its opening pages, presents us with the vivid picture of the witch Gormola MacNeill, while *The Jewel of Seven Stars* ranks second only to *Dracula* as Stoker's most compelling novel. Like that work, it is a supernatural detective story, with elements of the locked-room mystery. No doubt Stoker had read the early Sherlock Holmes tales by Sir Arthur Conan Doyle to good effect as they appeared in the *Strand Magazine* in the 1890s. Like Holmes in a similar situation, a character in *The Jewel of Seven Stars*, Dr. Winchester, makes the momentous pronouncement: "I have exhausted all human and natural possibilities of the case, and am beginning to fall back on superhuman and supernatural possibilities" (127). There is even a quasi-science-fictional element, in that the jewel of the title has been extracted from an aerolite. Like many later Victorians, Stoker saw in the radical advances of science during his time a means to defeat superstition once and for all. Van Helsing and his band use every scientific means at their disposal to combat the overwhelming power of the vampire, and the Egyptologist Abel Trelawny suggests something similar when he ponders the possibility that the ancient Egyptians might have known and used the properties of radium. His so-called Great Experiment—the magical resurrection of the mummified pharaoh-queen—constitutes some of the most awe-filled pages in Stoker's entire output.

Henry Irving died, fittingly, the very night after he triumphantly performed the lead role in Tennyson's play *Becket*, on 13 October 1905. Stoker spent the next several months writing the reverential memoir, *Personal Memories of Henry Irving* (1906). In the year that book was published, he suffered a stroke and was thereafter compelled to write with a magnifying glass. Nevertheless, now freed at last from being merely an appendage to a great man, Stoker determined to pursue a full-time literary career at last—a decision forced upon him by his increasing need for revenue. Aside from writing a substantial quantity of journalism, he generated two late novels, *The Lady of the Shroud* (1909) and *The Lair of the White Worm* (1911). The former, although tantalising in its suggestion that the strange female visitor who repeatedly visits Rupert Sent Leger at his castle in a fictitious eastern European country may be a vampire, proves to be an adventure novel with political overtones. Like *Dracula,* it is written in a documentary style, with letters, diaries, and other manuscripts designed to enhance verisimilitude and immediacy of effect. *The Lair of the White Worm* was written in a scant three months in 1911, but its rapidity of composition should not lead us to devalue it; in fact, it can take its place with *Dracula* and *The Jewel of Seven Stars* as the third of Stoker's supernatural triumphs. Like those novels, it is a supernatural detective story, and Stoker is careful to lay the clues that allow us to identify the sinister Lady Arabella March as something very different from the refined aristocrat she claims to be.

Bram Stoker died on 20 April 1912, five days after the *Titanic* disaster. The story of his widow Florence's jealous guarding of his literary properties—in particular, her lawsuit against F. W. Murnau, whose masterful film *Nosferatu* (1922) was loosely based on *Dracula,* forcing the film to be withdrawn from circulation and not seen for decades—is well known. She did permit dramatic adaptations of *Dracula* by Hamilton Deane (1924) and John Balderston (1930), the latter of which was famously adapted for the 1931 film starring Bela Lugosi. That the figure of Dracula—whether it be the somewhat stiff villain of Lugosi's portrayal or the suave seducer in Frank Langella's rendition—has become so universal a symbol of both the attraction and the repulsion of the supernatural hero is a testament to the learning and the creativity of its creator, Bram Stoker, whose decades in the theatre taught him how to mould a charismatic and dynamic figure who can captivate audiences on paper, on the boards, and in celluloid.

Works Cited

Belford, Barbara. *Bram Stoker: A Biography of the Author of* Dracula. New York: Knopf, 1996.

Daniels, Les. *Living in Fear: A History of Horror in the Mass Media.* New York: Scribner's, 1975.

Stoker, Bram. *Dracula.* 1897. New York: Modern Library, n.d.

———. *The Jewel of Seven Stars.* 1903. New York: Harper & Brothers, 1904.

———. *The Lady of the Shroud.* 1909. London: Egoist Press, 2014.

Mary E. Wilkins Freeman:
The Domestic Ghost

The weird work of Mary E. Wilkins Freeman (1852–1930) is a direct outgrowth of the extensive and multifaceted mainstream work that gained her an impressive reputation during her lifetime. Although firmly ensconced in the American literary canon, Freeman today is not as well-known or as highly regarded as other women writers of her period—Edith Wharton, Charlotte Perkins Gilman, and her longtime friend Sarah Orne Jewett (all of whom, incidentally, wrote weird fiction)—to say nothing of such male figures as Henry James, Theodore Dreiser, or William Dean Howells. But in her day she was an immensely popular and critically acclaimed writer, and it could be argued that her prolific array of novels, stories, poems, and other work laid the groundwork for the women writers who came in her wake. The weird was only a slim segment of her overall output, but in many ways it has stood the test of time somewhat better than her mainstream work.

Mary Ella (later Eleanor) Wilkins was born in Randolph, Massachusetts, on 31 October 1852, to Warren and Eleanor Wilkins. A strict religious upbringing in the Congregational sect of Protestant Christianity was inculcated in her by her father, a faith that "required a conversion experience, a public demonstration of grace received" (Reichardt 5). The faith also stipulated that "each person's sins and degree of grace were the concern of the entire community" (Westbrook 59). There is considerable evidence in Freeman's stories that she rebelled as best she could against this overbearing doctrine, and several works warn against the dangers of religious fanaticism. Freeman was aware of a family tradition that pointed to an ancestor, Bray Wilkins, who contrived to have his own grandson hanged as a witch during the Salem witch trials.

Mary was sickly as a child, and her family was beset by troubles and tragedies during her early years. A brother, born in 1853, died in 1858. More seriously, a sister, Anna, born in 1859, to whom Mary appears to have been very close, died in 1876. As a result of all this, Mary stayed physically and emotionally close to her mother—a bond reflected in any number of later stories. This closeness was augmented by the relative failure of her father to secure financial security for his family. When she was fifteen, the family moved to Brattleboro, Vermont; but her father, alternating between carpentry and the selling of dry goods, failed to prosper in either occupation. He wished Mary to marry young, for economic reasons—to be blunt, he simply wished her off his hands and under the responsibility of a husband, so that he would have one fewer mouth to feed.

Mary, for her part, did not begin attending school until the age of seven. But she was a diligent reader and soon took to writing, producing her first known literary work, a poem, at the age of fourteen. She attended Brattleboro High School and, in 1870, enrolled at Mount Holyoke Female Seminary (which Emily Dickinson had previously attended). But she remained there only a year, leaving (in her own words) "a nervous wreck" (cited in Glasser 18).

The family's financial distresses forced it to move in 1877 into the home of the Rev. Thomas Pickman Tyler, with whose son, Hanson (a sailor), Mary seems to have had some kind of brief romance dating to as early as 1873. Tyler had rejected her—or, at any rate, put off indefinitely any plans for marriage or a long-term relationship as he returned to sea; later he married another woman. Mary in some sense used her longing for Tyler as an excuse not to marry, something she clearly did not wish at this time to do.

Further tragedies afflicted the family. After Anna's death in 1876, Mary's father died in 1883 and her mother in 1886. Mary had taken up residence in 1883 with a childhood friend, Mary Wales, back in

Randolph, and lived with her until 1902. This involvement was without doubt the closest personal relationship she ever had in her life, surpassing that of the man she later married. The question will inevitably rise as to whether the relationship was in any way lesbian—a question that is now unanswerable. A comment in one story, "The Tree of Knowledge" (1900), might provide a clue: "The tenderness of one woman for another is farther reaching in detail than that of a man, because it is given with a fuller understanding of needs" (cited in Glasser 154). Mary for her part seemed entirely content to adopt the pejorative term "spinster," allowing Wales to be a kind of "wife" for her while she herself devoted all her energies to writing.

Mary had begun writing seriously as early as 1874, and her first professional sale (a poem) had occurred in 1881; the next year, she published her first short story. Throughout her life she devoted herself to the short story, writing nearly 250 of them in a career that spanned more than four decades; of these, 147 were collected in fifteen collections during her lifetime. She did write novels—fourteen of them[1]—but few of them were regarded as highly as her short stories, and several are little more than potboilers. She published in many of the popular magazines of the day—not just "women's" magazines such as *Harper's Bazaar*, but also such distinguished general periodicals such as *Harper's* and the *Atlantic Monthly*. Her first story collection, *A Humble Romance and Other Stories*, appeared in 1887, and her most famous collection, *A New England Nun and Other Stories*, was published in 1891. She went on to publish thirteen more collections down to 1918.

Mary met her eventual husband, Charles Freeman, in 1892. They became informally engaged as early as 1897, but disagreements over the next several years resulted in a separation and a long delay in the marriage, which did not occur until 1 January 1902. By this time Mary

---

1. One other novel, *An Alabaster Box* (1917), was written in collaboration with Florence Morse Kingsley. Another was a round-robin novel, *The Whole Family* (1908), in which Freeman wrote a chapter; other contributors included William Dean Howells and Henry James.

was an acclaimed author, and the course of her troubled romance with Freeman was widely reported in newspapers. Freeman himself was a physician, but never practiced; instead, he tried his hand at business, but was as unsuccessful at it as Mary's father had been. Upon their marriage, they settled in Charles's home in Metuchen, New Jersey.

Some scholars have contended that the marriage began happily but deteriorated as Charles's varied troubles overwhelmed him; but her most recent biographer, Leah Blatt Glasser, casts doubt upon this notion. It appears that, as a woman nearly fifty years of age entering upon marriage for the first time, she was initially to be taken with the *institution* of marriage (she quickly changed her name to Mary E. Wilkins Freeman and insisted that this name be used on her subsequent publications) without being notably happy in her own union with a man who did not seem very well suited to her. Charles Freeman, by some accounts, was a dictatorial man who insisted that his wife keep on writing chiefly or solely for the income it brought in. He also began drinking heavily, and his losing an election for mayor of Metuchen in 1907 could not have bolstered his self-esteem. He was hospitalised for alcoholism in 1909, and from this point on he went from bad to worse. He later became a drug addict, entering a sanitarium in 1919. He was then placed in the New Jersey State Hospital for the Insane in 1920, but he escaped from it after a few weeks. On 23 August 1921, he was committed to the New Jersey State Hospital, but Mary acquiesced to his departure about six weeks later, at which time she obtained a legal separation from him. Charles died on 7 March 1923.

Charles attempted to take revenge upon what he believed to be a wife who had failed to support him through his difficulties by writing a will in which the great proportion of his assets, amounting to some $225,000 (it is unclear whether this sum included Mary's own earnings from her writing; probably it did), to a chauffeur with whom he had struck up an acquaintance, leaving Mary the sum of $1. Both Mary and Charles's sisters challenged the terms of the will, and after years of litigation it was finally overturned; Mary was awarded $78,000. By this time Mary herself had fallen into poor health, and her writing career was largely over; she died on 13 March 1930.

Mary E. Wilkins Freeman was the recipient of some impressive awards during her lifetime. Aside from her wide publications in leading (and highly remunerative) magazines of the day and by prestigious book publishers, she won a contest between herself and a British writer, Max Pemberton, sponsored by the *New York Herald*: her novel, *The Shoulders of Atlas* (1908), won a readers' poll and was awarded the substantial sum of $5,000. More impressively, her work was praised by such critics as William Dean Howells and William Lyon Phelps, and, although she was initially rejected for entry into the National Institute of Arts and Letters for the sole reason that she was a woman, she was later among the first four women elected to that body (the others being Agnes Repplier, Margeret Deland, and Edith Wharton). The bronze doors of the institute, in New York City, bear the inscription: "Dedicated to the Memory of Mary E. Wilkins Freeman and the Women Writers of America."

Freeman's literary work has often been disparaged as being merely "local colour" or regionalist writing, although it is undeniably true that many of her tales and novels draw upon her deep knowledge of New England history, tradition, and folkways; it has also been criticised for focusing exclusively on domesticity and for depicting women characters as adhering to the narrow and constrained limits that American society of that time insisted upon for women and girls. But recent feminist criticism has accurately detected clear elements of revolt against the stifling of female ambition and the advocacy of a kind of social and psychological independence by women against male domination, however mildly and covertly this is exhibited in some of her work. Freeman herself was indomitable in pursuing a literary career for herself and in refusing for many years to submit herself to a man as a mere wife or housekeeper. One of her most celebrated stories, "A New England Nun" (1891), forcefully tells of a woman who glories in her "spinsterhood" after she has rejected marriage to an obviously unsuitable man.

The novel *Pembroke* (1894) presents a highly unflattering portrayal of two pig-headed men whose dispute results in a long delay in marriage for one of the participants. Another novel, *Madelon* (1896), somewhat flamboyantly focuses on the "aggressive sexuality and potential for violence" (Glasser 126) of its protagonist, a woman who has half French-Canadian and half Native American.

Freeman's eighteen weird tales display many of the elements running through her mainstream work while at the same time introducing supernatural or quasi-supernatural elements that underscore their central themes. Several tales are, despite their outward conventionality and the relative restraint of their supernatural manifestations, surprisingly forward-looking in their implications and may well have influenced later work in the field.

The supernatural, for Freeman, is intimately connected with the complexities of family dynamics that were the focus of her mainstream writing. In particular, the status of women—the young single woman, the married woman with or without children, the elderly "spinster" or widow—are the focus of numerous tales and reflect her conflicted attitudes toward the place of women in the family unit and in society as a whole. In her first weird tale, "A Symphony in Lavender" (1883), a young woman has a precognitive dream in which she almost gives a lilac to a young man—a metaphor for the woman's sexual submission to the man. Her resistance signals her refusal—a refusal that Freeman herself manifestly felt—to undergo the psychic and social subordination that such a submission would, at that period in history, have necessitated. A similar story, but one considerably broader in scope, is "The Prism" (1901), where the "fairies" that the protagonist, Diantha, sees in a prism are symbolic of the sense of freedom—both social and imaginative—that she feels as an unattached woman; her burial of the prism upon her marriage is a transparent metaphor for her reluctant decision to yield to the conventional happiness of the married state.

"Luella Miller" (1902) is a strikingly advanced tale of a psychic vampire—a woman who sucks the life out of those who seek to help her. Here the trope of the "helpless female" is given an ingenious supernatural dimension. One wonders whether this tale exerted an influence on such later works as H. P. Lovecraft's "The Shunned House" (1924)–where a similar psychic vampirism is manifested, although the root cause is very different–or even on Fritz Leiber's classic tale "The Girl with the Hungry Eyes" (1949), where the sexual element that is only implicit in Freeman's story is brought to the fore.

Children occupy a powerful presence in a number of Freeman's weird tales; their innocence and fragility were compelling emotional issues in this childless author. "A Gentle Ghost" (1889) is one of her most touching tales–a powerful portrayal, in its depiction of a child ghost, of the loneliness the child must have felt upon the death of her family. Here is one of numerous instances where Freeman correctly determined that a supernatural element enhanced the emotive power of the social message she was delivering; and in this case, at least, a "happy" ending proves to be satisfying to the reader. "The School-Teacher's Story" (1894), a hitherto uncollected tale, shows us the transformation of a hardened, embittered schoolteacher as she encounters the ghost of a child who had died fifty years earlier. The tale seems markedly similar to August Derleth's story "The Dark Boy" (1957), although it seems unlikely that Derleth could have read it.

"The Wind in the Rose-Bush" (1902) is one of six ghost stories that Freeman was apparently commissioned to write for the popular magazine *Everybody's*; these six tales were subsequently collected in the notable volume *The Wind in the Rose-Bush and Other Stories of the Supernatural* (1903). This is one of Freeman's most searing depictions of child abuse. The gradual accretion of bizarre details–focused on the anomalous wind that runs through a rose-bush outside a house when there is no wind– creates an incredible atmosphere of cumulative horror, even if the cause of the manifestation (a woman's deliberate neglect of her stepdaughter, which caused her to die) is not difficult to detect. Ultimately, the horror focuses on the stepmother, who in spite of her air of bluff offhandedness is in fact consumed with terror at every moment.

"The Lost Ghost" (1903) is another effective melding of horror and pathos, where again the central message—a little girl who died of starvation as a result of her mother's neglect—is powerfully expressed, and where again a "happy" ending (the child-ghost unites with the spirit of a recently deceased woman who had expressed sympathy for her) is by no means adventitious.

"The Southwest Chamber" (1903) is one of the longest of Freeman's weird tales and one of the most effective. It vividly embodies her belief that horror can most plausibly emerge out of the commonplace: here the supernatural is manifested in such ordinary objects as a chintz bedcover, a nightcap, and an old-fashioned dress. As the narrator expounds:

> This apparent contradiction of the reasonable as manifested in such a commonplace thing as a chintz of a bed-hanging affected this ordinary un-imaginative woman as no ghostly appearance could have done. Those red roses on the yellow ground were to her much more ghastly than any strange figure clad in the white robes of the grave entering the room. (148)

This idea could have been enunciated by Richard Matheson or even Stephen King, both of whom strove to return terror to the mundane as a reaction to the "cosmic horror" of Lovecraft and his disciples, who they felt had made weirdness a bit too remote from ordinary life.

Another story of approximately the same sort is "The Shadows on the Wall" (1903), which appears to have become something of a signature weird tale of Freeman's, although several other stories are probably superior when judged by purely aesthetic criteria. But this tale certainly embodies the uniquely claustrophobic and domestic terror that she pioneered, where the unchanging shadow on a wall, indicative of a man's violent death at the hands of his brother, creates a grim atmosphere of claustrophobia and weirdness. If the tale proves to be, in the ultimate sense, only a simple tale of supernatural revenge, its execution and attention to detail are nonetheless admirable.

The figure of the witch fascinated Freeman—not because she had the slightest belief that witches with supernatural powers ever existed, but because she knew that accusations of witchcraft were commonly hurled (by men) against women who refused to maintain their appropriately subservient place in the social hierarchy. The late tale "The Witch's Daughter" (1910) is perhaps typical—a touching story of a suspected witch who tries to practise witchcraft to bring her daughter's lover back, but who (as the narrative makes abundantly clear) succeeds in her task without any supernatural aid.

That tale is set in the period soon after the Salem witch trials in Massachusetts, but several other tales actually set during the witch trials convey Freeman's horror at the fanaticism and irrationality that allowed the authorities of Salem to execute nearly twenty suspected witches (most of them women) on the flimsiest of testimony from unreliable sources. The early tale "The Little Maid at the Door" (1892) poignantly depicts the human cost of this fanaticism, where a little girl whose relatives were dragged away and killed as witches starves to death and appears as a ghost only to the woman who drives by and expresses sympathy for her.

That story sets the stage for *Giles Corey, Yeoman* (1892), which was written on the two hundredth anniversary of the Salem witch trials. This play does not contain anything supernatural; indeed, its very premise is that there were no witches in Salem and that their trial and execution were instances of appalling injustice and cruelty. But the depiction of religious madness that sees witches at every turn—and which also impels two women, one young and one old, to believe that they actually are witches—creates a vivid sense of pseudo-supernaturalism. True horror of a physical sort enters when the title character, who had initially suspected his own wife of witchcraft but who later comes to realise the folly of his belief, is himself pressed to death for refusing to testify. Freeman drew upon authentic sources for her play—her chief reference was Charles W. Upham's two-volume treatise, *Salem Witchcraft* (1866)—and the names of several central characters (including the magistrates John Hathorne and Jonathan Corwin, the sanctimonious minister Matthew Parris, and Giles Corey himself) are taken from the historical record.

"Silence" (1893) is something of a follow-up to Freeman's historical witch stories. This tale, set during the French and Indian War (1754–63), depicts the lingering effects of the witchcraft panic in the figure of Goody Crane, a witchlike character with possibly precognitive powers. Although she is by no means the focus of the narrative, her possibly supernatural gifts render this one of the most delicate and elusive of Freeman's weird tales. And we can hardly overlook the uncollected story "The White Witch" (1893), a Christmas whimsy that seeks to chastise children who are not sufficiently grateful for the presents they receive.

Perhaps the most imaginative of Freeman's weird stories is "The Hall Bedroom" (1903), a tale that she surprisingly did not collect in any of her own volumes of short stories. This remarkable narrative goes well beyond the conventional "haunted house" or "haunted room" motif of several of her other tales, proposing a character's supernatural access to a hidden room of seemingly infinite extent that had been sealed off for decades or centuries—a scenario strikingly similar to Lovecraft's "The Dreams in the Witch House" (1932), although it seems unlikely that Lovecraft could have read Freeman's story before writing his own. One is also reminded of Joseph Payne Brennan's "Canavan's Back Yard" (1958), where the back yard of a house also seems to be of infinite extent. The manifestly sexual dreams or hallucinations experienced by the male protagonist is also something of a bold departure for Freeman.

Rounding out Freeman's weird work is "The Vacant Lot" (1902), a relatively conventional tale of revenants, and "The Jade Bracelet" (1918), a late tale that effectively posits a haunted bracelet that, when worn, reveals the murder of its previous owner.

Reactions to Freeman's weird work have been somewhat mixed over the years. It is perhaps not surprising that H. P. Lovecraft—a fellow New Englander and a writer also drawn to the long and sinister history of his native region—spoke highly of Freeman. His brief analysis in "Supernatural Horror in Literature" (1927) is worth quoting in full:

> Horror material of authentic force may be found in the work of the
> New England realist Mary E. Wilkins; whose volume of short tales, *The
> Wind in the Rose-Bush*, contains a number of noteworthy achievements. In
> "The Shadows on the Wall" we are shewn with consummate skill the re-
> sponse of a staid New England household to uncanny tragedy; and the
> sourceless shadow of the poisoned brother well prepares us for the climac-
> tic moment when the shadow of the secret murderer, who has killed him-
> self in a neighbouring city, suddenly appears beside it. (70)

And yet, even so sympathetic a critic as Perry D. Westbrook, whose
monograph on Freeman—first published in 1967 and issued in a
revised edition in 1988—produced the following incredibly wrong-
headed assessment of the stories in *The Wind in the Rose-Bush*:

> Deficient in suspense and atmosphere, these stories rely on generally ludi-
> crous devices for their interest: persistently appearing shadows on a wall;
> items of a dead woman's wardrobe that shuttle in and out of a closet in
> the chamber in which she died; spectral laundry hanging in a vacant lot
> near a haunted house; a rose blossom that detaches itself from a bush and
> comes to rest on a dead girl's bed. Indeed, in some cases Freeman seems to
> be striving for humor, though not very successfully. (111)

But in more recent years, and especially as feminist critics have
embraced Freeman as a quiet advocate of their cause, her supernatural
work has come to be more highly regarded. Both Leah Blatt Glasser
(219–26) and Mary R. Reichardt (67–74) have supplied illuminating
interpretations of her weird work, although in some instances these
authors do not seem entirely comfortable or familiar with the rhetoric
of weird fiction. The most exhaustive analysis is a lengthy paper by
noted supernatural critic Benjamin F. Fisher, published in 1996.[2]

---

2. Benjamin F. Fisher, "Transitions from Victorian to Modern: The Supernatural
Stories of Mary Wilkins Freeman and Edith Wharton," in *American Supernatural
Fiction: From Edith Wharton to the* Weird Tales *Writers*, ed. Douglas Robillard (New
York: Garland, 1996), 3–42. This and other articles are cited in Jack G. Voller's
"Mary Wilkins Freeman," in *Gothic Writers: A Critical and Bibliographical Guide*,
ed. Douglass H. Thomson, Jack G. Voller, and Frederick S. Frank (Westport, CT:
Greenwood Press, 2002), 120–24.

In 1974, Arkham House published Freeman's *Collected Ghost Stories*. The title, as in many similar cases, is deliberately ambiguous: the adjective "collected" can either stand as a synonym for "complete" or (as is likely in this instance) merely indicate what the editor decided to collect for this edition. The editor was clearly not Edward Wagenknecht, who wrote a brief and not particularly helpful introduction;[3] its compiler was probably August Derleth, even though the volume appeared three years after Derleth's death. As another writer who was deeply tied to the history and topography of his native state (Wisconsin), he would be expected to have sympathy with a writer like Freeman. *Collected Ghost Stories* included eleven tales: the six from *The Wind in the Rose-Bush*; "A Symphony in Lavender" and "A Far-away Melody" from *A Humble Romance* (1887); "A Gentle Ghost" from *A New England Nun* (1891); and two uncollected stories, "The Hall Bedroom" and "The Jade Bracelet." The arrangement was haphazard, with no regard for chronology or theme.

Freeman's weird work, seemingly conventional and written in prose that at times appears to be almost of childlike simplicity, nonetheless contains depths of feeling, complexity of theme and motif, and skilful handling of supernatural elements that more flamboyant authors in our field would envy. That Freeman devoted even a slim proportion of her bountiful output to the weird is something that devotees of the form should welcome; and her ability to enhance social and domestic traumas by means of deft supernatural touches is a lesson in how to make weird fiction aesthetically relevant to human concerns rather than being a mere exercise in bloodletting and grue.

---

3. "Since I am introducing the present volume without having myself edited it, I cannot of my own knowledge swear that there is nothing of a supernatural character anywhere—say, among the numerous uncollected stories—which has not been caught between these covers." Edward Wagenknecht, "Introduction" to *Collected Ghost Stories* ix.

Works Cited

Freeman, Mary E. Wilkins. *Collected Ghost Stories*. Sauk City, WI: Arkham House, 1974.

Glasser, Leah Blatt. *In a Closet Hidden: The Life and Work of Mary E. Wilkins Freeman*. Amherst: University of Massachusetts Press, 1996.

Lovecraft, H. P. *The Annotated Supernatural Horror in Literature*. Ed. S. T. Joshi. New York: Hippocampus Press, rev. ed. 2012.

Reichardt, Mary R. *Mary Wilkins Freeman: A Study of Her Short Fiction*. New York: Twayne, 1997.

Westbrook, Perry D. *Mary Wilkins Freeman*. Boston: Twayne, rev. ed. 1988.

E. Nesbit: Lying Awake in the Dark

To say that the life of E. Nesbit was eventful would be putting it mildly. Her life-span covered some of the most traumatic years of English (and Western) history, from the end of the Victorian era through World War I and into the Roaring Twenties; and her tumultuous personal relationships—with her siblings, her husband, several lovers, numerous friends and colleagues, and her five children (three natural-born, two adopted)—created such turmoil at various stages of her life that one wonders how she managed to get as much writing done as she did. But she did produce an immense quantity of work—poems, stories, articles, sketches, and most of all an array of children's books that established her as one of the pioneering writers in that field. That she managed, along the way, to write a brace of splendid weird tales was in some ways a lucky accident.

Edith Nesbit was born on 15 August 1858, in Kennington, a district of South London. She was the fourth child of Sarah and John Collis Nesbit. John ran a small agricultural college, but he died unexpectedly in 1862. Sarah managed to take over the administration of the college and ran it successfully for several years. But Edith's older daughter, Mary (called Minnie), contracted tuberculosis in 1866; as a means of alleviating her condition, her mother took the family to the coastal town of Brighton, where Edith (usually called Daisy as a child) attended a private school run by a Mrs. Arthur; she later attended a boarding school in Stamford, in Lincolnshire. Both these brief educational stints were unhappy experiences for Edith, as she endured harsh discipline and suffered from homesickness. In 1867 her mother took the family to France for an extended trip, and Mary spent months learning French. The family later went on to Spain. After a brief return to England, the Nesbits settled in the town of Dinan, in Brittany, where Edith was enrolled for a short time in a school run by an Ursuline convent; still later, she was sent to study at a school run by Moravian sisters in Düsseldorf. (One thinks of Algernon Blackwood, who was enrolled for a year [1885–86] in a school run by the Moravian Brotherhood in Königsfeld.) But at the outbreak of the Franco-Prussian War in 1870, the Nesbits were obliged to return to England.

Edith's first literary work was a poem that she wrote at the age of eleven. She wrote poetry extensively in the years 1872–75, when the family was living in Halstead, Kent. These were among the happiest years of Edith's early life. The earliest known publication of her work was a poem that appeared in *Good Words* (the periodical formerly run by Charles Dickens) in December 1876.

Financial difficulties forced the family to move from Halstead to Islington. It was in 1877 that Edith met her future husband, Hubert Bland. At this time she was engaged to a bank clerk named Stuart Smith; but by 1878 she had freed herself from Smith and become engaged to Hubert. Bland was himself engaged to another woman, Maggie Doran, and in fact later had a child by her. He continued to see—and be intimate with—Maggie for years or decades after his marriage to Edith. Edith's mother did not approve of the association with Hubert, chiefly because his own job prospects seemed doubtful. He himself was for a time a bank clerk, but then put his modest resources into various businesses, none of which were notably successful. The sexual irregularities that dogged both Edith's and Hubert's adult life were on display at the time of their marriage on 22 April 1880: exactly two months later, on 22 June, she gave birth to her first son, Paul.

For the entirety of their married life, the Blands lived in various rented quarters in various London suburbs; even at the height of Edith's literary success, in the first decade of the twentieth century, they never purchased a house. In the years following her marriage, Edith began writing stories prolifically for magazines; she also made extra income by making hand-painted greeting cards. A daughter, Mary Iris, was born on 2 December 1881. Hubert at first collaborated with Edith on her stories and other work, but later established himself as a distinguished journalist and reviewer. Both of them were founding members of the Fabian Society, the moderate socialist organisation that established itself in 1883–84 and advocated gradual conversion from capitalism to socialism. Edith, however, did not become entirely "advanced" in her thinking; she retained vestiges of her Anglican religious upbringing and also maintained a residual belief in traditional social and economic roles for women, even though she herself did not conform to those roles herself, frequently earning far more income than her husband. In her views on women, which included a vehement objection to woman suffrage, she was probably influenced in part by her strong-willed and dogmatic husband, who frequently spoke out on the subject.

A third child, Fabian, was born on 8 January 1885. Later that year, her first book—a novel written with Hubert, *The Prophet's Mantle*—appeared. This was a complex work in the Victorian manner, featuring a multitude of characters and incidents in the manner of Dickens. But it was through her socialist connexions that Edith and Hubert became acquainted with some of the most notable literary figures of the day. She first met George Bernard Shaw in 1884 at a meeting of the Fabian Society. The most peculiar relation Edith ever established was with Alice Hoatson, an editor at *Sylvia's Home Journal,* where some of her early work appeared. Edith professed great fondness for Alice; but Alice quickly became Hubert's mistress and eventually bore him two children. The first of these, Rosamund, was born in 1886; at this time, Alice moved in with the Blands, and they raised Rosamund as if she were a child of theirs. In part this was done to shield Alice from the social ostracism she would have encountered as an unwed mother; but the arrangement also had the advantage of allowing Alice to be a kind of "wife" to both Edith and Hubert, tending to the children while both the others focused on their writing.

But the complex and emotionally wrenching situation must have

been a strain for Edith, and matters were not helped when she gave
birth to a stillborn child in early 1886. Edith had by this time
developed an infatuation with Shaw, and at least initially he responded
in kind. Whether they actually became intimate is a matter of doubt,
but there is no denying that Edith suggested that she and Shaw run
away together. Shaw, who himself was married at the time, began
pulling away from Edith and later denied that he had ever had any
kind of affair with her. Meanwhile, Edith was fully aware of Hubert's
sexual relations with Alice; whether she knew that he was also
continuing his relations with Maggie Doran is not clear, but there were
any number of outbursts in the family, in part spurred by Edith's
penchant for self-dramatisation.

Edith herself developed relations (which may or may not have included a sexual element) with any number of younger men, the first of
whom was a man named Noel Griffith, whom she met in 1887; later,
she had a brief affair with the poet Richard Le Gallienne. Friendships
of a more orthodox sort also developed with such writers as Olive
Schreiner (*The Story of an African Farm*, 1883), Laurence Housman (a
widely published novelist and the brother of A. E. Housman), and
others. The British literary scene of the time was a relatively small one,
and leading writers quickly became acquainted with one another and
maintained contact through numerous gatherings, soirées, and other
events. Edith herself enjoyed being the hostess of many parties thrown
for literary and other friends throughout her adult life.

Nesbit had published several books of poetry in the later 1880s,
and for decades she considered herself chiefly a poet; she was disappointed that her poetry was not more highly regarded, but its chief
deficiency is its fundamental unoriginality, as it is largely derived from
her enthusiastic reading of the Brownings and other poets of the day.
By the early 1890s, Nesbit gradually turned to prose; spurred on by an
editor, Robert Ellice Mack, she took to writing children's stories. Much
work during this period was cowritten with Oswald Barron, another
younger man with whom Nesbit carried on a languid affair for years.

Two books that are of direct interest to us appeared in 1893: *Grim Tales* and *Something Wrong*. The former consists entirely of weird tales, originally published in such leading magazines as *Temple Bar*, *Argosy*, *Longman's*, and the like. The latter, although one reviewer referred to it as containing stories written "in the manner of Edgar Allan Poe," in fact contains only one weird specimen, "Hurst of Hurstcote." These books attracted little interest, but that could not be said for *The Story of the Treasure Seekers* (1899), the first of her books about the rambunctious Bastable family. It was an immediate success and remained so throughout Nesbit's lifetime, having been reprinted fifteen times through 1928. The significance of the book lies in the realism of its treatment of childhood pleasures and traumas; in these and other books about the Bastable family, Nesbit largely eschewed the benign fantasy that often made children's books seem insubstantial or remote from reality.

Nesbit did write a number of stories and novels for adults, including such a bold work as *The Secret of Kyriels* (1899), a novel frankly dealing with female sexuality. Her affair with Bernard Shaw was transmuted into the novel *Daphne in Fitzroy Street* (1909). But it was her children's books that won her fame and fortune, including *The Wouldbegoods* (1901), *Five Children and It* (1902), *The New Treasure Seekers* (1904), *The Phoenix and the Carpet* (1904), *The Railway Children* (1906), *The Enchanted Castle* (1907), and others. Some of these books address the grim social realities of the day, such as poverty, imprisonment, race prejudice, and the like. Several of them also have a significant fantasy element: *The Five Children and It*, basically a work about her own children, also involves a curious creature called the psammead; *The Enchanted Castle* introduces us to horrible creatures called the Ugly-Wuglies and perhaps constitutes the closest Nesbit came to writing a horror tale for children. Many of these books first appeared as serials in the *Strand Magazine*, which paid the unprecedented amount of £30 per episode; for many years the *Strand* published a Nesbit story in every issue.

Nesbit's personal life continued to be traumatic even in the course of the celebrity she acquired in the first decade of the twentieth century. A second child, John, was born to Alice on 6 October 1899. Then, in 1900, her fifteen-year-old son Fabian died as a result of a botched operation to remove adenoids. In that year Hubert joined the Catholic Church, and a few years later Edith joined him. It is not clear what changes this conversion created in either their personal life or their literary work.

Then there was their involvement with H. G. Wells. The couple had first met Wells in 1902, as he was himself an ardent socialist. But around 1908 Wells developed an infatuation with Edith's adopted daughter Rosamund, who was twenty-two at the time; although Wells was married and twenty years her senior, the two tried to run away together, but were stopped at a train station in London. An enormous row ensued, and of course the Blands' association with Wells was permanently terminated. Wells gained his revenge by maliciously depicting a couple clearly based on the Blands in his novel *The New Machiavelli* (1911). Shaw had a field day writing satirical letters on the whole imbroglio.

Nesbit continued to develop acquaintances with notable writers, including E. M. Forster and the young Lord Dunsany. She not only admired Dunsany's stories of ethereal fantasy (she published some of them in a short-lived periodical, the *Neolith* [1907–08], an exquisite example of handset type and fine printing) but was captivated by a week-long stay with Lord and Lady Dunsany at Dunsany Castle in Ireland. But Edith's "great decade" of writing ended ominously when, in 1910, Hubert suffered a detached retina and became virtually blind; he began relying even more heavily on Alice to continue his literary work, and he seemed to be growing apart from his nominal wife. Edith's association with the *Strand* ended in 1913, and her last children's book was *Wet Magic* (1913); this led to money shortages for the family. The Blands had, since 1899, been staying in a large house called Well Hall, Eltham, in the borough of Greenwich; but although the spacious house and generous acreage were an ideal place for the Blands to write, it became increasingly expensive to maintain.

Hubert Bland died on 14 April 1914. Alice continued living with Edith, although relations were apparently quite strained. When the war broke out in August, Nesbit quickly edited a volume of *Battle Songs* (1914) as a patriotic gesture; her occasionally ferocious anti-German fulminations in letters alienated some of her literary associates. In 1915 she received a Civil List pension from the British government for her services to literature; but it amounted to only £60 a year (Arthur Machen, in 1931, received a Civil List pension of £100 a year) and was not enough to offset her financial difficulties. She was forced to take in paying guests (which she alternately referred to in letters as "P.G.'s" or, more unkindly, "pigs") and also sold produce from her garden; for a time she tried to raise chickens, but they all perished from disease.

It was, then, something of a blessing that, in 1916, she met Thomas Terry Tucker (nicknamed "the Skipper"), a marine engineer about two years her elder; he began to help Edith around the house and estate. He was immediately taken with her and proposed marriage; at first she declined, but then she acceded, marrying him on 20 February 1917. Although he was of equable temper and habitually deferential to his wife (as the domineering Hubert had never been), Tucker evoked opposition from Edith's children, chiefly because he was not a "gentleman": the social gulf between this rough-hewn working-class man and his elegant, refined, literarily accomplished wife bothered them, although Edith himself seemed unconcerned about the matter and was genuinely in love with him. Soon after the marriage Alice Hoatson was pointedly asked to leave the household: with the children grown up and the strange bond—Hubert—that had united them gone, her role in the family was at an end.

Through Thomas's influence, Edith decided at last to give up Well Hall; they purchased a small cottage near the town of St. Mary in the Marsh, a village in Kent, where one of her neighbours was the young Noël Coward. By this time Edith herself was in poor health, thanks to a chronic smoking habit (at one period she smoked forty cigarettes a day). For the last two years of her life she suffered painfully from what was probably lung cancer, and she died on 4 May 1924. Her funeral was attended by, among others, Lord and Lady Dunsany.

E. Nesbit's work as a children's writer justifies the bold comment by her most recent biographer, Julia Briggs, that she "is the first modern writer for children" (xi). Her weird tales were essentially a sideline, but she revealed a remarkable range in the eighteen tales that can be considered weird; indeed, these tales come close to exhibiting the full scope of themes, motifs, and approaches of the weird literature of the period.

Many of the most gripping elements in Nesbit's weird stories derive from her own terrors and phobias, many of them dating to her earliest years. She attested to both a fear of the dark and a fear of the dead, and these two conceptions figure largely in her weird work. She spoke of them at length in a serial, My School-Days, published in the Girl's Own Paper in 1896-97. Here is an account of the fears she experienced during her initial trip to France in 1867:

> I lay awake in the dark, the light from the oil lamp in the street came through the Persiennes and fell in bright bars on the wall. As I grew drowsier I seemed to read there in letters of fire "Débit de Tabac".
> Then I fell asleep, and dreamed that my father's ghost came to me, and implored me to have the horrible French inscription erased from his tomb—"for I was an Englishman," he said.
> Then I woke, rigid with terror, and finally summoned courage to creep across the corridor to my mother's room and seek refuge in her arms. I am particular to mention this dream because it is the first remembrance I have of any terror of the dead, or of the supernatural. I do not at all know how it had its rise . . . (My School-Days, Part III; cited in Briggs 12–13)

Another nightmare—this time about mummies that she saw in the catacombs of Bordeaux—also affected her:

> The mummies of Bordeaux were the crowning horror of my childish life; it is to them, I think, more than to any other thing, that I owe nights and nights of anguish and horror, long years of bitterest fear and dread. All the

other fears could have been effaced, but the shock of that night branded in on my brain and I never forgot it. For many years I could not bring myself to go about any house in the dark, and long after I was a grown woman I was tortured, in the dark watches, by imagination and memory, who rose strong and united, overpowering my will and my reason as utterly as in my baby days. (*My School-Days*, Part V; cited in Briggs 13–14)

A passage like this makes one wonder why Nesbit wrote no tales explicitly involving mummies. This passage appears in an entire chapter of *My School-Days* devoted to the mummies of Bordeaux; this and an earlier chapter, on her fear of the dark, are so striking that they are worth including as an appendix to this book.

As noted, Nesbit assembled an entire volume of weird tales early in her career, *Grim Tales* (1893); she reprinted all but one of them ("The Mass for the Dead"), along with "Hurst of Hurstcote" (from *Something Wrong*, 1893) and other, uncollected tales in the seminal volume *Fear* (1910). A number of weird tales appeared subsequent to this book, but they were not gathered in any volumes during her lifetime.

Several of Nesbit's earliest weird stories effect a union between weirdness and romance in an effective manner. These tales use the supernatural as a metaphor for underscoring moral or social conceptions facing us in our everyday lives. "John Charrington's Wedding" (1891), for example, tells of a man who speaks of the virtues of persistence in affairs of the heart—so it is not at all unexpected that he keeps the appointment for his wedding, even after his death. "The Ebony Frame" (1891) poignantly tells of a man's love for the ghost of a woman whom his ancestor knew in the past—but this scenario is a transparent metaphor for his dissatisfaction with the woman he is courting in real life. Somewhat similar, although less emotionally intense, is "Uncle Abraham's Romance" (1893), a brief tale of a man who loves a female ghost. "The Mass for the Dead" (1892), although generally excluded from collections of Nesbit's weird work, does seem to have a subtle but clearly traceable supernatural element, especially when the two lovers at the centre of the tale both hear an organ playing the mass for the dead when it later becomes evident that no organ was playing at the time.

Here again a difficult emotional situation—the tortured love triangle where two men are vying for a woman's affections—is given a supernatural dimension. Much the same could be said for "From the Dark," a tragic tale of love and death with an ambiguously supernatural ending.

"The Mystery of the Semi-Detached" (1893) once again focuses on domestic issues, but is the somewhat predictable tale of a man who has a vision of his fiancée's throat being cut—a vision that turns out to be a glimpse of the future involving another person entirely. Perhaps the grimmest—and certainly the most celebrated—of Nesbit's weird tales is "Man-Size in Marble" (1893), where we are shown nothing less than a full-fledged rape of a woman by a stone statue. Julia Briggs maintains that the tale was likely influenced by Prosper Mérimée's classic tale of a living statue, "La Vénus d'Ille" ("The Venus of Ille," 1837), and this is probable. We must admire the artistry whereby the confirmation of the supernatural element is withheld until the final line of the story.

Continuing the theme of domestic horror is "Hurst of Hurscote" (1893), where a man conducts an experiment whereby he hypnotises his wife so that her soul remains in her body even after her death. One might have thought that this story was influenced by Arthur Machen's "The Great God Pan" or "The Inmost Light," both of which record similar experiments by male scientists on women (the latter actually hints that a woman's soul has been transferred into a gem); but Machen's tales were published a year after Nesbit's.

Nesbit appears to have written—or, at any rate, published—no weird tales between the years 1893 and 1905. During much of this period, of course, she was focused on writing her ever more popular children's books and stories. When she returned to the weird tale, her focus had shifted somewhat. "The Power of Darkness" (1905) naturally emphasises her own fear of the dark, and does so effectively in spite of the hackneyed premise (two men dare each other to spend a night in a spooky waxworks museum). The delineation of psychological terror is grimly powerful, and the dispelling of the supernatural is managed without a sense of deflation or trickery. The same cannot quite be said for "The

Head" (1907), a predictable non-supernatural tale of revenge and sadism. "In the Dark" (1910), however, is another powerful depiction of the psychological effects of terror; the ending seems to explode the supernatural manifestation, but ambiguities remain. "Number 17" (1910) is unusual in Nesbit's work in being a comic weird tale—but again, an ending that seems to dispel the supernatural only ends up leaving the matter in doubt and uncertainty.

The variety of Nesbit's weird work is highlighted by "The New Samson" (1909), which perhaps can best be characterised as an action thriller with an underlying element of psychological (but not supernatural) terror. Here a couple strives with great effort to save thousands of innocent lives from death at the hands of a dead architect who contrived to cause a theatre to collapse after his death. A somewhat implausible final twist underscores the element of petty revenge inherent in the tale.

A kind of proto-science-fictional element enters into two tales about secret and mysterious drugs, "The Three Drugs" (1908) and "The Five Senses" (1910). The former is again an interesting mix of a suspense/thriller scenario and supernaturalism, where a scientist hopes to have found a combination of drugs that will turn a person into a superman. The latter story tells of a scientist who has invented a series of drugs that will acutely enhance all five senses at once—apparently even after death.

Nesbit's latest weird tales would seem to be mere rehashes of earlier works, but there are points of interest in them nonetheless. "The Haunted House" (1915) appears to rework the motif of "The Three Drugs" in its depiction of a scientist who claims to have found a formula (by mingling the blood of the four chief races of humanity) to achieve immortality. A pseudo-supernatural conclusion concludes the tale effectively. "The Pavilion" (1915) reprises the central theme of "The Power of Darkness": here a pavilion is thought to be haunted, and two men battling for the love of a woman dare each other to spend a night there. This time, however, a supernatural conclusion is most emphatically at play.

It can be seen that E. Nesbit's weird work spans a wide range of subgenres—the ghost story, the "explained supernatural" (where the supernatural is suggested but explained away by natural means), the supernatural or non-supernatural thriller, the tale of psychological horror, the tale of ambiguous supernaturalism, and even some quasi-science-fiction narratives. Many of these subgenres would be developed extensively by later writers in the field, but Nesbit's contributions can hold their own with any work by either her predecessors or her successors. She was able to transmute her early fears of death and the dark into powerful weird tales where the emotions of love, revenge, rivalry, and hatred are elaborated with telling psychological insight and elaborated with vivid supernatural effects. Weird writing never constituted a major element in Nesbit's extensive literary work, but the tales she did write in this genre are among the most distinguished of their time.

Works Cited

Briggs, Julia. A Woman of Passion: The Life of E. Nesbit, 1858–1924. London: Hutchinson, 1987.

[Unsigned.] [Review of Something Wrong.] Spectator (18 November 1893): 37.

Edna W. Underwood: Dear Dead Women

We are grateful to Carol Wood Craine, author of the monograph *Mrs. Underwood: Linguist, Littérateuse* (1965), for virtually all the information that exists about the prolific author, poet, and translator Edna Worthley Underwood (1873-1961), who enjoyed something of a reputation in the 1910s and 1920s but whose work had fallen into obscurity long before her death at an advanced age. Craine made good use of the mass of Underwood's papers that the library of Fort Hays Kansas State College (now Fort Hays State University) had acquired—a collection that includes manuscripts, letters both to and from Underwood, scrapbooks, and much other matter.

Among connoisseurs of the weird, the supernatural, and the decadent, few are aware of Underwood's solitary collection of short fiction, *A Book of Dear Dead Women* (1911), and even fewer of the long novella "An Orchid of Asia," which lay unreprinted for ninety years after its appearance in a magazine. You will seek for her in vain in such reference works as Donald Tuck's *Encyclopedia of Science Fiction and Fantasy through 1968* (1968-74), Jack Sullivan's *The Penguin Encyclopedia of Horror and the Supernatural* (1986), and David Pringle's *Horror, Ghost and Gothic Writers* (1998), although the tireless E. F. Bleiler does include her in his *Guide to Supernatural Fiction* (1983). Mike Ashley's *The Supernatural Index* (1995) indicates that none of her stories had been reprinted in anthology down to the early 1990s, and this dearth can be extended to the present day.

Born in Maine in January 1873, Edna Worthley could boast English descendants extending back to the well-known sixteenth-century poet Henry Howard, Earl of Surrey. Her own upbringing, however, would seem to have inclined her toward any career except writing. She received no schooling as a child, but did attend school sporadically when her family moved to Kansas in 1884. Her thirst for learning, however, led her to undertake extensive self-instruction; with some assistance from a Swiss teacher, Arnold Jeannerett, she began learning several languages on her own, including Latin and several of the major European languages. She actually read Shakespeare and Poe first in German translations. In the end she mastered ten modern languages as well as Latin, and this erudition held her in good stead later in her career.

She began attendance at Garfield University in Wichita, Kansas, but later transferred to Michigan State University in Ann Arbor, where she received a B.A. in 1892. Returning to Kansas, she taught in a public school for three years before being dismissed on a trumped-up charge: she refused to give up reading the yellow-bound foreign-language books that she habitually carried with her, which her superiors believed to be "wicked books" of a possibly pornographic nature. The frontier mentality of Kansas Presbyterians was hostile to the sort of learning Underwood embodied, as she herself admitted:

> I was always vexed that Presbyterianism thrived upon sand. It was connected, in my mind, with unloveliness, both of matter and spirit. There was never a surface that reflected so bitterly the light, as the white front of that church. It had three sharp points, in a row, that stuck up ready and willing to impale sinners. The priests of Presbyterianism are stormy and iron hearted. (Quoted in Craine 20)

After marrying Earl Underwood in August 1897, Edna moved first to Kansas City, then to New York City, where her husband accepted a job in a jewellery firm. The bustling cosmopolitanism of that metropolis manifestly suited her, and she spent much of the rest of her life there. She immediately plunged into literary activity, writing poetry, plays, filmscripts, and other matter. Although her first published book was a collaborative translation of a work by Nikolai Gogol in 1903, the first published book that bore her name as author was *A Book of Dear Dead Women*, only one of whose stories—"The Painter of Dead Women"

(*Smart Set*, January 1910)—had been previously published in a magazine. It is remarkable that a relatively unknown writer succeeded in selling a book of short stories to a major publisher (Little, Brown of Boston). The publisher's letter of acceptance is of interest:

> We have read the manuscript you kindly left with us and are much impressed with the originality and fantastic quality of the stories. At the same time a publisher has courage who attempts at this time to bring out a volume of short stories, for such a book seldom has much sale. We would, however, like to issue this book with the idea that you could later let us have for publication a story of sufficient length to make a volume, and the present book would help to make your name better known. (Quoted in Craine 22)

How refreshing to see a mainstream publisher actually welcoming a volume of tales of "fantastic quality"! But Little, Brown's desire for a novel is also evident. In the event, Underwood did not publish any subsequent work with Little, Brown, probably because the story collection did not in fact sell well, as the publisher had predicted, even though it received on the whole favourable reviews. The *Philadelphia Press* noted that the stories had "something of the fantastically imaginative power of Hawthorne, combined with a gorgeousness of imagery that a writer fresh from the puritanical traditions could hardly have attained to" (quoted in Craine 36). The *New York Herald* accurately stated: "Her invention is remarkable . . . her sense of beauty and power are quite extraordinary. To those who love beautiful things and beautiful thoughts, it will appeal."

And yet, with the sole exception of "An Orchid of Asia," Underwood apparently wrote no more short stories. "Orchid" itself was the product of two years' study of orchids, begun as early as 1914. It appeared in the magazine *Asia* for August and September 1920. Two years earlier, she had sent the manuscript of the story to Luther Burbank, the botanist and horticulturist; he commented:

> The narrative is beautiful from beginning to end. . . . The first criticism I could make in reading your work is that it might give much more time on the development of plant life on the earth with great advantage to the

work; the second is where the dream commences. It is a pity you should make it cruel. . . . Altogether you have used your imagination to the fullest extent in creating the new orchid. (Quoted in Craine 23)

Evidently Burbank did not appreciate the use of his beloved orchids as the "villains" of a horror tale!

Although Underwood did publish a book of poetry, *The Garden of Desire* (1913), with the prestigious publisher Mitchell Kennerley, she belatedly took the advice of her early publisher and turned to the writing of novels. These are, however, for the most part historical novels, drawing heavily upon the languages she had learned, the extensive travel she had undertaken (usually in conjunction with her husband's business, Underwood acting as his translator), and her thorough grounding in history. *The Whirlwind* (1918) is a novel about Catherine II of Russia and set the stage for what she called The New World Trilogy—*The Penitent* (1922), about Alexander I; *The Passion Flower* (1924), about Nicholas I and Alexander Pushkin; and *The Pageant-Maker*, a novel that was planned but for some reason never completed or published. These novels were all issued by Houghton Mifflin and garnered generally favourable reviews; but by the mid- to late 1920s Underwood had made a decision to turn to poetry and translation.

By this time she had already issued translations from Russian and the Slavic languages (*Short Stories from the Balkans*, 1919), as well as translations from Persian (*Songs of Hafiz*, 1917) and Japanese (*Moons of Nippon*, 1919). Now she produced numerous translations from the Chinese, including the eighth-century poet Tu Fu (now rendered as Du Fu); these translations were made in collaboration with Chi-Hwang Chu. By the early 1930s she had turned to translating from the Spanish, including poets of Mexico, Haiti, and South America. It would be difficult to find an American writer who exhibits a greater facility in the translation of so many varied languages.

I have not had access to Underwood's poetry, issued in several small volumes by the specialty publisher Thomas Bird Mosher. It would appear, from examples quoted in Craine's monograph, that

Underwood adhered to traditional rhyme and metre from beginning to end, including her last published volume, *Maine Summers: Sonnets to My Mother* (1940), written to commemorate her mother's death. None of the verse appears even remotely weird, although *Egyptian Twilights* (1928), according to Craine, "comprises two poems, one a legend of the Priest of the Goddess Mut, the other an impressionistic picture of ancient Abydos and its statues" (43).

By 1940 Underwood appears to have given up both writing and translating. She was content to live alternately in New York and in a home in Arkansas City, Kansas. Her husband died on 5 September 1944, and Underwood herself was placed in a sanitarium in 1953, evidently the victim of dementia. She died on 14 June 1961.

What reputation Underwood is likely to have as a writer may rest on her solitary short story collection, *A Book of Dear Dead Women*, and "An Orchid of Asia." The chief feature of these stories is a sensitivity to aesthetic beauty in many forms, especially painting ("The Painter of Dead Women") and music ("Liszt's Concerto Pathétique," "The House of Gauze"). In many ways it could be said that Underwood adhered rigidly to Oscar Wilde's imperishable dictum in the preface to *The Picture of Dorian Gray*—"The artist is the creator of beautiful things"— and that the fantasy or weird element that enters almost incidentally into some of her tales does so only to enhance the atmosphere of ethereal beauty that Underwood is manifestly attempting to create. "The Painter of Dead Women" might be said to be on the borderline of the weird in its suggestion that a painter has devised a poison that will keep women in a state of undecaying beauty (a theme that may have been derived from Robert W. Chambers's exquisite story "The Mask," in *The King in Yellow*, 1895). More central to the weird tradition is "The Mirror of La Granja," about a soul entrapped in a mirror.

Underwood's two great triumphs of supernaturalism are unquestionably "The Opal Isles" and "An Orchid of Asia." Both are set in the South Seas—it is not certain whether Underwood had actually voyaged there, although she later travelled to the Caribbean, Panama, and all across Europe—and both have a distinctive atmosphere of horror in which beauty is inextricably mingled. The former tale also seems to have an uncanny similarity to the television show *The Prisoner* in its tale of a Frenchman shipwrecked on a remote island. In regard to the latter, there was some talk of turning it into a movie, but Underwood and the magazine *Asia* (which wished to commission a screenplay) could not agree on financial terms, so the project came to nothing. Even as a silent film, it could have been a striking production.

Of Underwood's non-supernatural tales, several are noteworthy, ranging from the grim *conte cruel* "The Sacred Relics of Saint Euthymius" to the delicate "Liszt's Concerto Pathétique," in which the concerto induces a bizarre hallucination. Several of the stories, including "Saint Euthymius" and "Sister Seraphine," appear to exhibit a certain hostility to organised Christianity, although this element is stood on its head in "The King," the last story in *A Book of Dear Dead Women.* "The House of Gauze," a story about Mozart, may perhaps reveal a certain naïveté that in some senses infuses all the stories, while "One of Napoleon's Loves" is a pure historical tale that anticipates her novels of a decade later.

It would be an exaggeration to claim that Underwood's work is a significant contribution to weird literature, but there is no denying its distinctiveness, elegance, and charm. The mingling of beauty and terror that is the hallmark of her best work links it with the writing of several of her contemporaries, including Oscar Wilde, Lafcadio Hearn, Lord Dunsany, and Robert W. Chambers; it could well have been a legacy of the Yellow Nineties in which Underwood's first literary experiments were evidently made. That she did not persist in the writing of tales of the supernatural is our misfortune, but the tales she did leave behind are sufficient testimony to her unique literary gifts.

Works Cited

Craine, Carol Wood. *Mrs. Underwood: Linguist, Littérateuse.* Hays: Fort Hays Kansas State College, 1965.

Things in the Weeds: The Supernatural in Hodgson's Short Stories

William Hope Hodgson's substantial output of short stories appears to have received short shrift from readers and critics alike, and for reasons that are not entirely clear. To be sure, Hodgson's four novels are all so distinctive of their kind—and, at a time when the "horror novel" was by no means a recognisable commodity, so noteworthy as harbingers of things to come—that they have perhaps justifiably attracted a significant proportion of the critical attention given to Hodgson. The mere fact that he wrote short stories with such prodigality and made relatively little attempt to gather them in collections—only four, *Carnacki the Ghost-Finder* (1913), *Men of the Deep Waters* (1914), *The Luck of the Strong* (1916), and *Captain Gault* (1917), appeared in his lifetime, and only a small proportion of this material was reprinted in such later volumes as *Deep Waters* (1967) and *Out of the Storm* (1975)—has made an assessment of his short fiction an unusually difficult prospect. Only now, with the publication by Night Shade Books of Hodgson's *Collected Fiction*,[1] is it becoming possible to gauge the full extent of Hodgson's work as a short story writer beyond such anthology chestnuts as "The Voice in the Night" or the well-known Carnacki stories.

That work has both its virtues and its drawbacks. Like many short story writers, Hodgson wrote a bit too much, and his tales are in some

---

1. In spite of certain deficiencies—notably an unacceptably high number of typographical errors and an absence of the highest professional standards of text editing and copyediting—this edition does make available a substantial proportion of Hodgson's short stories in a convenient edition, and it will be cited here where possible, under the abbreviation *CF*.

instances marred by repetitiousnes of conception, slipshod writing, and a certain monotony of setting, as he overused the sea topos that forms the most recognisable feature of his overall output. Hodgson appears to have had a relatively small body of distinctive short story ideas, and he often wrote several tales on the same basic premise with only slight variations in tone, setting, and execution. Moreover, his tales fall into several discrete categories, with relatively little overlap. The Carnacki stories, utilising the "psychic detective" scenario popularised by Algernon Blackwood's *John Silence–Physician Extraordinary* (1908), form a class by themselves, as do the lesser-known Captain Gault stories, recounting the adventures of that genial smuggler. Other tales are purely stories of adventure, whether on sea or land. But a substantial residue feature the core element that infuses at least three of his four novels (*The Night Land* being put aside as an unclassifiable cosmic fantasy): the supernatural. More specifically, a number of short stories provocatively address whether the supernatural does or does not come into play, and do so in such a way as to fall variously into such rubrics as the clearly supernatural, the "explained supernatural" (where purportedly supernatural phenomena are explained away as the product of trickery or of perceptual error on the part of the protagonists), the ambiguously supernatural (where it is not possible to determine whether the apparently supernatural phenomena are actually supernatural or the products of mental aberration),[2] and even a few proto-science fiction specimens.

That the great proportion of Hodgson's tales, of whatever type, take place in a maritime setting suggests that Hodgson saw in such a setting a convenient means for effecting that "willing suspension of disbelief" so critical to the success of a supernatural tale. Because the sea—especially in its more remote stretches, as in the immensities of the Atlantic or Pacific Ocean—is a relatively unknown quantity to most

---

2. Henry James's *The Turn of the Screw* (1898) has been thought to be a prototypical example of this mode; but see my discussion in *Unutterable Horror* (296–99), where I maintain that the tale is, and is meant to be perceived as, supernatural.

readers, and because of the known existence of unusual creatures lurking in the depths of the ocean, a sea setting can be the locus of horrors that, on land, might appear too incredible for belief. "I will expose, in all its hideous nakedness, the death-side of the sea" (*CF* 3.180), says the narrator of "Out of the Storm" (1909)—a statement that is emblematic of much of Hodgson's work. In "The Stone Ship" (1914) we learn that "some mighty strange things do happen at sea, and always will while the world lasts" (*CF* 3.299). The technique is no different in kind from other weird writers' use of remote locales—Blackwood's employment of the Canadian wilderness in "The Wendigo" and other tales; Lovecraft's setting many of his tales in the backwoods of New England or, in *At the Mountains of Madness*, in the frozen wastes of Antarctica—and Hodgson incorporates within his zone of mystery not only the inaccessible reaches of the sea itself but those hapless islands of humanity, ships, that dare to venture upon it.

One of the means by which Hodgson seeks to convey a sense of the supernatural, even if in the end the supernatural does not actually come into play, is by the seemingly elementary use of the word *Thing*. The fact that he would use such titles as "The Thing in the Weeds" and "The Thing Invisible" points to the importance of this formulation in his aesthetic of the weird. What might seem like a kind of cop-out—an inability or unwillingness to describe in detail the entity in question—becomes instead a device for the segregation of the non-human (or the no-longer-human), or even the non-animal, from the known animate species that populate the earth. It is exactly the *indefinability* of the "Things" encountered by Hodgson's protagonists that is the source of terror in these tales; they inspire fear because, at least initially, they resist easy classification within the realm of biology, and their almost uniform aggressiveness and hostility to humanity renders them a far from abstract intellectual conundrum.

To be sure, Hodgson is variously successful at conveying the inimical qualities of his "Things." In the early tale "A Tropical Horror" (1905) an immense monster that comes on board the deck of a ship is labelled a "Thing" (CF 3.146), but later it is identified as a "serpent" (3.147). It is not entirely clear whether the serpent is actually a supernatural entity or merely a large sea-snake: Hodgson, as frequently in his tales and novels, relies on the increased dramatic pace of his narrative—many of his tales become adventure stories in which frenetic action must be taken against the hostile force, whether natural or supernatural, that is menacing the protagonists—to distract the reader from questioning too closely the reality or plausibility of the entity in question. In "A Tropical Horror" the entire absence of any plausible rationale for the serpent's existence renders the tale unconvincing and preposterous. Similarly, in "The Call in the Dawn" (1920) the "Thing" (CF 1.227) encountered by a ship in the Sargasso Sea proves to be "some kind of devil-fish or octopus" (1.227)—presumably non-supernatural, even if "The thing was enormous" (1.228).

The Sargasso Sea stories, indeed, engage in a subtle dance between supernaturalism and non-supernaturalism. In several tales the super-natural does not appear to come into play, unless we are to assume that the very existence of this weed-choked realm is itself a supernatural phenomenon, a matter directly addressed in "The Call in the Dawn":

> To those who have cast doubt upon the reality of the great Sargasso Sea, asserting that the romantic features of this remarkable sea of weed have been greatly exaggerated, I would point out that this mass of weed lurking in the central parts of the Atlantic Ocean is a fluctuating quantity, not confined strictly to an area, but moving bodily for many hundred of miles according to storm and prevailing winds, though always within certain limits. (CF 1.221)

This pseudo-scientific explanation is, in fact, not especially helpful, but it suggests that there is a kind of double remoteness associated with the site—not only is it in an unknown stretch of the Atlantic Ocean (where, theoretically, almost anything can breed and emerge), but those all-pervading weeds themselves provide an added layer of obscurity beneath which "Things" can lurk. In the two-part "From the Tideless Sea" (1906-07) we learn that "There was some dread Thing hidden within the weed" (CF 1.148), but this turns out to be an octopus. The hapless Arthur Samuel Philips, who, with his wife, is trapped aboard a derelict caught in the weeds, states, "I have grown to believe this world of desolation capable of holding any horror, as well it might" (1.156); but there is little justification for his alarm until he discovers that a pig that he had on board has been killed by "some monstrous thing" (1.165). But even this baleful entity proves to be "a gigantic crab, so vast in size that I had not conceived so huge a monster existed" (1.172). But when Philips, seeing an entire herd of crabs large and small, remarks that "the mystery [was] solved" and that "with the solution, departed the superstitious terror which had suffocated me" (1.172), we are to understand that no actual supernatural phenomenon has occurred.

Something similar happens in the other Sargasso Sea stories. In "The Mystery of the Derelict" (1907) the derelict encountered by the crew of the *Tarawak* proves to be filled with "giant rats" (CF 1.184), but no suggestion of supernaturalism is necessarily conveyed by this description. At the end of the story the narrator reflects on the matter:

> . . . of the rats that evidently dwelt in [the derelict], I have no reasonable explanation to offer. Whether they were true ship's rats, or a species that is to be found in the weed-haunted plains and islets of the Sargasso Sea, I cannot say. It may be that they are the descendants of rats that lived in ships long centuries lost in the weed-sea, and which have learned to live among the weed, forming new characteristics, and developing fresh powers and instincts. (1.186)

The implication is that the existence of these rats could be encompassed by science, if sufficient information about their nature and origins were available.

"The Thing in the Weeds" (1912) opens with the dramatic statement, "This is an extraordinary tale" (CF 1.187), which might lead one to suspect supernaturalism, as might the later comment that "out there in the darkness there surely lurked some Thing of monstrousness" (1.191). The narrator, looking out over the prow of his ship at night, contemplates the situation: "I remember how the lamps made just two yellow glares in the mist, ineffectual, yet serving somehow to make extraordinarily plain the vastitude of the night and the *possibilities of the dark*" (1.193). Hodgson's emphasis on that last phrase suggests that, just as anything can be imagined coming out of the sea, so can horrors of all sorts be conceived to emerge from the darkness. Indeed, in this tale the monster is much more frequently *heard* and *smelled* before it is actually *seen*. When it finally makes itself visible, it proves to be nothing more than a giant "squid" (1.198), one that is dispatched with guns and knives. The same fate overtakes the aquatic creature in "The Finding of the *Graiken*" (1913), which is finally identified as a cuttlefish (CF 1.219).

The ambiguity of the ontological status of Hodgson's monsters—are they supernatural or natural?—is maintained in a great many of his non-Sargasso Sea stories as well. "The Silent Ship"—evidently a variant ending of *The Ghost Pirates*—presents entities that are manifestly humanoid but, also, manifestly supernatural, in keeping with the nautical ghosts of the novel: "I saw Things coming out of the water alongside the silent ship. Things like men, they were, only you could see the ship's side through them, and they had a strange, misty, unreal look" (CF 1.138). In "The Stone Ship" (1914) the eponymous ship appears to be the locus of a succession of supernatural phenomena: members of the crew that lands on the ship seem to see immense faces peering at them underwater, are pursued by what seem to be strings of red hair, and the like. But the narrator, Duprey, systematically explains all these phenomena: the strings of red hair prove to be nothing more than "some kind of big-hairy sea-caterpillar" (CF 1.302), while the faces are those of drowned men whose tissues have been swollen by what is explicitly noted as a "natural process" (1.303). All this lends credence to Duprey's expostulation, "The natural wonders of the sea, beat all made-up yarns that ever were!" (1.301).

An exquisite ambiguity as to the nature of the supernatural phenomenon is maintained in "The Haunted *Pampero*" (1918). Captain Tom Pemberton agrees to take the *Pampero,* a ship that has a bad reputation, on a commercial voyage. His derision at the notion that the ship is cursed ("She's no more haunted than I am!" [CF 1.377]) does not reassure his wife, who insists on accompanying him. Shortly after a man, Tarpin, is picked up as a castaway, strange things begin to happen on the *Pampero*: the pigs on the ship are attacked, and appear to be suffering from shark-bites; a mysterious snarling creature appears to be on board. There is some suggestion that the entity is after the captain's wife; and there is the further suggestion that Tarpin is a kind of shape-shifter. After the latest attack, Tarpin is missing—and something is seen swimming away from the ship: "He saw the Thing again. The fish had two tails—or they might have been legs" (1.389). In the end the matter remains unresolved: the narrator quotes from an unnamed writer who has written about the phenomena aboard the *Pampero*, and who suggested that Tarpin might have been a "sea ghoul"—"some abnormal thing out of the profound deeps" (1.390). And yet, this writer also maintains that

> he did not believe the *Pampero* to be "haunted." It was, he held, simple chance that had associated a long tale of ill-luck with the vessel in question; and that the thing which had happened could have happened as easily to any other vessel which might have met and picked up the grim occupant of the derelict whaleboat. (1.391)

And the final bit of supernatural deflation comes from Pemberton's recollection that "the marlinspike which Tarpin always carried was sharpened much to the shape of a shark's tooth" (1.391).

Another sea legend is recounted in "The Mystery of the Water-Logged Ship" (1911)—the legend of the sailor's light. The captain of the *White Hart* explains:

> "It's always give as a warnin'. My father, as was fifty-five year at sea, an' died there, seen it three times, an' if he hadn't took notice he'd have smashed up his shop every time. He always said it was the spirits of them that's drowned warnin' the sailors. I half believes it, you know, and half don't." (CF 2.357)

This legend appears to be, at the start, the only way to explain the lights seen on an apparently abandoned derelict in the North Atlantic. Later, as further bizarre phenomena occur, another member of the crew states, "There's something devilish aboard that craft, you mark my word; but whether carnal weapons is any use, the Lord He knows. I don't" (2.362). Certainly, something awesome and mysterious appears to be involved, especially when five members of the *White Hart*'s crew disappear. But here the resolution of supernaturalism is traced not to unusual natural phenomena but to human trickery: it is discovered that the derelict has a secret underground compartment where its crew had been hiding, having robbed an immense quantity of gold bullion from another ship. The crew was deliberately staging the lights and other mysterious events to scare off potential detection.

Quite similar is "The Ghosts of the *Glen Doon*" (1911), whose very title suggests the supernatural. But the opening sentence of the story— "The *Glen Doon* was reputed to be haunted—whatever that somewhat vague and much abused term may mean" (CF 1.369)—already equivocates on the matter. The *Glen Doon* had capsized and was anchored in San Francisco Bay. Larry Chaucer accepts a bet to spend a night aboard the ship. He hears a strange tapping or hammering on board the ship, then disappears. His father, the chief of police, investigates: "He had no belief at all in the supernatural" (1.377), and quickly gets to the bottom of the affair: the ship has a hollow steel mast that leads down to a large room, formed by a series of boilers, housing counterfeiters.

It is, however, difficult to deny that the entities in "Demons of the Sea" (1923) are supernatural. The narrator writes:

> . . . crawling about the barque's deck were the most horrible creatures I had ever seen. . . . Their bodies had something of the shape of a seal's, but of a dead, unhealthy white. The lower part of the body ended in a sort of double-curved tail on which they appeared to be able to shuffle about. In place of arms they had two long, snaky feelers, at the ends of which were two very human-like hands equipped with talons instead of nails. Fearsome indeed were these parodies of human beings! (CF 1.479–80)

These loathsome entities are dispatched—or, at any rate, dispersed—with cutlasses and pistols; but the fact that they are not entirely extirpated makes the narrator ponder uneasily: "Perchance on some dark, fog-bound night, a ship in that wilderness of waters may hear cries and sounds beyond those of the wailing of the winds. Then let them look too it; for it may be that the demons of the sea are near them" (1.482).

The two Captain Jat stories are of some interest in this context. Told from the point of view of Pibby Tawles, a cabin-boy for whom the gruff captain has developed a fondness, the tales appear merely accounts of adventure on the high seas, as Captain Jat searches for treasure in far-off corners of the world. In "The Island of the Ud" (1912) Jat comes to that island, whose name he explicitly declares to mean "Devil" (CF 2.423). Pibby and Jat first hear "a far, faint inhuman howling" (2.421), then see "something that was half a woman and half something else" (2.421). Later several of these women are seen; a later description is striking:

> They had faces so flat as to be almost featureless. At first, if he thought at all, he supposed that they were wearing some kind of mask; but as they ran, the nearest woman opened her mouth and howled, the same disgusting sound that he had heard earlier that night. As she howled, she brandished both the hand that held the torch, and the other hand, above her head. But she had no hands; her arms ended in enormous claws, like the claws of a giant crab. (2.422)

This seems spectacular enough, but later Pibby "saw plainly that [the claws] were no more than cast-off shells of some huge sea-reptile" (2.428). But just as the supernaturalism of the tale seems to be deflated, Pibby sees another sight: "But the second woman gave him a horrible feeling; he could not see where her arms ended and the claws began" (2.428). And there the matter is left unresolved: do these women merely put on the claws of some sea creature for the purpose of frightening their enemies, or do their arms actually grow into claws? Much the same ambiguity is maintained in "The Adventure of the Headland" (1912), in which Jat and Pibby encounter creatures called Iils, or sacred dogs "near big as donkeys" (CF 2.450), as Jat remarks. Other creatures found running with the dogs, who "whined and snarled like dogs, yet certainly were not dogs" (2.452), prove to be the priests of the cult, covered with dog-skins and running on all fours.

There is little reason to doubt that "The Voice in the Night" (1907) is Hodgson's most accomplished tale of supernatural horror. What distinguishes this story, aside from the gradualness and subtlety of its supernatural manifestation, is an element of religious criticism that is rare in Hodgson's work. We learn that the protagonist—named only John—and his fiancée (never named), having survived the sinking of the *Albatross* (a name that immediately recalls Coleridge's *The Rime of the Ancient Mariner*, a poem of supernatural horror that is itself heavily laden with religious imagery), find themselves stranded on a lagoon. Initially they "thanked God" (CF 3.160) for their apparent salvation, especially when they found that there were edible foodstuffs on a foundered ship near the lagoon, at which point John "thanked God in my heart for His goodness" (3.161). But the lagoon is nearly entirely covered with a curious grey fungus, which also grows and on the foundered ship. A short time later a bit of the fungus is found growing on John's fiancée's hand—then on John's own face. At this point the couple seem resigned to their fate ("God would do with us what was His will" [3.163]), but after several months in which their food has been reduced to virtually nothing, the woman takes to eating the fungus. Later John encounters a hideous creature—perhaps a man—covered with the fungus. Finally, John capitulates and eats some of the fungus himself. . . . As in Lovecraft's "The Colour out of Space" (1927), which features a somewhat analogous phenomenon, we are left to wonder at both the physical and the psychological degradation of the couple—and we are not surprised that John, in seeking help from a ship that has sailed nearby, refuses to allow the crew members to catch a glimpse of him. What is puzzling, however, is John's insistence that "it is God's wish that we should tell to you all that we have suffered" (3.159). The motivations of a god who would allow the creatures of his special care to experience such a loathsome fate can only be wondered at.

"Out of the Storm" is somewhat similar in its implicit religious criticism. A scientist has apparently managed to establish some kind of mental communication with a man who is on board a sinking ship. This man sees "the tentacles of some enormous Horror" (CF 3.180) and, in his terror, delivers a rebuke to God: "Oh! God, art Thou indeed God? Canst Thou sit above and watch calmly that which I have just seen? Nay! Thou art no God! Thou art weak and puny beside this foul *Thing* which Thou didst create in Thy lusty youth. *It* is *now* God—and I am one of its children" (3.180). Although the man later admits that he has blasphemed (3.182), it is his condemnation, not his sheepish apology, that remains in our minds.

"The Derelict" (1912) appears to be somewhat of an expansion or revision of "The Voice in the Night." Whereas in the earlier story the exact biological status of the grey fungus is never clarified (is it animate? or is it merely a kind of virus or plague?), "The Derelict" is much more explicit. What appears to be a kind of half-animate mould is found on an ancient derelict:

> All about him, the mould was in active movement. His feet had sunk out of sight. The stuff appeared to be *lapping* at his legs; and abruptly his bare flesh showed. The hideous stuff had rent his trouser-legs away, as if they were paper. He gave out a simply sickening scream, and, with a vast effort, wrenched one leg free. It was partly destroyed. The next instant he pitched face downward, and the stuff heaped itself upon him, as if it were actually alive, with a dreadful savage life. It was simply infernal. (CF 3.249)

Horrible as this is, it is not the end of the story. The culmination occurs when the strange noises accompanying the horrors on the derelict—specifically a "Thud! Thud! Thud!" heard at regular intervals—are explained: they are the beating of the heart of the derelict itself, which by some means has become a living entity. In the end a doctor who had introduced the narrative concludes that it exemplifies his notion that "so eager [is] the Life-Force to express itself, that I am convinced it would, if given the right Conditions, make itself manifest even through so hopeless-seeming a medium as a simple block of sawn wood" (3.235). In the case of the derelict, the doctor continues,

> "If we could know exactly what that old vessel had originally been loaded with, and the juxtaposition of the various articles of her cargo, plus the heat and time she had endured, plus one or two other only guessable quantities, we should have solved the chemistry of the Life-Force, gentlemen. Not necessarily the *origin,* mind you; but, at least, we should have taken a big step on the way." (3.257)

Whether this pseudo-scientific explanation is convincing is not to the point; the gesture of making such an explanation at all is what matters. Just as in some of the Sargasso Sea stories, we are led to believe that it is merely the absence of adequate scientific information that prevents the seemingly supernatural phenomena from being entirely explained in natural terms.

A different kind of "scientific" explanation is found in a number of the stories involving Thomas Carnacki, the psychic detective—but it is an explanation based largely upon unconvincing occultist presuppositions. Although perhaps the best known of Hodgson's short stories, the Carnacki tales as a group do not rank high in his overall output, as they are marred by the crude stylistic formulae customary in popular fiction—the mechanical use of a recurring character, a verbose drawing out of the plot beyond its natural parameters, certain irritating habits of speech by Carnacki himself (especially his repeated query, "Can you understand?" when dealing with apparent supernaturalism), the contrived use of occultist mumbo-jumbo ("electric pentacles," the "Saaamaaa Ritual," etc.), and so forth. That Hodgson was attempting to capitalise on the success of Blackwood's best-selling *John Silence* (1908) is evident, as the Carnacki tales began appearing in the *Idler* only two years after the appearance of that volume.

And yet, where the Carnacki tales gain their interest is in their constant fluctuating, exactly as Hodgson's other tales do, between supernaturalism and non-supernaturalism. In "The Thing Invisible," Carnacki declares that "I am as big a sceptic concerning the truth of ghost tales as any man you are likely to meet" (CF 2.138). Carnacki goes on to say that he is an "unprejudiced sceptic," by which he means that "I am not given to either believing or disbelieving things 'on principle', as I have found many idiots prone to be . . . I view all reported 'hauntings' as un-proven until I have examined into them; and I am bound to admit that ninety-nine cases in a hundred turn out to be sheer bosh and fancy" (2.138). The proportion is not by any means quite that high in the nine Carnacki tales, but a surprising number of them resolve themselves non-supernaturally: in "The Thing Invisible" it turns out that the dagger that has apparently hurled itself through the air and nearly killed a man has been operated by a secret mechanism; in "The House among the Laurels" the seemingly supernatural phenomena in a deserted castle have been staged by a group of squatters who may have lived in the place for years; "The Find" is an explicitly non-supernatural story of a forged rare book. Conversely, "The Gateway of the Monster," "The Whistling Room," "The Haunted *Jarvee*," and "The Hog" are unequivocally supernatural, although several are spoiled by incomprehensible occultist pseudo-science.

This leaves the two stories, "The Searcher of the End House" and "The Horse of the Invisible," in which *many* but not *all* of the "super-natural" phenomena are resolved naturally: Carnacki, at the end of both stories, insists that a slim residue of genuine supernaturalism may still remain. The first tale is set in a house being rented by Carnacki himself and his mother; and it is plagued with strange odours, inexpli-cable rappings, and so forth. Although Carnacki discovers that many of the occurrences were engendered by a Captain Tobias, a smuggler, he is unable to identify Tobias as the source of the most striking phenome-na—the ghosts of a woman and a child, seen variously by Carnacki him-self and others. Carnacki is compelled to conclude: "I can only suppose that *fear* was in every case the key, as I might say, which opened the senses to an awareness of the presence of the Woman" (CF 2.230). Similarly, in "The Horse of the Invisible," while it is determined that a man named Parsket has dressed up as a horse in order to scare away a naval officer named Beaumont who is engaged to Miss Hisgins (Parsket being in love with her himself), Carnacki believes that "there was something more at work than [Parsket's] sham-haunting" (CF 2.252) and concludes tentatively that "Parsket had produced what I might term a kind of 'induced haunting,' a kind of induced simulation of his mental conceptions, due to his desperate thoughts and broodings" (2.254). The suggestion in both stories is that intense emotions can of themselves produce quasi-supernatural phenomena even when other phenomena are convincingly explained away as the product of deceit and trickery.

In other tales by Hodgson we find the pseudo-supernatural ("The Goddess of Death" [1904], in which the apparent movement of a marble statue of Kali is explained away as a mechanical contrivance), the mystical ("The Riven Night," in which spirits of the dead are seen in a purple fog), a touching religious fantasy ("The Valley of Lost Children," which explains what happens to little children who die prematurely), and even a curious proto-science fiction tale to prove a religious point ("The Baumoff Explosive"). The posthumously published "The Room of Fear" appears to be one of Hodgson's earliest tales, and is a gripping narrative of the effects of fear upon a small boy who is made to sleep in a lonely bedroom and is terrified of the shadows he encounters there. In many ways this story is emblematic of the entire corpus of Hodgson's short fiction, which exhibits the manifold effects of fear upon the varied protagonists—ranging from grizzled sea captains to learned scientists, from hapless passengers adrift on derelicts to uneducated and superstitious sailors—who people his tales.

Even if few of the short stories can be said to have the substantive effect of his novels, especially such a fantastic epic as *The Night Land*, and even if they are marred by a certain repetitiveness of setting and incident, the best of Hodgson's tales comprise an important contribution to the literature of terror; and in large part they gain their significance by exhibiting a multiplicity of gradations between pure non-supernaturalism and pure supernaturalism, with some of the most provocative of them failing to resolve definitively into the one mode or the other. While the obscurity into which much of Hodgson's work fell for a generation following his death may have precluded its exercising a notable influence upon his successors in the weird tale, the refusal of that work to fade away bespeaks an inner core of aesthetic merit that augurs well for its endurance.

Works Cited

Hodgson, William Hope. *The Boats of the "Glen Carrig" and Other Nautical Adventures.* The Collected Fiction of William Hope Hodgson, Volume 1. Ed. Jeremy Lassen. San Francisco: Night Shade Books, 2003. [CF 1]

———. *The House on the Borderland and Other Mysterious Pieces.* The Collected Fiction of William Hope Hodgson, Volume 2. Ed. Jeremy Lassen. San Francisco: Night Shade Books, 2004. [CF 2.]

———. *The Ghost Pirates and Other Revenants of the Sea.* The Collected Fiction of William Hope Hodgson, Volume 3. Ed. Jeremy Lassen. San Francisco: Night Shade Books, 2005. [CF 3.]

Joshi, S. T. *Unutterable Horror: A History of Supernatural Fiction.* Hornsea, UK: PS Publishing, 2012; rpt. New York: Hippocampus Press, 2014. 2 vols.

II. The Era of Lovecraft

M. R. James and the Classic Ghost Story

In one sense, it is exceptionally odd that M. R. James (1862–1936) would become the leading twentieth-century author of ghost stories; in another sense—especially when we consider the sort of ghost stories James came to write—it seems eminently natural and inevitable. James led a double, perhaps a triple, life—first as one of the most distinguished scholars of medieval manuscripts and early Christianity of his time, second as a noted professor and administrator at Cambridge University and then at Eton College, and finally as a writer of ghost stories. It is no surprise that only that last body of work continues to attract the attention and fascination of readers worldwide: James's scholarship, although fundamentally sound, has now been largely superseded, and in any event its audience is necessarily limited to a small cadre of the learned, whereas the ghost stories are of universal appeal and have never been surpassed by those many authors who have chosen to pay them tribute by imitation.

Montague Rhodes James was born on 1 August 1862, at the vicarage of Goodnestone, in Kent, the fourth child and third son of Herbert and Mary Emily James. Three years later Herbert was transferred to Livermere Hall, near Bury St. Edmunds in Suffolk, a home that remained in the James family until Herbert's death in 1909, and remained close to M. R. James's heart long after that.[1] Herbert had fallen under the influence of the evangelical movement of the time, but there is little evidence that his children became doctrinaire or fundamentalist in

---

1. A photograph of Livermere Hall can be found in Norman Scarfe, "The Strangeness Present: M. R. James's Suffolk," *Country Life* No. 4655 (6 November 1986): 1416.

their religion; indeed, it was a lasting disappointment for Herbert when Montague eventually decided not to pursue holy orders.

The young Montague received his education first at Temple Grove preparatory school (1873-76), then Eton College (1876-82), where he gained a lifelong attachment to his tutor, Henry Elford Luxmoore. Luxmoore may have seen in James—who was already exhibiting an interest in what might be called biblical archaeology (notably the apocryphal books of the Old and New Testament and the apocalyptic literature of the early Middle Ages)—the wide-ranging scholar that he did not have the opportunity to be. At the same time, Eton also saw James's initial interest in the ghost story. In a letter to his parents he speaks of stumbling upon the work of the mediaeval writer Walter Map (whose *De Nugis Curialium* James would later edit and translate), "which contains some extraordinary stories about Ghosts, Vampires, Woodnymphs etc." (cifted in Pfaff 28). His reading of the Irish supernaturalist Joseph Sheridan Le Fanu, who would remain his favourite writer of horror tales, also dates to his Eton days. There is evidence that he wrote—or, at any rate, told—his first ghost stories as early as 1878; certainly, by 1880, when the *Eton Rambler* published his essay on "Ghost Stories," his interest was well established.

But for the time being, scholarship was paramount. It was inevitable that, after graduating from Eton, James would advance to King's College, Cambridge: for centuries King's had been a closed corporation reserved exclusively for graduates of Eton, and even after the reforms of 1861 it was still largely an Etonian preserve. James's years as a collegian at King's (1882-87) saw the flowering of his interest in biblical curiosa, mediaeval manuscripts, and church history. This work only continued when he was successively named Fellow (1887), Dean (1889), and finally Tutor (1900) of King's. His first scholarly article had been published as early as 1879, but beginning in 1887 he commenced a series of publications—books, monographs, editions, articles, and reviews—that would not cease until his death. In 1893 James also became the director of the Fitzwilliam Museum at Cambridge, a post he would hold until 1908.

How exactly James found the time for all this work, let alone the writing of ghost stories, was a puzzle to friends and colleagues alike, especially when one considers James's other interests—his devotion to Dickens, P. G. Wodehouse, and Conan Doyle's Sherlock Holmes stories; his interest in card games and crossword puzzles; and, of course, the abundant conviviality he showed to friends, students, and almost any others who came within his horizon. A charming and often-told anecdote gets to the heart of the matter:

> When Monty was in his early thirties, Lord Acton came here [to King's] ... "You know Montague James?" he asked a King's man. "Yes, I know him." "Is it true that he is ready to spend every evening playing games or talking with undergraduates?" "Yes, the evenings and more." "And do you know that in knowledge of MSS he is already third or fourth in Europe?" "I am interested to hear you say so, Sir." "Then how does he manage it?" "We have not yet found out." (Cited in Cox 101)

The matter becomes even more baffling when we consider the extensive travel in which James engaged from as early as 1892, when he took his first bicycle tour of the Continent. From 1895 to 1914 he took at least one trip to France a year, chiefly for the purpose of examining mediaeval cathedrals; he would later maintain that he had personally seen 141 out of the 143 extant cathedrals in France. Trips to Scandinavia followed in 1899 and 1900.

James's ghost stories were manifestly an amusement of his lighter hours, although they need not be esteemed lightly on that account. We may date the commencement of his supernatural writing to the rather frivolous tale "A Night in King's College Chapel" (probably written in 1892), but it was not long before he produced weightier work. A celebrated meeting of the Chitchat Society (a literary and social group at Cambridge) on 28 October 1893, saw James read his two earliest ghost stories, "Canon Alberic's Scrap-book" and "Lost Hearts." Thus began a long tradition, extending well in the 1920s, when James would read drafts of his tales to a succession of friends, collegians, and other groups, usually at Christmas time. Although these first two stories were published in magazines in 1895, James would very likely not have considered book publication of his tales had not a close friend, James McBryde, undertaken the task of illustrating several of them. McBryde's sudden death in 1904, after completing only four illustrations, appears to have led James to issue *Ghost-Stories of an Antiquary* (1904) as a tribute to his friend's memory.

A year after this volume came out, James was made Provost of King's College. It proved to be a difficult assignment: not only had he been selected only after two others had declined the post, but the tedium of administrative work began to weigh upon his temperament. It was also at this time that a struggle between the "pious" and the "ungodly" began to emerge for control of Cambridge's intellectual culture; James, manifestly on the side of the "pious," was notably uncharitable toward such of his "ungodly" Cambridge colleagues as James George Frazer and Bertrand Russell. The war years were particularly stressful: Cambridge seemed emptied of its finest youths, many of whom (such as Rupert Brooke, whose participation in Cambridge theatricals had attracted James's admiration) left their bodies on the battlefields of France. Although a second volume of tales, *More Ghost Stories of an Antiquary*, appeared in 1911, along with an array of impressive scholarly works, this was a markedly unhappy time in James's life.

The return to Eton in 1918, this time as Provost, could only have been a relief. As Provost of King's, James had been criticised for failing to be an intellectual pioneer; his scholarship seemed increasingly remote and unrelated to present-day concerns. A close friend, A. C. Benson, who had known James since his Eton days, wrote somewhat uncharitably in his diary: "his mind is the mind of a nice child—he hates and fears all problems, all speculation; all originality or novelty of view. His spirit is both timid and unadventurous" (cited in Cox 125). Eton was, however, exactly the place for James: his instinctive empathy with the enchantments and travails of schoolboy life, the unaffectedly avuncular or even grandfatherly air he exhibited, and the prodigious learning that he carried so unassumingly were perfectly suited to the education of British youth. Administrative mundanities were safely in the hands of a head master; James, although he faced the terror of dining with the King and Queen once every year, could devote himself wholly to nurturing his charges with quiet encouragement.

It was during his Provostship that his two final collections of ghost stories, *A Thin Ghost* (1919) and *A Warning to the Curious* (1925), appeared, followed by the gathering of all four volumes, plus a few additional tales, as *The Collected Ghost Stories of M. R. James* (1931). Such important works of scholarship as *The Apocryphal New Testament* (1924), and such popular works as *The Wanderings and Homes of Manuscripts* (1919) and *Abbeys* (1925), also appeared. James's learning of the Danish language paid dividends when he translated some of Hans Christian Andersen's fairy tales into English in 1930. In 1925 he completed the prodigious task—begun informally as early as 1884—of cataloguing all the manuscripts of the Cambridge colleges. Honours were showered upon him in later life: he became a trustee of the British Museum in 1925; he was awarded honorary degrees from Oxford (1927) and Cambridge (1934); and, as a capstone, in 1930 he received the Order of Merit from King George V. James's later years were plagued with increasing ill health, and he died on 12 June 1936. His headstone bears the words of Ephesians 2:19: "No longer a sojourner, but a fellow citizen with the saints and of the household of God."

It would be easy to pass off James's ghost stories as light-hearted amusements; James himself lends some credence to this view in many of his own remarks. Indeed, many scholars on James have unwittingly belittled his work by asserting that "His stories are straightforward tales of terror and the supernatural, utterly devoid of any deeper meaning" (Penzoldt 191), or that "his fiction . . . was simply the bagatelle for an idle hour, the construction of a delicate edifice of suspense with which to entertain the young people whose company he so much enjoyed" (Briggs 125). To be sure, a more exhaustive study of James's life and scholarly work will shed additional light on some of the telling autobiographical elements in the stories—his wide-ranging travels as the source of the authentic local colour in such stories as "Canon Alberic's Scrap-book" or "Number 13"; his pathological fear of spiders in "The Ash-Tree"; the extraordinary re-creation of mediaeval Latin in the opening of "The Treasure of Abbot Thomas" and of a seventeenth-century trial in "Martin's Close"—but even this does not get us close to the philosophical thrust of the ghost stories.

Richard William Pfaff maintained, correctly, that "Writers on ghost stories . . . fail not so much in praising MRJ's stories too little—indeed, it might be argued that if anything the tendency is to overpraise them as a whole—but in paying little or no attention to the really remarkable thing about them, the brilliance of the antiquarian background" (415). But Pfaff himself may not have been quite as precise in this formulation as one might wish; for it is not merely the "antiquarian background" (which, in one sense, is merely utilised to create a patina of veri-similitude) that is remarkable, but the purpose to which James puts it. James was sufficiently well-read in the traditions of supernatural fiction to know that terror is most effective when emerging from the depths of history. Where he differed from his predecessors—especially the Gothic novelists of the late eighteenth and early nineteenth centuries, who actually set their works in the mediaeval era in order to enhance the reader's suspension of disbelief in the supernatural manifestations they exhibited—was in suggesting the pervasiveness of the past's influence upon the present: his tales, generally set only a few decades prior to their date of writing, establish a continuity between past and present in which the present is entirely engulfed and rendered fleeting and ineffectual in the face of the heavy cultural burden of prior centuries. Martin Hughes gets close to this idea when he writes: "the premiss of antiquarian stories is that records and relics are very important: when properly studied they are extremely revealing of all aspects of life in the past; moreover what they reveal is still important now" (81).

In conveying this conception, James's protagonists are of central importance. It is a truism to say that James never engages in any detailed psychological analysis of the antiquarians who are the driving force of his tales: they are, in one sense, merely stand-ins for himself—uniformly male, scholarly, somewhat unworldly, and engaged in investigating the past largely to satisfy curiosity. Jack Sullivan has remarked of these figures:

> The characters are antiquaries, not merely because the past enthralls them, but because the present is a near vacuum. They surround themselves with rarefied paraphernalia from the past—engravings, rare books, altars, tombs, coins, and even such things as doll's houses and ancient whistles—seemingly because they cannot connect with anything in the present. (75)

There may not be sufficient textual evidence to support this interpretation, but it is provocative nonetheless. What has, however, gone largely unnoticed is that there is a subtle but unmistakable progression between these seemingly "innocent" characters (all of whom bring doom upon themselves by actively seeking to probe into ancient secrets that they know full well may be dangerous) and the avowedly "evil" figures who people some of James's most memorable tales. The redoubtable Mr. Abney in "Lost Hearts," who seeks prolonged life by eating the still-beating hearts of little children, is described as "a man wrapped up in his books," while Karswell, in "Casting the Runes," is merely a scholar gone wrong—one who is so embittered at his failure to gain recognition as a man of learning that he turns to occultism as an act of revenge. It may be worth noting that the motif of supernatural revenge, very common in James's stories, may itself have been a product of his own scholarly interests, specifically his interest in apocalyptic literature. Early in his career he had noted that this literature "operates on the principle that the punishment should fit the crime, with much attention to the often gory details by which this principle is worked out" (cited in Pfaff 109).

It is here, I believe, that James's ghost stories, his antiquarian scholarship, and his religion become inextricably fused. Shane Leslie, a longtime friend of James, made the seemingly startling remark that "his belief in ghosts marched parallel with his religion" (45), although he does not elucidate the statement. Another friend, Stephen Gaselee, has portrayed James's religion as follows:

> He was a man of simple and deep religious feeling. Learned biblical scholar as he was, he did not think much of the "higher criticism", at any rate when it was destructive; and I have heard him say that the biblical documents were subjected to criticism not only unfair in itself, but of a kind that no one would ever have dreamed of applying to the secular literary remains of antiquity. (429–30)

That last sentence is of the highest importance; for although James may not have been a dogmatic or fundamentalist Christian, his hostility to the intellectual ferment of his time in matters of religion—the shockwaves following Darwin's *Origin of Species* (1859); the "Higher Criticism" that showed the evolution of biblical texts over centuries and made it increasingly unlikely that they were direct revelations from God; the gradual but inexorable shift of intellectual opinion from unquestioned piety to agnosticism and even atheism—is evident. In his ghost stories, James uses such devices as occultism (the perversion of religion into impious magic and sorcery) and the misuse or misconstrual of biblical passages as a warning on the dangers of straying from orthodoxy. The Bible's own warnings on the dangers of being tempted by Satan are so frequent that it can easily lead the weak or the vicious—such as James Wilson, the redoubtable landowner of "Mr. Humphreys and His Inheritance"—into becoming one of the Devil's party.

So much attention has been given to the technique of James's ghost stories that insufficient attention has been paid to their deeper meanings. This is particularly the case with James's ghosts. H. P. Lovecraft wrote pungently:

> In inventing a new type of ghost, he has departed considerably from the conventional Gothic tradition; for where the older stock ghosts were pale and stately, and apprehended chiefly through the sense of sight, the average James ghost is lean, dwarfish, and hairy—a sluggish, hellish nightabomination midway betwixt beast and man—and usually *touched* before it is *seen*. (92)

All this is very entertaining and, indeed, by no means off the mark; but Lovecraft fails to probe the true symbolism of James's ghosts. They are "lean, dwarfish, and hairy" because they thus embody the *primitivism* that stands in stark contrast to the learned, rational, sceptical antiquarians who, for James, represented the pinnacle of human achievement. It is not insignificant that Somerton, in "The Treasure of Abbot Thomas," "screamed out . . . like a beast" when encountering the horror in the well: contact with the primitive reduces even the most civilised to the level of the subhuman.

Related to this whole motif is James's array of lower-class characters. The fractured and dialectical English in which these characters speak or write is, in one sense, a reflection of James's well-known penchant for mimicry; but it cannot be denied that there is a certain element of malice in his relentless exhibition of their intellectual failings. The illiteracy of Somerton's valet in "The Treasure of Abbot Thomas"; the malapropisms of the bailiff, Mr. Cooper, in "Mr. Humphreys and His Inheritance"; the ignorance of the hapless librarian in "The Tractate Middoth"—all these and other characters are made figures of fun, the butt of jests from a man whose own learning was unassailable. And yet, they frequently occupy pivotal places in the narrative: by representing a kind of middle ground between the scholarly protagonists and the aggressively savage ghosts, they frequently sense the presence of the supernatural more quickly and more instinctively than their excessively learned betters can bring themselves to do.

Another aspect of James's characterisation is his women characters—or, rather, their virtual absence from his tales. Even in his own lifetime James, the lifelong bachelor, suffered from accusations of misogyny: in 1896 he opposed the granting of degrees to women at Cambridge, and in 1916–17 he attacked with unwonted viciousness a paper on comparative religion by Jane Harrison in the *Classical Review* that he regarded as disrespectful to Scripture. Several women appear to have pursued James for his hand in marriage, but he resisted each time. James's defenders point to his cordial friendships with any number of women, notably Gwendolen McBryde, the widow of his friend James McBryde; but the world of James's fiction is as devoid of significant female characters as H. P. Lovecraft's. This need not be regarded as a flaw: James was not writing mimetic fiction that claimed to present a well-rounded portrayal of society at large. He was writing of what he knew—the world of (male) antiquarian scholarship. And yet, the sardonic view of marriage that we find in such a story as "The Rose Garden," or the annoying Lady Waldrop in "Mr. Humphreys and His Inheritance," seems to go a bit beyond mere whimsy. What, then, are we to make of the fact that several of the ghosts in James's tales create fear through a hideous parody of affection? Who can forget the thing in the well in "The Treasure of Abbot Thomas," which "slipped forward on to my chest, and *put its arms round my neck*" (James's emphasis)?

And yet, it may well be said that for James, as Austin Warren has observed, "It is places, not persons, which are hauntable" (98). In this sense, "Number 13," otherwise as far as possible from the standard "antiquarian ghost story" that James initiated, is prototypical in its display of a haunted hotel room. Although the locus of horror in James is chiefly situated in cathedrals, abbeys, and other sites where centuries of religious tradition have engendered an inevitable backlash of unorthodoxy among a select band of heretics, horror can also manifest itself in any locale where the long reach of history has had free play—a rose garden, a hedge maze, even a library. The mundanity of these settings is vital to James's methodology of the ghost story, which (as he wrote in the preface to his second collection) is designed to elicit the reader's awareness that "If I'm not careful, something of this kind may happen to me!"

It is generally agreed that the tales in M. R. James's final two collections of ghost stories, *A Thin Ghost and Others* (1919) and *A Warning to the Curious* (1925), to say nothing of the stories that he gathered only in his *Collected Ghost Stories* (1931) or did not collect at all, are generally inferior to those of his two landmark volumes, *Ghost-Stories of an Antiquary* and *More Ghost Stories of an Antiquary*. And yet, for a writer as accomplished as James, even his lesser work—and this includes essays, fragments, and even letters—remains of compelling interest. In his final two decades of life, scholarship and administrative burdens remained paramount in his sphere of interests—it was, after all, at this time that he produced such monuments as his edition of *The Apocryphal New Testament* (1924) and his translation of the fairy tales of Hans Christian Andersen from the Danish (1930)—but the writing of ghost stories (which James acknowledged was the only type of fiction he cared to write) was more than the production of an idle hour.

A *Thin Ghost and Others* appeared shortly after James became Provost of Eton in 1918—an occasion on which he received congratulations from Thomas Hardy, A. E. Housman, the Archbishop of Canterbury, and other notables. The war was over, much to James's relief; there is some evidence that he felt a certain guilt at pursuing arcane scholarship at King's College, Cambridge, while others were dying in the battlefields of Europe. Unlike the stories in his first two collections, which take for their settings a large segment of the European continent, from France and Germany to Sweden and Denmark, his later tales stay pretty close to home. All are set in England, most of them in out-of-the-way rustic sites where disproof of the supernatural phenomena on display is difficult. It is as if James himself, after spending much of his youth and early adulthood in wide-ranging travels for scholarly and antiquarian purposes, felt the need to re-establish his roots with the country of his birth—especially with the rural countryside, where he manifestly felt far more at home than in the frenetic megalopolis of London. The extraordinary felicity that James displayed in devising fictitious names for his settings is enviable: it requires a careful consultation of a gazeteer of England to determine that none of the sites mentioned in "A View from a Hill"—Fulnaker Abbey, Oldbourne Church, Lambsfield, Wanstone, Ackford, and Thorfield—have any existence except in James's imagination.

But to say that the names of James's locales are fictitious is one thing; it is a very different thing to say that they are purely imaginary. His extensive travels, by foot and by bicycle, throughout his native land had rendered every county familiar. It does not, perhaps, take much effort to determine that Seaburgh, in "A Warning to the Curious," is a thin disguise for Aldeburgh, in Suffolk, or that, in "The Uncommon Prayer-book," the imaginary towns of Stanford St. Thomas and Stanford Magdalene are probably based upon Stanford on Teme and Stanford Bridge, in Hereford and Worcester. What all this suggests is that James was becoming increasingly disinclined to mask the autobiographical details that form the core of genuine experience at the foundation of many of his tales. This feature may be exhibited most clearly in some of the tales he gathered only in his *Collected Ghost Stories* or did not collect, or publish, at all. It is scarcely to be denied that James himself is the narrator of "Wailing Well," a tale that sent shivers through the Boy Scout troop to whom he read it in 1927; "The Fenstanton Witch," although set in the eighteenth century, draws clearly upon James's intimate familiarity with the history and topography of King's College, where he was successively a King's Scholar, Fellow, Dean, and Provost.

James's later tales appear to display a fascination with the *technique* of the ghost story—specifically, with the attempt to render the supernatural plausible in light of the increasingly militant materialism and secularism (exhibited such such Cambridge thinkers as Lytton Strachey, John Maynard Keynes, and Bertrand Russell) that was dominating intellectual thought in his day. Naïve exhibitions of ghosts and vampires were clearly out of the question; extreme indirection now had to be employed. This focus on technique perhaps reaches its apex in "Two Doctors," which even so devoted a partisan as Michael Cox calls "one of Monty's least successful stories" (*Casting the Runes* 143). And yet, this story hardly deserves the bad press it has received, for it proves to be an extraordinarily clever supernatural detective story (James was devoted to mystery and detective tales, to the extent that in one of his articles on ghost stories he makes a casual and unexplained reference to Captain Hastings, the sidekick of Agatha Christie's Hercule Poirot) in which all the pieces of the puzzle are laid out for the reader clever enough to place them in their correct sequence and bestow upon them their correct significance.

Another device much used by James in his later tales to create verisimilitude, and to overcome the hard-headed sceptic's natural incredulity in the face of the supernatural, was narrative distancing. This device is carried perhaps to excess in such a tale as "The Residence at Whitminster," in which a first-person narrator, acting as a kind of editor, redacts the notes of a Dr. Ashton, letters by Mary Oldys (the niece of Henry Oldys, Dr. Ashton's successor at the collegiate church at Whitminster), the diary of a Mr. Spearman (Mary's fiancée), and other documents, all in the effort to present with the utmost indirectness, and with what politicians might later term plausible deniability, the supernatural phenomena on display.

It is possible that this obsession with technique was the result of James's exhaustive study of the history and theory of the ghostly tale, a work chiefly undertaken in the 1920s as a concomitant to his fascination with one of the leading Victorian practitioners of the weird tale, Joseph Sheridan Le Fanu (1814–1873). James testifies that he pored through entire runs of such periodicals as the *Dublin University Magazine* and *All the Year Round* in the hunt for previously unattributed works by Le Fanu; and although he erred in a few cases, his work did result in the addition of several tales to the Le Fanu corpus, as exemplified by James's landmark edition of Le Fanu's *Madam Crowl's Ghost and Other Tales of Mystery* (1923). It is very likely that this work led James to reformulate, or at any rate refine, his own nebulous views on what constitutes a ghost story and how it should best be told.

His first words on the matter occur in the brief preface to *More Ghost Stories of an Antiquary* (*Count Magnus* 255–56). Here, in a very short space, he manages to outline three principles of ghost story writing: 1) "the setting should be fairly familiar and the majority of the characters and their talk such as you may meet or hear any day"; 2) "the ghost should be malevolent or odious"; 3) "the technical terms of 'occultism' . . . tend to put the mere ghost story . . . upon a quasi-scientific plane, and to call into play faculties quite other than imaginative." In his later writings on the ghost story—such as his introduction to V. H. Collins's *Ghosts and Marvels* (1924), "Some Remarks on Ghost Stories" (1929), and "Ghosts—Treat Them Gently!" (1931)—James does not so much revise as lend further nuance to these principles.

And yet, there is a question as to how faithfully James himself adhered to his own dicta when writing ghost stories. The notion of "familiarity," especially as regards characterisation and setting (both of time and of place), was for James a matter of some elasticity. Although he remarks that a setting as remote as the twelfth or thirteenth century is not likely to induce a reader to remark, "If I'm not careful, something of this kind may happen to me!," we quickly see that any number of James's tales are set, or at least begin, in the seventeenth, eighteenth, or early nineteenth century. James of course does not require absolute contemporaneity: he does remark in the introduction to *Ghosts and Marvels* that

> For the ghost story a slight haze of distance is desirable. "Thirty years ago," "Not long before the war," are very proper openings. If a really remote date be chosen, there is more than one way of bringing the reader in contact with it. The finding of documents about it can be made plausible; or you may begin with your apparition and go back over the years to tell the cause of it; or . . . you may set the scene directly in the desired epoch, which I think is hardest to do with success. (*Haunted Dolls' House* 248)

It can readily be seen that James has adopted each of these options in his various tales. And yet, I believe that James's own antiquarianism allowed him to believe that even the seventeenth century was a period of relative recency that requires only the citing of certain telling historical details to elicit the reader's sense of vital reality. Whether the passing of another full century since the writing of James's earliest ghost stories—and, perhaps more significantly, the collapse of historical learning even on the part of many readers who claim to be well educated—has rendered this conception a bit more dubious is something for which James cannot be held responsible.

But James exemplified brilliantly in his own work his corresponding principles of "atmosphere and a nicely managed crescendo." He goes on to state: "Let us, then, be introduced to the actors in a placid way; let us see them going about their ordinary business, undisturbed by forebodings, pleased with their surroundings, and into this calm environment let the ominous thing put out its head, unobtrusively at first, and then more insistently, until it holds the stage" (*Haunted Dolls' House* 248). Here James may have been combating the luridness that he censured in many of the Gothic novels of the late eighteenth and early nineteenth centuries—a luridness whose recrudescence he would also censure in some of the pulp magazine fiction of the 1920s and 1930s. Curiously, James's enunciation of this principle places him strikingly in accord with the dominant tendency of post-World War II horror fiction, when such writers as Ray Bradbury, Shirley Jackson, and Richard Matheson chose to emphasise the ordinariness of their characters as they encounter the supernatural, in conscious contrast to what came to be regarded as the over-the-top flamboyancy of H. P. Lovecraft and his disciples. It could well be said that this principle has now been carried somewhat to excess in the best-selling work of Stephen King, Peter Straub, and Dean Koontz, who are so focused on the mundane lives of their mundane characters that the supernatural phenomenon—which, one would suppose, is the *raison d'être* of their work—is given short shrift.

As it is, James found himself increasingly critical of much of the supernatural literature of both his predecessors and his contemporaries. His disdain for Poe's masterwork, "Ligeia," is scarcely concealed by the remark: "Evidently in many people's judgments it ranks as a classic" (*Haunted Dolls' House* 250). In "Some Remarks on Ghost Stories" the drumbeat of negativity continues: after lavishing praise upon the Victorians, especially Le Fanu, James finds that Bram Stoker's *Dracula* "suffers by excess"; that his friend E. F. Benson "sins occasionally by stepping over the line of legitimate horridness"; that Ambrose Bierce is "sometimes unpardonable"; that the psychic detective stories of Algernon Blackwood and of K. and Hesketh Pearson err by overreliance on occultism; and so on and so forth (*Haunted Dolls' House* 258–59). But James reserves his greatest condemnation for the material contained in the *Not at Night* anthologies assembled by Christine Campbell Thomson, most of which derived from the American pulp magazine *Weird Tales*: "These [stories] are merely nauseating, and it is very easy to be nauseating" (*Haunted Dolls' House* 259) In fact, James is probably largely on target here: present-day devotees of pulp fiction only make themselves ridiculous by defending its literary worth *in toto* instead of the tiny fraction of work (chiefly the tales of Lovecraft, Clark Ashton Smith, Robert E. Howard, Henry S. Whitehead, and a very few others) that can legitimately be said to rise above the general level of formulaic hackwork.

But James lets down his hair entirely in a private letter not meant for publication—one he wrote to Nicholas Davies on 12 January 1928, shortly after receiving W. Paul Cook's magazine *The Recluse* (1927), containing H. P. Lovecraft's historical treatise "Supernatural Horror in Literature," which featured several glowing pages on James himself ("An M. R. James Letter"). Beginning by remarking that Lovecraft's "style is of the most offensive," James goes on to condemn Matthew Gregory Lewis's *The Monk* (it "is really not fit to be read"), Mary Shelley's *Frankenstein* (which "fails to impress me as it should"), Edward Bulwer-Lytton's "The Haunted and the Haunters" (which is "boomed above its merits"), Bierce (who "to my thinking oversteps the mark"), Robert W. Chambers (whose supernatural novels "are horrid & nasty"), Arthur Machen (who "has a nasty after-taste: rather a foul mind I think, but clever as they make 'em"), and so on. In general, "the moderns are apt to be either woolly or too nasty for me."

James, certainly, is entitled to his opinions, but it is evident that his emphasis on reticence and indirection has betrayed him into wholesale condemnations of authors and works that have far more merit than he was willing to acknowledge. James remained devoted to the ghostly tales of such writers as H. Russell Wakefield, A. M. Burrage, Walter de la Mare, and their congeners; the one American he seems to have appreciated unreservedly is Mary E. Wilkins Freeman, author of *The

Wind in the Rose-Bush and Other Stories of the Supernatural (1903), as richly evocative of the history and landscape of New England as James's own tales are of those of England. His distaste for any admixture of sexual imagery in the supernatural tale is what no doubt led him to condemn Arthur Machen, whose "The Great God Pan" evoked the outrage of many other critics as the outpouring of a foul mind.

And yet, on this whole issue, James himself may not have followed his own counsel as strictly as he seemed to fancy. There is no denying a certain element of "horridness" in much of James's own work, however artfully and indirectly it is conveyed. From beginning to end of his career as a writer of ghost stories he could unleash such hideous displays as the following:

> On the left side of his chest there opened a black and gaping rent; and there fell upon Stephen's brain, rather than upon his ear, the impression of one of those hungry and desolate cries that he had heard resounding over the woods of Aswarby all that evening. ("Lost Hearts")

> . . . they saw a round body covered with fire—the size of a man's head—appear very suddenly, then seem to collapse and fall back. This, five or six times; then a similar ball leapt into the air and fell on the grass, where after a moment it lay still. The Bishop went as near as he dared to it, and saw—what but the remains of an enormous spider, veinous and scarred! ("The Ash-Tree")

> "I was conscious of a most horrible smell of mould, and of a cold kind of face pressed against my own, and moving slowly over it, and of several—I don't know how many—legs or arms or tentacles or something clinging to my body. I screamed out . . . like a beast, and fell away backward from the step on which I stood . . ." ("The Treasure of Abbot Thomas")

> But in the chalk pit it was that poor Uncle Henry's body was found, with a sack over the head, the throat horribly mangled. It was a peaked corner of the sack sticking out of the soil that attracted attention. I cannot bring myself to write in greater detail. ("The Story of a Disappearance and an Appearance")

> You don't need to be told that he was dead. . . . His mouth was full of sand and stones, and his teeth and jaws were broken to bits. I only glanced once at his face. ("A Warning to the Curious")

Have scarecrows bare bony feet? Do their heads loll on to their shoulders? Have they iron collars and links of chain about their necks? Can they get up and move, if never so stiffly, across a floor, with wagging head and arms close at their sides? and shiver? ("Rats")

Of course, it is unjust to rip out these passages from their contexts; they are no doubt what James specified as the culmination of a "nicely managed crescendo." And even here, the reticence that James so valued comes into play: the simple sentences "I cannot bring myself to write in greater detail" and "I only glanced once at his face" evoke far more horror than any amount of blood-and-thunder grisliness ever could, and one can be assured that, had James lived another two or three generations, he would have emphatically bestowed his mark of approval on such masters of subtlety as Robert Aickman, Ramsey Campbell, T. E. D. Klein, and Thomas Ligotti rather than on their noisier contemporaries, Dennis Wheatley, Stephen King, John Saul, and Clive Barker. In horror fiction, less is almost always more, and even the most florid word-painting (or, in film, special-effects violence and grue) pales in comparison to what the sensitive imagination can envision when properly stimulated.

M. R. James would no doubt have been surprised at the literary legacy he fostered. This legacy is exhibited not so much in the work of those friends and colleagues of James who tended to produce uninspired pastiches of his style and manner—E. G. Swain (*The Stoneground Ghost Tales*, 1912), Arthur Gray (*Tedious Brief Tales of Granta and Gramarye*, 1919), R. H. Malden (*Nine Ghosts*, 1942), A. N. L. Munby (*The Alabaster Hand*, 1949)—as in certain other writers who used the antiquarian ghost story as the springboard for imaginative creations of their own. The three Benson brothers—A. C., E. F., and R. H.—all wrote supernatural tales, and E. F. was present at the legendary meeting of the Chitchat Society in 1893 when James read his first tales (Lubbock 38); but the tales of E. F. Benson, the best of the three, although not written with quite the meticulous precision of James's, tend to be of broader range and theme.

It can by no means be claimed that such writers as Walter de la Mare, L. P. Hartley, Oliver Onions, L. T. C. Rolt, Russell Kirk, or Robert Aickman are in any sense merely imitators of James; indeed, one suspects that the greater emphasis that many of these writers place upon the psychological analysis of ghostly phenomena, especially as they affect the victim of them, is a direct result of James's apparent lack of interest in this regard. In any event, one would like to think that James—whose views of his predecessors and contemporaries in the realm of supernatural fiction were not always charitable—would have taken some pride in the tradition he instigated, for all his deprecation of his own work as merely an exercise in pleasant shudder-coining. There is much to be said for the scholarly reserve, indirection, and subtlety of James's tales, so strikingly in contrast to the loud, brash, and frequently vulgar effusions that clutter the supernatural field today. That his stories have survived a century or more while those of his noisier successors seem destined to lapse into merited oblivion should itself be regarded as "a warning to the curious."

Aside from H. P. Lovecraft, no writer of supernatural fiction has achieved such celebrity on such a relatively small body of work as M. R. James. Even the least of his ghost stories exhibits a craftsmanship and attention to detail that must be the envy of more hasty and prolific scriveners, while the fertility of conception that allowed him to ring so many ingenious changes upon the one topos of the ghost or revenant can only elicit our admiration. James and his disciples have attracted a small cadre of devotees intent on preserving their work, if only by means of the small press, and, more valuably, on explicating its smallest particulars. But James's ghost stories are far more than the property of a coterie: by revealing to the full the possibilities of aesthetic achievement in the tale of supernatural horror, they become a contribution to the literature of the ages.

Works Cited

Briggs, Julia. *Night Visitors: The Rise and Fall of the English Ghost Story.* London: Faber & Faber, 1977.

Cox, Michael. *M. R. James: An Informal Portrait.* London: Oxford University Press, 1983.

Gaselee, Stephen. "Montague Rhodes James." *Proceedings of the British Academy* 22 (1936): 418–33.

Hughes, Martin. "A Maze of Secrets in a Story by M. R. James." *Durham University Journal* 85 (January 1993): 73–98.

James. M. R. *Casting the Runes and Other Ghost Stories.* Ed. Michael Cox. London: Oxford University Press, 1987.

—————. *Count Magnus and Other Ghost Stories.* Ed. S. T. Joshi. New York: Penguin, 2005.

———. *The Haunted Dolls' House and Other Ghost Stories.* Ed. S. T. Joshi. New York: Penguin, 2006.

———. "An M. R. James Letter." In *A Pleasing Terror: The Complete Supernatural Writings of M. R. James.* Ed. Barbara and Christopher Roden. Ashcroft, BC: Ash-Tree Press, 2001. 638–43.

Leslie, Shane. "Montague Rhodes James." *Quarterly Review* 304 (January 1966): 45–56.

Lovecraft, H. P. *The Annotated Supernatural Horror in Literature.* Ed. S. T. Joshi. New York: Hippocampus Press, 2nd ed. 2012.

Lubbock, S. G. *A Memoir of Montague Rhodes James.* Cambridge: Cambridge University Press, 1939.

Penzoldt, Peter. *The Supernatural in Fiction.* London: Peter Nevill, 1952.

Pfaff, Richard William. *Montague Rhodes James.* London: Scolar Press, 1980.

Sullivan, Jack. *Elegant Nightmares: The English Ghost Story from Le Fanu to Blackwood.* Athens: Ohio University Press, 1978.

Warren, Austin. "The Marvels of M. R. James, Antiquary." In *Connections.* Ann Arbor: University of Michigan Press, 1970. 86–107.

Some Notes on Lord Dunsany

I. The Pegāna Mythos

When H. P. Lovecraft wrote, somewhat extravagantly, that Lord Dunsany's "point of view is the most truly cosmic of any held in the literature of any period," he was manifestly referring to the first two of Dunsany's collections of tales, *The Gods of Pegāna* (1905) and *Time and the Gods* (1906). These two volumes form a compelling aesthetic unity. Along with three later stories, they constitute what might be termed a "Pegāna Mythos"–Dunsany's creation of a fully realised imaginary realm, complete with gods, demigods, priests, and worshippers.

If one considers the first twenty-six years of the life of Edward John Moreton Drax Plunkett (1878–1957), who in 1899 became the 18th Lord Dunsany upon the death of his father, one might be pardoned for doubting that he would become the pioneering fantaisiste of his generation. Born of an ancient aristocratic line that could trace its ancestry in Ireland to the twelfth century and its peerage to the fifteenth, Dunsany seemed in his youth and adolescence nothing but a scion of the idle rich. He had published only one mediocre poem, "Rhymes from a Suburb" (*Pall Mall Magazine*, September 1897), and showed little interest in literature, in spite of being tutored by the poet Stephen Phillips prior to his entering Sandhurst, a military school for the English aristocracy.

But in 1904 three notable events occurred. First, Dunsany wedded Lady Beatrice Villiers (daughter of the Earl of Jersey), and they would have a long and happy marriage that would last until Dunsany's death. Second, he ran for Parliament on the Conservative ticket; fortunately for literature, he lost. Third, he wrote *The Gods of Pegāna*.

Since Dunsany had no literary reputation, he had to pay for the publication of the book by Elkin Mathews. But its unexpected *succès d'estime*—augmented by a glowing review by the poet Edward Thomas—assured Dunsany's standing, and he would never have to subsidise the publication of his work for the next fifty years. Indeed, in those fifty years Dunsany probably became one of the most widely published authors in English literature, appearing in every conceivable magazine from the *Atlantic Monthly* to *Ellery Queen's Mystery Magazine* and publishing thirteen novels, seventeen story collections, forty-one plays, eight volumes of poetry, and a variety of essays and miscellany. Hundreds of stories, essays, and poems remain uncollected to this day.

What is the significance of *The Gods of Pegāna*? Why create an entirely new ersatz mythology? There is no real parallel for such an undertaking in the entire range of previous literature, and at the very least the invention of a new religion suggests some discomfort on the part of the author with the religion to which he was born. As an Anglo-Irish aristocrat, Dunsany presumably absorbed the Protestant teachings of his family, but he appears to have been singularly devoid of conventional religious belief. His biographer Mark Amory (40) reports that Dunsany read Friedrich Nietzsche in 1904, the very time he was writing his first book, and perhaps that is the only clue we need.

The Gods of Pegāna is an instantiation of the quintessential act of fantasy: the creation of a new world. Dunsany has simply carried the procedure one step further than any of his conceivable predecessors—William Beckford (*Vathek*), William Morris with his mediaeval fantasies—by inventing an entire cosmogony. But this act is not meant frivolously or whimsically. In effect, Dunsany infuses his new realm with his own philosophical predilections, and these predilections—although expressed in the most gorgeously evocative of prose-poetry—are of a very modern, even radical, sort.

At the very opening of *The Gods of Pegāna* Dunsany asserts that time has no beginning nor end, and that space is equally infinite. These are strange conceptions for an orthodox religionist to assert, but they are exactly in accord with the findings of nineteenth-century science. The god Kib is the creator of all earth life, but he created men out of beasts—exactly as Darwin established.

Is it a paradox for an apparent atheist like Dunsany to create a multiplicity of gods and other semi-divine forces? Quite the contrary, for *The Gods of Pegāna* might be thought an instance of *aesthetic animism*. Animism—the act of endowing a quasi-human consciousness and will to natural forces—is prototypical of primitive man. A river runs downstream; therefore, there must be a force compelling it to do so. A tree grows; therefore, there must be a force or god in the tree that is producing this growth. Of course, Dunsany is no primitive, nor does he expect his readers to be; this is where the aesthetic element comes into play. By this assertion of animism Dunsany is urging his readers to see the world anew, with the fresh, unjaded eyes of a child or a primitive, so that we may all re-establish the bond with the natural world that modern civilisation—particularly with the advent of mechanisation—seems to be dissolving. When speaking, in his poignant autobiography *Patches of Sunlight* (1938), of how he came to be a writer, he tells of seeing a hare in a garden:

> If ever I have written of Pan, out in the evening, as though I had really seen him, it is mostly a memory of that hare. If I thought that I was a gifted individual whose inspirations came sheer from outside earth and transcended common things, I should not write this book; but I believe that the wildest flights of the fancies of any of us have their homes with Mother Earth. (9)

One other key quotation applies specifically to *The Gods of Pegāna* and *Time and the Gods*, when Dunsany notes his inability to master Greek in school, which

> left me with a curious longing for the mighty lore of the Greeks, of which I had had glimpses like a child seeing wonderful flowers through the shut gates of a garden; and it may have been the retirement of the Greek gods from my vision after I left Eton that eventually drove me to satisfy some such longing by making gods unto myself, as I did in my first two books. (30)

Certainly, the polytheism of Pegāna is more akin to Graeco-Roman mythology than to Christianity, as is the intimate way in which the gods participate directly in human affairs.

In Pegāna, the gods are a terrible force. One of the most chilling lines in all literature, perhaps, is the simple utterance of the gods in "Of How Imbaun Met Zodrak": "Let Us call up a man before Us that We may laugh in Pegāna." The gods even punish the hubris of demigods—the rivers Eimēs, Zānēs, and Segastrion—who go beyond their domain and flood the hills and plains. And when the King of Runazar made statues of the gods with his face upon them, the gods decreed not merely that the king should not be, but that he should never even have been. (Lovecraft found this so piquant a conception that he alluded to it in *The Case of Charles Dexter Ward*, in reference to the obliteration of the memory of Joseph Curwen.)

Yet in *Time and the Gods* even the gods begin to feel fear as well as dispensing it, and it is Time that is their great enemy, something even they cannot battle. After all, they know that their very existence is fleeting and tentative: they exist only as the dreams of the ultimate god, Māna-Yood-Sushāī, who is lulled to sleep by the constant drumming of Skarl the Drummer and who will one day wake and banish all creation.

Time and the Gods makes Dunsany's hostility to conventional religion still clearer than *The Gods of Pegāna*. In that first volume, Imbaun the priest had shrewdly remarked, "Wherefore have the people chosen prophets but that they should speak the hopes of the people, and tell the people that their hopes be true?" Imbaun goes on to speak of the afterlife in terms manifestly resembling those in which a Christian might describe heaven, but Imbaun knows it is merely a benign fable. In *Time and the Gods*, however, religion becomes a force of evil. "The Sorrow of Search" is a simple parable of the errors of religion. In "For the Honour of the Gods" a once-happy people, devoid of religion, are persuaded to worship gods and to fight in their name, but this brings nothing but death and the destruction of their civilisation. As for "The Relenting of Sarnidac," which speaks of how a lame dwarf, seeing the gods forsaking the earth and following them, is himself mistaken for a god and worshipped: how can we not think of the accidental and haphazard way in which unworthy and (spiritually) deformed entities are made into gods?

The three stories that Dunsany gathered under the title "Beyond the Fields We Know" in *Tales of Three Hemispheres* (1919) contain the only other references to the locales and entities of Pegāna in all his work. These three tales perhaps clarify—or, conversely, muddle even further—Dunsany's conception of the distinction between dream and reality. His early tales as a whole are oftentimes carelessly referred to as dream-fantasies, but very few of them are explicitly presented as such. Instead, they purport to be "true" accounts of incidents in the life of a civilisation in the dawn of time. Yet, in *The Gods of Pegāna*, we read of Yoharneth-Lahai, who sends out little dreams and fancies to human beings at night; but only Māna-Yood-Sushāī knows whether these dreams be false and the events of the waking world be true, or vice versa. Lovecraft echoes this conception in a slightly different context in "Beyond the Wall of Sleep": "Sometimes I believe that this less material life [of dreams] is our truer life, and that our vain presence on the terraqueous globe is itself the secondary or merely virtual phenomenon."

"Idle Days on the Yann" is, for the first time in Dunsany's work, an explicit dream-fantasy, as the narrator leaves the realm of Ireland and enters a dream-world—not, apparently, of his own imagining, but a kind of general realm to which all dreamers have access. (Lovecraft again follows Dunsany on this point in *The Dream-Quest of Unknown Kadath*.) In "The Shop in Go-by Street," the narrator wishes to enter the dream-world once more, but appears unable to do so by actual dreaming. He is informed of a shop in London through whose back door he can have access to the realm he seeks; when he enters that door, he finds that the boat on which he had sailed down the river Yann is in decaying ruins. Evidently dream-time and real time do not function in unison.

Then, in "The Avenger of Perdóndaris," even stranger things occur.

Once again passing through the shop door, he encounters an old witch who suggests that London itself is a dream for those in the dreamworld. Fantasy and imagination become merely a matter of perspective, and—in a possible anticipation of his later work—Dunsany suggests that he can find wonder even in what he previously took to be prosaic reality. The astounding statement of the narrator, as he yearns to return to the London he had previously found so wearisome—"I'm tired of the Lands of Dream"—is a herald of Dunsany's own repudiation of imagined worlds and his rediscovery of the imaginative stimulus of his native land of Ireland in such novels as *The Curse of the Wise Woman* (1933) and *The Story of Mona Sheehy* (1939).

But in these early works reality is wholly and delightfully banished, and we appear to be in a realm whose only reason for existence is the evocation of beauty and terror. There is every reason to believe that, throughout the whole of his life, Dunsany acknowledged the truth of Oscar Wilde's bon mot—"The artist is the creator of beautiful things"— and sought to embody it in his work.

This is not the place for any detailed examination of the influence of Dunsany upon H. P Lovecraft. Suffice it to say here that Lovecraft found these early works of Dunsany so overwhelming (*A Dreamer's Tales* [1910], the first book of Dunsany's that Lovecraft read, "arrested [him] as with an electric shock") that he immediately lapsed into that pitfall so keenly noted by C. L. Moore: "No one can imitate Dunsany, and almost everyone who's ever read him has tried."[1] Yet it is of some note that the very feature that Lovecraft found most stimulating in these tales—cosmicism, or the suggestion of the infinite reaches of time and space and the resulting insignificance of all human life and endeavour— is exactly what Lovecraft chose not to imitate in the bulk of his own "Dunsanian fantasies," with the exception of "The Other Gods." Lovecraft must have realised that Dunsany had written works so perfect

---

1. C. L. Moore to H. P. Lovecraft, 30 January 1936 (ms., John Hay Library, Brown University).

of their kind that imitation was fruitless; when he came to incorporate cosmicism into his own writing, he did so in those realistic tales where it takes on a very different form from that found in *The Gods of Pegāna* and *Time and the Gods*.

Lord Dunsany's career began a decade before Lovecraft's and continued two decades beyond Lovecraft's death, yet it is largely through Lovecraft that we continue to remember the Irish writer. Perhaps, then, it is now time to appreciate Dunsany in his own right as a master fantaisiste whose prodigal imagination was equalled by few, whose prose style was a model of affecting simplicity, and whose bold philosophical vision remains challenging to the present day. Those readers who hearken to the siren's song of Dunsany's tales, novels, and plays will find an inexhaustible treasure-trove of wonder for their delectation.

II. Jorkens

There is a certain injustice in the fact that Lord Dunsany is best known for the shimmering tales of exotic fantasy embodied in his early volumes, from *The Gods of Pegāna* (1905) to *Tales of Three Hemispheres* (1919), and including such landmark works as *A Dreamer's Tales* (1910) and *The Book of Wonder* (1912). It is these works that come to mind when we employ the adjective "Dunsanian," and it is these works that influenced such later writers as H. P. Lovecraft, Fritz Leiber, and J. R. R. Tolkien. And yet, Dunsany's literary career extended a full three and a half decades after the definitive end of this early phase of high fantasy, and it would be unjust not to give at least some consideration to the very diverse work—novels, short stories, plays, essays, poetry—that he produced during this fertile period. One of the most distinctive bodies of work that he generated at this time were five published volumes (with a sixth prepared but not published at the time of his death) of tales involving the clubman Joseph Jorkens.

The Jorkens tales came at a critical moment in Dunsany's career. After *Tales of Three Hemispheres*—itself a relatively weak volume of heterogeneous minor tales, designed chiefly to capitalise on his new-found celebrity, especially in the United States—he was clearly unsure how to proceed as a writer. It took another three years for him to publish his first novel, the engaging but relatively slight *Chronicles of Rodriguez* (1922), followed two years later by the masterful fantasy *The King of Elfland's Daughter* (1924). Dunsany's career as a novelist was launched; but what of his work as a short story writer? He published no short stories at all in the years 1921–25, even though he had published nearly 250 in the period 1905–20. Had his inspiration for short fiction dried up? It would appear so; but then he wrote "The Tale of the Abu Laheeb," the first of 127 Jorkens stories collected in five volumes. Dunsany writes of this tale in his second autobiography, *While the Sirens Slept* (1944), while discussing a hunting expedition in Africa:

> It was from material gathered on this journey that on the 29th and 30th of March, 1925, I wrote a tale called *The Tale Of The Abu Laheeb*. There was in this tale more description of the upper reaches of the White Nile or of the Bahr-el-Gazal than I have given here; indeed the whole setting of that fantastic story may be regarded as accurately true to life, though not the tale itself. I mention this short story and its date, because it was the first time that I told of the wanderings of a character that I called Jorkens. He was my reply to some earlier suggestion that I should write of my journeys after big game and, being still reluctant to do this, I had invented a drunken old man who, whenever he could cadge a drink at a club, told tales of his travels. When in addition to his other failings I made him a liar, I felt that at least there could be nothing boastful about my stories. (78)

There are a number of interesting points here, not the least of which is the curious fact that "The Tale of the Abu Laheeb" took more than a year to find print, appearing in the *Atlantic Monthly* only in July 1926. Dunsany, perhaps unwittingly, suggests here that the bulk of the Jorkens tales were designed solely to reflect his worldwide travels— chiefly as a big-game hunter, beginning as early as 1909—and this suggestion is fostered by the titles of the first two Jorkens books, *The Travel Tales of Mr. Joseph Jorkens* (1931) and *Jorkens Remembers Africa* (1934). And yet, not only does the former volume—which, somewhat artificially, is arranged in chapters, as if it were a novel—include several tales told by other characters altogether, but the latter is by no means restricted in its setting to Africa. What is more significant, Dunsany gives no clue that the Jorkens tales emphasise, in their generally light-hearted manner, important themes and issues that dominate his entire literary work. Many of the Jorkens tales may seem like nothing more than clever *jeux d'esprit* (the very name Jorkens is perhaps meant to evoke the word "joke"), but they underscore messages that were close to Dunsany's heart.

Dunsany's plain admission in *While the Sirens Slept* that Jorkens was a "liar" is of interest, for of course it is exactly our inability to determine whether Jorkens is in fact fibbing or not that creates much of the delight in these tales. Definitive proof is always just out of reach. When one Murcote first gives the narrator (who may or may not be Dunsany) some background information on the clubman and his outlandish stories, the narrator says, "I see . . . a bit of a liar." Murcote immediately responds: "That's rather hard." This is not an actual denial that Jorkens is a liar, just a suggestion that calling him one is a bit cruel and tactless. Other members of the Billiards Club—notably Jorkens's nemesis, Terbut (who of course envies Jorkens because he himself has never set foot out of England)—are not so charitable; and in "The Bare Truth" someone pointedly confronts Jorkens with the challenge, "Jorkens, have you ever told the truth in your life?" to which Jorkens blandly replies, "Yes, once."

While it is true that such stories as "The Tale of the Abu Laheeb," "What Jorkens Has to Put Up With," and "The Golden Gods" do reflect quite accurately Dunsany's far-flung travels, especially in the Sahara, there are more significant issues at stake in many of the tales. The preface to *Travel Tales* is worth considering in this regard, even though it too is written with a certain wry flippancy. Here the narrator outlines two motives for telling these tales: they may "advance the progress of Science" or, conversely, they may "add something of strangeness to parts of our planet, just as it was tending to grow too familiar." Two more contradictory rationales could scarcely be imagined; and yet, it becomes clear that the latter is really what Dunsany is getting at—and, indeed, what he was striving for in the course of his entire work.

One of the chief means by which the world was being robbed of "strangeness" was industrialism. The dominance of the machine was something Dunsany never tired of lambasting; perhaps his most poignant utterance occurs in the essay "Romance and the Modern Stage" (1911):

> For our age is full of new problems that we have not as yet found time to understand, that bewilder us and absorb us, the gift of matter enthroned and endowed by man with life; I mean iron vitalised by steam, and rushing from city to city and owning men for its slaves. I know of the boons that machinery has conferred on man, all tyrants have boons to confer, but service to the dynasty of steam and steel is a hard service and gives little leisure to fancy to flit from field to field. (830)

And so we have the poignant Jorkens tale "The Witch of the Willows," who indicts our entire civilisation with the pregnant comment, "They're going all the wrong way"—the way of machinery. And we also have the curious tale "The Electric King," in which an American electricity magnate seeks in vain to find solace for a recurring nightmare. I believe this tale is a parable inspired by the life of Samuel Insull (1859-1938), a London-born associate of Thomas Alva Edison who came to the United States in 1881 and, over the next forty years, revolutionised both the technology and the economics of electric power in this country. Insull's fortunes suffered a collapse in the early years of the Depression. (There is, however, no suggestion that Insull was afflicted with the psychological traumas Dunsany attributes to his character.)

For Dunsany, man's yielding to machinery has engendered an alienation with the natural world, and so that world may take occasion to rebel against his dominance. This is the thrust of perhaps the most chilling of the Jorkens tales, "The Walk to Lingham"—where Jorkens, carelessly cheering the cutting down of a poplar tree, finds that that poplar's fellows may be relentlessly stalking him as he walks down a lonely road. The political metaphors with which this story concludes— "I knew at once that there had been no revolution," Jorkens states in relief, as he finds no poplars surrounding the pub into which he has taken refuge—underscores the message: the plant world has not (yet) rebelled against man, but perhaps may do so in the future. All this makes one recall Dunsany's final, and most exhaustive, treatment of the struggle between man and machine—the novel *The Last Revolution* (1954).

"The Witch of the Willows" makes clear that Dunsany occasionally used the Jorkens stories to return to that early, prose-poetic manner that had won him so many enthralled readers. It is no accident that the story brings to mind several of Dunsany's earlier tales, especially "The Avenger of Perdóndaris" (in *Tales of Three Hemispheres*), in which a witch who resides on the borderland of reality and dream challenges the protagonist to cross over from the one realm to the other. Jorkens, faced with a similar choice, opts for the familiarity of our everyday world—and then spends the rest of his life regretting it. "In the Garden of Memories" is another exquisite story, telling of memories coming to life, while "The Golden Gods" reflects even more closely—and perhaps even parodies—some of the themes in Dunsany's early tales, especially those in *The Book of Wonder* where redoubtable gods take grisly vengeance upon those rash mortals who seek to rob them.

"A Large Diamond" is one of several tales in which Jorkens comes close to making a fabulous fortune, only to be thwarted at the last; others of this type are "The Pearly Beach" and "A Mystery of the East." These scenarios underscore an important structural element in the Jorkens stories: they must end in such a way that proof or disproof of the events they relate can never be forthcoming. If Jorkens actually had made a fortune by one means or another, then that would validate the truth of his account; but because he has not done so, we are left wondering whether the events he speaks of really occurred. Similarly, in "Earth's Secret" Jorkens claims to have secured the formula for making gold, but unfortunately loses it; in "What Jorkens Has to Put Up With" he appears to have returned with a unicorn's horn, but a single word by another member casts doubt upon the object; and most delightfully of all, in "Mrs. Jorkens" we find that the clubman has actually married a mermaid—but regrettably she swims out to sea not long after the ceremony. And in "A Queer Island," can we really believe that Jorkens has come upon a modern-day Circe who has turned men into animals? Everything in this story is told with the most exquisite plausibility and circumstantiality—it would be so easy to believe what Jorkens says (or, rather, to accept the inference Jorkens manifestly wishes us to accept) . . . but can we?

From this perspective, the most remarkable of the early Jorkens tales is "Our Distant Cousins," in which Jorkens himself yields the narrative to a friend, Terner, who relates a spectacular voyage to Mars. Let it pass that the mechanism by which Terner claims to have reached the red planet is entirely implausible; the heart of the story is its suggestion that the humanlike denizens of Mars are *not* the dominant entities on the planet. The implication is clear: is our own control of the earth secure or permanent? Dunsany produces a delightful sequel to this story in "The Slugly Beast."

The first two Jorkens volumes display a remarkable fertility of imagination; clearly Dunsany had found a new voice—or, at any rate, a new way of saying the many things he had to say. The stories proved immediately popular with both readers and critics, if reviews by Basil Davenport and Graham Greene are any gauge. It is no surprise that much of the rest of Dunsany's short-story writing career was devoted to Jorkens, and the remaining volumes present an even greater diversity of subject, theme, and tone. The Jorkens tales may never displace *The Gods of Pegāna* or *A Dreamer's Tales* as the books a Dunsany devotee turns to first, but they present surprising satisfactions of their own; and they are stories that no true connoisseur of the bizarre can afford to be without.

Jorkens Has a Large Whiskey is perhaps the rarest of the five published Jorkens collections. Appearing a year after the commencement of World War II, in September 1940, it was issued under the severe paper rationing that lasted for years after the war; and, although the London edition was reprinted in December 1940, it was never published in the United States. The same cannot, of course, be said for *The Fourth Book of Jorkens* (1947), which was one of the early publications of August Derleth's fledgling small press, Arkham House. Some have believed that the Arkham House edition of 1948 is the actual first edition, but in fact the London firm of Jarrolds issued the book in December 1947, although that edition is undated.

The stories in these two collections, nearly sixty in number, testify to the extent to which the chronicles of Joseph Jorkens had come to dominate Dunsany's short-story output during the period 1935–47: in this interval Dunsany published just under 120 short stories, so that fully half of his production consisted of Jorkens tales—and many of the remainder were light whimsies published in *Punch*. It is no surprise that, after *Tales of Three Hemispheres* (1919), Dunsany issued no non-Jorkens short story collections until two late volumes, *The Man Who Ate the Phoenix* (1949) and *The Little Tales of Smethers* (1952).

The stories in the third and fourth Jorkens books are perhaps not as substantial—or not as consistently substantial—as those in the first two volumes, but they present a wealth of interesting matter. The proportion of stories that suggest the supernatural has decreased, and many of the tales merely exhibit Jorkens engaging in various forms of trickery (as in "Jorkens' Revenge," when he bets his hapless nemesis, Terbut, that the distance between Westminster Bridge and Blackfriars Bridge in London is longer than the distance between Blackfriars Bridge and Westminster Bridge—and wins the bet) or in thrilling adventures and hair-raising escapes (as in "Jorkens Leaves Prison").

The number of stories relating to Jorkens's winning and losing fortunes makes one wonder whether the worldwide depression of the 1930s had any effect upon Dunsany's imagination. Indeed, "Jorkens in High Finance" is nothing but a clever riff on Britain's abandonment of the gold standard, an event that was seen as epochal and revolutionary at the time. The insouciance with which, in "The Ivory Poacher," Jorkens aids and abets a poacher smuggling ivory out of Africa suggests his belief that any means of making money was, in this critical period, fair game.

A trilogy of tales in *Jorkens Has a Large Whiskey*—"The Grecian Singer," "The Development of the Rillswood Estate," and "A Doubtful Story"—

resurrects figures from Greek mythology and thrusts them into the present day, with surprisingly poignant results. Pan, when transplanted from the groves of Hellas to the bustle of London in "A Doubtful Story," expresses a plangent need for "green things" and "quiet," dwelling in misery until he is rescued by a Valkyrie. The 1930s was the period when Dunsany wrote two of his strongest novels about the conflict between Nature and civilisation, *The Curse of the Wise Woman* (1933) and *The Story of Mona Sheehy* (1939), and even in his light-hearted Jorkens tales he could scarcely stay away from a theme so central to his thought.

"Elephant Shooting" is a tale representative of another central theme in Dunsany's work—or, perhaps, a variant of the same Nature-vs.-civilisation theme. This variant might be called "humanity-vs.-the-animals," and it can be expressed at its simplest by the depiction of a human consciousness occupying the body of an animal and perceiving its greater harmony with the natural world—as in *My Talks with Dean Spanley* (1936) and that lost classic of fantasy, *The Strange Journeys of Colonel Polders* (1950)—and, in a more pungent manner, the potential rebellion of animals against the domination of mankind, as in the plays *Lord Adrian* (1933) and *The Use of Man* (in *Plays for Earth and Air*, 1937). In "Elephant Shooting," Dunsany—although himself a vigorous and unashamed hunter—allows the elephant to outwit his human foe, so that the story's title becomes a nasty pun.

"The Invention of Dr. Caber" introduces another and much more dangerous nemesis to Jorkens than the harmless and easily bamboozled Terbut; and although, in "The Strange Drug of Dr. Caber," Caber actually assists the government in disposing of a German spy, in "The Cleverness of Dr. Caber" he has devised a device so dangerous that permanent imprisonment is the only solution. He is just one of a succession of fiendish villains whose potential for destroying the very fabric of the world or the universe makes them far greater threats than ordinary criminals, as in "Jorkens Handles a Big Property," where a man threatens to divert the Gulf Stream and bring eternal winter to the British Isles.

The tales in *The Fourth Book of Jorkens*, for all their apparent frivolity, occasionally have unwontedly grim undercurrents. "A Life's Work," although seemingly a clever send-up of the meaninglessness of political platforms and parties, can also be read as a deeply pessimistic fable on the futility of human endeavour. Then there is the pathetic man who, in "Lost," is "lost in time," suffering a far greater torment than the protagonist of Dunsany's great play *If* (1921), who himself went back in time and experienced a dismal enough fate. "Jarton's Disease" tells of a man destroyed by his own mind, while "The Warning" speaks balefully of the emerging dominance of machines over humanity, a theme that found exhaustive expression in Dunsany's late novel, *The Last Revolution* (1951). And what of "The Rebuff," where the inhabitants of Mars tell us contemptuously to go hang ourselves?

"Strategy at the Billiards Club" is one of several late stories in Dunsany's work dealing with the atomic bomb. Clearly the dropping of the bomb on Hiroshima and Nagasaki was a traumatic event for Dunsany: he was in the midst of writing a series of lectures, *A Glimpse from a Watch Tower* (1946), when he heard news of the event, and his reaction can be gauged by the harrowing words he uttered:

> Strange, strange news came to us to-day. We have just heard of the atomic bomb. . . . Henceforth we are like children in a powder-factory. We have found out how to turn atoms into energy. The world is full of atoms, and henceforth they are explosive. It is even possible that clever people like us have existed upon planets of other stars, and that they became too clever and set light to their planet and exploded its parent star. (41, 47)

Is it any wonder that Dunsany's last, unpublished novel, *The Pleasures of a Futuroscope*, deals with the effects of a nuclear holocaust that has virtually depopulated the world?

But if Dunsany found in the Jorkens tales a means of treating the most serious subjects, he also found them a means of expressing his boundless stores of cleverness, wit, and imagination. "A Deal with the Devil," with its ingenious—one is almost inclined to say its diabolically clever—confirmation that one can never get the better of Old Nick; "The Development of the Rillswood Estate," with its inimitable satire on middle-class respectability; "Jorkens in Witch Wood," one of several tales that find Jorkens in Dunsany's native Ireland—these and all the other tales in these two volumes speak eloquently of the continuing vigour of Dunsany's literary output in his sixth and seventh decades of life, in a career that, by 1947, had already spanned more than forty years. That a man who was close to seventy when *The Fourth Book of Jorkens* appeared would go on to write two further volumes of Jorkens tales in the decade of life left to him can only make us think of the imaginary clubman he created, who himself tramped through stories of three decades without showing the least signs of decreasing vitality.

Seven years elapsed between the publication of *The Fourth Book of Jorkens* (1947) and *Jorkens Borrows Another Whiskey* (1954). In that period Dunsany wrote more than 120 short stories, but that fifth Jorkens collection contains only 34, meaning that Dunsany was at last turning his attention away from his loquacious clubman to stories of widely differing sorts. It was in this period that he published his two final non-Jorkens story collections, *The Man Who Ate the Phoenix* (1949) and *The Little Tales of Smethers* (1952), although the tales in both those volumes extend over a wide chronological range, some dating as early as 1930. The eccentric tales of the self-effacing Smethers (which make up only a part of the collection bearing his name) recount the adventures of the detective Linley (we never learn his first name), including the classic "The Two Bottles of Relish" (1932), one of the most widely reprinted stories in modern literature. Ellery Queen thought highly enough of this volume to rank it among the essential books of detective stories in the English language. It was during this period, too, that Dunsany wrote, apparently in quick succession, his last three published novels: *The Strange Journeys of Colonel Polders* (1950), a forgotten classic of fantasy in its account of a bluff soldier whose soul is forced to occupy the bodies of a bewildering succession of animals; *The Last Revolution* (1951), a weak novel about machines revolting from human control; and *His Fellow Men* (1952), a curious, delicate, and altogether unclassifiable work about the need for religious toleration.

The very first tale in the fifth Jorkens collection, "The Two-Way War," points to another major work in Dunsany's oeuvre—his last novel, *The Pleasures of a Futuroscope*, which remained unpublished until nearly a half-century after his death in 1957. In all honesty, the Jorkens story, dealing with a man named Methery and his invention, the futuroscope, does not amount to much, nor does a brief unpublished sequel, "The Ultimate Goal." Dunsany clearly felt that the conception required far more extensive exposition, and around 1955 he did just that, producing a poignant, wistful novel about the appalling effects of a nuclear holocaust in the near future—a holocaust that results in the complete destruction of London (only a crater, later filled in by water from the Thames, remains where the great metropolis stood), with humanity reverting to a Stone Age existence. For Dunsany, however, this seeming tragedy proves to be a kind of boon, for it means that the few remaining human denizens of the globe have returned to a more natural life, close to Earth—the kind of life they had before machines became first our servants, then our soulless masters.

These complex conceptions—the threat of nuclear catastrophe; the need to restore our ties to the natural world; the dangers that scientific discovery unrestrained by moral concerns—run like a multicoloured thread throughout the stories of Dunsany's last two Jorkens books, which now includes *The Last Book of Jorkens*, a volume of twenty-two stories assembled by Dunsany prior to his death but never published until the special Night Shade edition of 2002. (The title is the editor's, as Dunsany had not chosen a title for the collection.) Throughout these two volumes the shadow of the atomic bomb looms—a shadow that Dunsany was by no means certain the human race was intellectually and spiritually capable of dispelling. The number of scientific megalomaniacs who seek, through immensely powerful inventions, to affect not merely the state of the world but of the universe is impressive: in "The New Moon" and "A Big Bang" we encounter men who wish to endow the earth with a second satellite; "Bringing Things Up to Date" and "A Modern Conqueror" display scientists seeking to kill all humanity by means of new diseases—something that strikes home deeply today with our fears of AIDS, SARS, and the Ebola virus; "A Conversation in Bond Street" suggests that the atomic bomb was known on other planets, to their detriment; "A Plaything of Our Betters" brings in the Greek gods to point a moral about the dangers of putting dangerous weaponry into the hands of those incapable of controlling it.

Along these same lines are a number of tales in which Jorkens is a spy on the other side of the Iron Curtain. With the elimination of the Nazis, Soviet Russia quickly emerged as the greatest threat to the West, and Dunsany has more than his share of fun with the potential dangers of espionage and Jorkens's narrow escapes from imprisonment or death. It is notable that in most of these stories—"Among the Neutrals," "A Rash Remark," "A Bit of Counter-Espionage," "Jorkens' Dilemma"—we actually don't know exactly what Jorkens is spying on, or what kind of information he is attempting to bring back to the British government. The mere fact of Jorkens's spying is enough to get the plot moving, for of course the real conundrum in these tales is not what Jorkens is doing but how he will escape.

Dunsany's belief that machines were both making us less human and separating us from the natural world is emphasised in several poignant tales. In "The Lost Invention" a man who has created artificial animals, even artificial grass, destroys the invention in horror at the loss of the familiar sheep and cattle from the English countryside. Somewhat too similar to this is "The Greatest Invention." Artificial intelligence is the focus of "An Eccentricity of Genius" and "Misadventure," and the light-hearted treatment here is rather more effective than in the excessively earnest novel *The Last Revolution*. "Which Way?" can perhaps be cited as well, with its ruminations on whether primitivism is in fact a superior manner of life than what we call civilisation.

Dunsany frequently expressed his concern about industrialism in a curious way—by the use of animals. Animals, prototypically, are close to Nature, and it is therefore no surprise that Dunsany regards their manner of life as in many ways superior to that of human beings. This is the burden of *The Strange Journeys of Colonel Polders*, and several Jorkens stories underscore the idea as well. "On Other Paths" brings to mind the earlier Jorkens story "Our Distant Cousins" in asking what it would be like if human beings were not the "top dogs" on this planet. In this case, dogs themselves are the top dogs. This story (like "The Verdict") can on one level be seen simply as an exposition of one of Dunsany's crochets— his horror of the practice of cutting off the tails of dogs and horses, a subject on which he dunned the London *Times* with repeated letters to the editor—but on another level it asks whether human beings really deserve their position of physical superiority on the earth.

A number of tales in the two final Jorkens books bring earlier stories to mind, as if Dunsany were attempting to recapture the panache and enthusiasm of his first accounts of the widely travelled raconteur. "The Unrecorded Test Match" is another delightful tale of cricket and a deal with the Devil, vividly echoing the early story "How Jembu Played for Cambridge" but sufficiently different in focus as to stand as an independent narrative. The very title of "An Idyll of the Sahara" recalls not only the early Jorkens but Dunsany's gorgeous prose-poetic tales of the 1910s. In "The Two Scientists" we travel to Africa—just as we did in *Jorkens Remembers Africa* (1934)—and encounter nothing less than a man-eating plant.

As with the third and fourth Jorkens volumes, the number of stories purporting to recount excursions into the supernatural declines steadily, as compared with the first two collections; but there are still some striking examples. "A Walk in the Night" and "A Friend of the Family" are effective ghost stories, while "The Lost Charm" is a haunting tale on the borderline of fantasy and science fiction. Also on the edge of the supernatural are the two final tales in the *Last Book*, "A Visitor" and "On the Wings of Song," which, in their delineation of the power of music, share a theme with the unpublished tale "A Meeting of Spirits."

If the supernatural is in short supply, then crime and murder appear in abundance. These last two Jorkens collections add their share of clever, ingenious, or implacable murderers, from the faceless Smith of "A Long Memory" to the jilted lover of "The Deal." Whether "A Fatal Mistake" deals with a criminal or a spy is unclear, but in either case his end is not pleasant. But the pinnacle is reached in "Not Guilty" (previously published under the title "Near the Back of Beyond"), one of the most gruesome crime stories ever written. The transition from these grim tales to the stories of clever con artists—notably "Letting Bygones Be Bygones" to "A Wonderful Day"—may seem quite a step down, but even in the latter Dunsany reveals such a shrewd insight into the foibles of his fellow human beings as to make them all too probable and believable.

A very different tale of a con artist is "Across the Colour Bar," certainly the most politically controversial story in *The Last Book of Jorkens*. It would be easy to accuse Dunsany of racism in this story, but a closer reading displays his keen awareness of the plight of African Americans and the long and bitter legacy of slavery in the United States. Possibly Dunsany was unaware of the highly charged nature of the subject to American readers, but no one can accuse him of a lack of sympathy with the hapless blacks in this tale.

The more than 150 tales of Joseph Jorkens represent a landmark in the history of weird fiction. Wondrously diverse but unified by their bland, phlegmatic protagonist; ranging from science fiction to the supernatural to crime to mere trickery; unfailingly clever, structurally impeccable, interspersed with surprising moments of prose-poetry, eloquence, pathos, and wistfulness; and all treading the very borderline between the almost-believable and the totally outrageous, the Jorkens tales comprise a body of fantastic writing of compulsive readability and inexhaustible ingenuity. Never repeating himself in more than thirty years of writing, Dunsany reveals such a prodigious fertility of imagination that he would be worth remembering had he written nothing but these six volumes of tales. To realise that he also wrote more than a dozen novels, more than 400 additional short stories, scores of plays, and hundreds of essays and poems is to gain a full appreciation of the towering literary achievement of this Irish master, whose half-century of writing has left an imperishable imprint upon the history of fantastic fiction.

III. Christianity and Paganism in Two Dunsany Novels

Lord Dunsany, although raised as a Protestant, was in all likelihood an atheist. While by no means being the dogged opponent of religious belief that his disciple H. P. Lovecraft was, Dunsany ultimately seems to have come to the conclusion that conventional Christianity was in league with the forces of modernism—specifically as exemplified in his greatest *bête noire*, mechanisation—in undermining that unity with the natural world which he felt to be only means by which human beings could justify their place in the world. Two of his novels, *The Blessing of Pan* (1927) and *The Curse of the Wise Woman* (1933), are devoted to probing the conflict between Christianity and paganism, which for Dunsany symbolised the even more significant conflict between nature and machinery.

The Blessing of Pan is unusual in the corpus of Dunsany's work by portraying an explicit conflict of two diametrically opposed religious visions of the world and of human life and society. The conflict is joined at the very outset—indeed, in the very title of the novel. In Dunsany's work as a whole, names and titles are of supreme importance, and this is especially the case here. In a Christian society, to speak of a "blessing" is an unambiguous reference to the beneficence offered by belief in Jesus Christ; but when that "blessing" is initiated by Pan, the prototype of paganism, we are in a different world altogether. And the fact that the chief (human) protagonist of the novel, Elderick Anwrel, is identified on the first page of the novel as a "clergyman" and a "vicar" sets up the leading players in the conflict right from the start.

Anwrel's name is worth pondering. Its extreme artificiality might place it in line with many other Dunsany names that are extremely rare, if indeed they have any existence in British nomenclature at all (Jorkens and Smethers are only two well-known examples); but here the artificiality is deliberately heightened. The fact that, as the representative of Christian culture in the small town of Wolding, he is given such a peculiar name seems designed to suggest Christianity's lack of vital re-lation to the community. Dunsany also devotes a full paragraph to the artificiality of his wife Augusta's name as well: "There are reasons for names like that: some gorgeous relative of other days, some splendid fancy crossing the mind of a parent, some imperious look perhaps, long ago, on the face of the child herself; there are always reasons" (10). She sides with her husband in his strange conflict until almost the end. Contrast these names with that of Arthur Davidson, the vicar who had preceded Anwrel in Wolding and who turns out to be the ultimate instigator of the movement toward paganism in the community: the rugged simplicity of his name stands in striking contrast to that of his successor.

The premise of the novel is simple. Davidson, about whom something seemed terribly wrong, seems to have infected the minds and hearts of the townspeople of Wolding in some inexplicable manner. As Anwrel, increasingly disturbed that the tunes played by seventeen-year-old Tommy Duffin are attracting a greater and greater number of people to head up to the hills to perform pagan ceremonies, investigates his predecessor, he finds hints of the appalling truth. Davidson—as an old woman, Mrs. Tichener, tells Anwrel—was once seen "dancing" (67) at night in the vicarage. This seemingly harmless peccadillo is the symbol for a much more alarming anomaly (alarming, at any rate, from Anwrel's perspective), for Mrs. Tichener goes on to say: "He [Davidson] had a joint, sir, below his spats as he danced" (69). Could Davidson have been a satyr, or Pan himself?

But Davidson is only the trigger for the events of the novel. He had conducted the marriage ceremony of the Duffins, and it is suggested that he had infused something of his spirit into their son, Tommy. Tommy, a dull, thick-witted youth, is nothing more than a receptacle—a conduit for the insidious infusion of paganism into the village. He knows not why he made his pipe, "an instrument he made out of bulrushes or some such weeds" (6), nor does he understand fully why he plays his tune up in the hills and why it has the influence it does. Anwrel himself is attracted to it:

> [It was] a clear wild tune so remote from the thoughts of man that it seemed to drift from ages and out of lands with which none of our race

has ever had any concern. More elfin than the blackbird, more magical than all nightingales, it thrilled the clergyman's heart with awful longings, which he could no more tell of in words than he could have put words to that tune. (8–9)

This is only one of many passages that suggest both the remote antiquity of the tune and its symbolising the identity of paganism with unspoiled Nature. Dunsany even remarks that "plainer minds, being close to natural, even to pagan, things responded to the marvel of that enchantment with an abandonment unknown even to him [Anwrel]" (25–26). Tommy himself is said to be like "some wild creature shut into a woodman's hut" (45).

The explicitly religious nature of the tune—and, by extension, the religious overtones of the conflict the novel exhibits—is emphasised in numerous passages. One of the first to be attracted to the tune, and to Tommy, is Lily, a young woman who serves as a maid for one of the residents of Wolding. She states flatly that the pipes were "sacred" (88); and, when some young men, offended that Tommy is luring all the young women of the village up to the hills, wish to follow him and exact some kind of vengeance, she calls their behaviour "outrageous and sacrilegious" (90). Anwrel, for his part, plainly declares the tune to be "heresy" (54). Later it is said: "Down in the village their thoughts went wandering awhile to far times and curious *rites*" (107; my emphasis). Other passages make the connection to paganism transparent: when the girls stare at the young men who wish to do Tommy harm, their glares are compared to "Medusa's powers" (109); Tommy himself is said to be "playing [tunes] like Apollo" (127). In the end, the young men end up being Tommy's followers.

The mention of rites is significant: what Tommy—and, in the end, all the other people of Wolding—wish to do is to conduct some kind of ceremony at the Old Stones, a megalithic structure near the village. It becomes apparent that some ceremony—a sacrifice—is to be held on the flat stone in the middle of the structure. Once Anwrel learns this, his attempts to curtail the villagers' descent into paganism is only redoubled.

It cannot, however, be emphasised too strongly that Anwrel is portrayed throughout the novel as a sympathetic character. Dunsany performs a striking feat here: we all know that his own sympathies lie with paganism—and the unity with nature that it entails—and yet the quest of Anwrel to halt its spread is looked upon as wholly admirable, albeit doomed to defeat. The entire novel is told from his perspective, and the repeated blows he suffers in his hopeless quest are depicted poignantly, as of a man tragically overwhelmed by an incalculably superior enemy.

The fact that Anwrel is, at the very outset, himself attracted to the tune suggests his own plangently human fallibility—he is scarcely different from the villagers whose spiritual needs he seeks in his quiet and humble way to satisfy. Indeed, at one point Anwrel himself is inclined to "dance fantastic dances" (82) when he hears the tune—exactly as his predecessor, Arthur Davidson, had done.

Anwrel appeals to ally after ally, only to find that they fail him. First he writes to his bishop a tentative letter outlining the situation; but lacking specificity as to the gravity of the situation, the letter only incites a bland reply by the bishop to take a week's vacation. This comes across almost as an order, and Anwrel and his wife dutifully spend a week in the conventional vacation town of Brighton. When they return, they find nothing changed; if anything, the influence of the tune has only grown. Anwrel contemplates writing a more urgent letter, telling that Tommy Duffin "has been affected to a terrible degree by some pre-natal influence from a perfectly shocking source" (75); but he cannot bring himself to mail the letter.

At only one point is our sympathy for Anwrel in danger of subsiding. He approaches Tommy's father at one point, speaking bluntly that the matter has come down to "witchcraft" and going on to say: "You know there are laws against that still on the statute-book" (99). This raises the baneful spectre of the infamous biblical passage "Thou shalt not suffer a witch to live" (Exodus 22:18), and of the witchcraft trials and hangings that stained several centuries of earlier British history. But Anwrel's warnings are weak, and there is little likelihood that he would be able to act upon them. When, after a time, Anwrel sees nearly all the people of the village going up to the hills to follow Tommy, he collapses "in tears" (129)—and we too feel his plight keenly, the plight of a man whose own religious faith may be crumbling.

Matters go from bad to worse. Anwrel decides to look up a man named Hetley, who had taken his place when Anwrel was in Brighton. Hetley had spent several days in Wolding, and he must have heard something about the tune and its baleful influence. But he is crestfallen when Hetley declares flatly: "I heard nothing" (149). Hetley is a formidable Greek scholar, but the period of his expertise is not the primitive era of Greek culture but the later, classical era: he is too scholarly, too civilised to have sensed the paganism inherent in the tune—and, by extension, the spiritual plight of the community. His subsequent suggestion to Anwrel that he encourage the young men of the village to play more cricket ("I have always found that spiritual things follow very closely the physical" [154], he says tritely) is worse than useless.

Finally Anwrel visits the bishop in person, but nothing comes of this either. It is at this time that Anwrel explicitly states to the bishop's chaplain that his parishioners "practise the rites of Pan instead of the Christian faith" (163). The chaplain's response is conventional: "Dear me . . . They shouldn't do that, of course" (163). But when Anwrel explains the matter to the bishop, the latter echoes Hetley's recommendation of more cricket.

Anwrel returns in despair to Wolding. He finds the tokens of civilisation crumbling one by one: the post is no longer being delivered; the hay is not being gathered in the fields; a maid is no longer cleaning the teapot. By these simple means does Dunsany convey the collapse of the fabric of civilised life. Even Augusta seems to be wavering. And yet, the villagers are still attending church on Sunday, and Anwrel is initially encouraged when he learns that Mrs. Duffin is continuing to teach Sunday school. But his encouragement turns to horror when he discovers that she is inculcating a strange catechism that sounds like "Egg, oh, pan, pan, tone, tone, lofone, R. K. D." (215). Dredging up the Greek he studied at Cambridge, he realises with terror that she is teaching them a sentence (quoted in Greek in the novel) that translates to: "I, Pan, king of all the Arcadian slopes"—"the accursed blessing of Pan!" (215).

At this point Dunsany addresses a point that many of his readers may have wondered about. Wolding seems to be an idyllic community that is itself in tune with the eternal rhythms of Nature. Why would Pan choose this place to make his inroad against Christianity? Once again, names are significant. Let us recall *The King of Elfland's Daughter* (1924): although there seems to be a stark contrast between the "real" world of Erl with the fantasy realm of Elfland, it does not take much scholarship to realise that *Erl* is German for "elf"—making the distinction between Erl and Elfland problematical indeed. Much the same can be said for *The Blessing of Pan*. Wolding itself—an imaginary village that has no corollary in actual English topography—is derived from *wold* (forest, woodland); and Dunsany notes plainly that it was "not harmed at all by anything that had changed the world in the restless nineteenth century" (217). It is, indeed, precisely because this village is "unspoiled" (219) that it serves as the launching-place for Pan. The young people are affected first, because the older residents are more attuned to the ways of civilised life: "the old have forgotten so much and the young have yet to learn" (120). But in the end, they go too.

In one of the most dramatic episodes in *The Blessing of Pan*, Anwrel decides to make one last plea to the sensibilities of his parishioners in a final sermon on a Sunday service. He first attempts to write a sermon "based on Holy Writ" (221), but is unable to do so: the limitations of Christian dogma in the face of pagan opposition are transparently displayed. Finally, Anwrel resorts to an extemporaneous sermon in which he pleads with his parishioners to remember the old ways to which they had grown accustomed: "the old ways were best . . . the faith of their fathers and of the old time before them" (227). Although his sermon seems at first to be working, he is dismayed to find that the people are leaving the church one by one. In the end only his wife, Augusta, remains; and then, shockingly, she too gets up and leaves. Later she tells him poignantly: "I stayed till you were finished" (251).

To whom can Anwrel turn? During his visit to the bishop, he had stumbled upon a crazy person named Perkin. If the scholarship and rationality of Hetley, the bishop, and others are unavailing, perhaps the madness of Perkin will be of some use. He sends a telegram to Perkin, pleading with him to come and help. Perkin finally does so, showing up at the end of Anwrel's final sermon. He declares flatly that the townspeople have exchanged one "illusion" (250) for another; and in the novel's most critical passage he discusses the matter with Anwrel:

> "Why, what does one need but illusions?" answered Perkin.
> "They're gone. I've lost them," said the vicar. "One cannot hold them all alone." He spread his hands to the emptiness of his room. "I've none to help me now."
> "Plenty of friends over there," said Perkin, pointing to Wold Hill. "Plenty of illusions."
> "But," gasped Anwrel, "but they're the enemy's!"
> "They're yours if you want them," said Perkin. (250)

Those words are prophetic. Anwrel, almost unaware of what he is doing, fashions an axe from an old palaeolith (he was in the habit of collecting them as a hobby) and goes up to the Old Stones. All the villagers are there. At dawn, he conducts the rite they have all been waiting for, sacrificing an old bull on the altar stone.

At this point Dunsany makes clear the message he had been suggesting all along—the identity of paganism with a repudiation of modern mechanised civilisation. For the villagers had "forsaken the ways of the nineteenth century"—adding, significantly, "and, for that matter, the ways of the last two thousand years" (261), thereby fusing civilisation with Christianity. The defeat of Christianity signifies the triumph of Nature and of the ancient past:

> Tommy Duffin's curious music that lured one away from the present, and that then seemed to wake up old memories that nobody guessed were there, seems to have come at a time when something sleeping within us first guessed that the way by which we were then progressing t'wards the

noise of machinery and the clamour of sellers, amidst which we live today, was a wearying way, and they turned from it. And turning from it they turned away from the folk that were beginning to live as we do. (274)

And yet, Dunsany cannot disguise his religious scepticism, as he states plainly that the pagan gods were themselves merely a part of "whatever might lurk in the vast space of man's ignorance" (272). Anwrel, for his part, is now happy in his resumed role of the villagers' spiritual guide—but from a pagan, not a Christian, orientation.

The Curse of the Wise Woman is a very different kind of novel. Here, the conflict between Christianity and paganism is only one strand of a rich tapestry that includes such other dichotomies as past vs. present, England vs. Ireland, Catholic vs. Protestant, and nature vs. civilisation. But as in The Blessing of Pan, the paganism/Christianity dichotomy is virtually identical with the nature/civilisation dichotomy.

In the simplest terms, The Curse of the Wise Woman—Dunsany's first "Irish" novel—is about a company, Peat Development (Ireland) Syndi-cate, that wishes to drain a bog near the imaginary town of Clonrue, Ireland: by compressing the peat with machinery, it can produce cheap coal. A "wise woman"—which the narrator makes plain is merely a euphemism for a "practising witch" (32)—is outraged at the plans. Summoning apparently supernatural powers, she causes an immense storm to destroy the company's machinery and put an end to its plans.

Interweaved with this relatively elementary conflict is a network of other tensions, focusing not only around the protagonist, Charles James Peridore, the son of a duke and the owner of a large estate in the area, but also his gamekeeper and "bog-watcher," Tommy Marlin, whose mother is the wise woman. It is the Marlins who specifically embody the paganism of the novel. Marlin himself is described at the outset as one who seemed "to be somehow akin to those forces that ruled, or blew over, the bog, and that cared nothing for man" (22)—the latter description always a positive thing in Dunsany's worldview. This deep sense of communion with nature on Marlin's part is enhanced by his devotion to the mythical Tir-nan-Og—an otherworldly realm in Irish myth analogous to Elysium or Valhalla. And yet, because Marlin has been saturated with traditional Catholic upbringing, he believes that this devotion is a "reserved sin"—which Peridore explains as meaning that "he had done something for which no parish priest could give absolution" (37). Marlin has, in effect, "preferred Tir-nan-Og to Heaven" (38), and he condemns himself for it while being unable to rid himself of the belief. And because Marlin thinks of Tir-nan-Og specifically because of the bog (42), Dunsany effects a union between paganism and nature on the one hand and Christianity and civilisation on the other.

Peridore, for his part, is close to nature in his own way. The first half of the novel is full of scenes of hunting—Peridore learning the methods of hunting snipe and geese from Marlin, and also engaging in a long fox hunt that takes him across miles of lovely Irish countryside—in a manner that may offend modern sensibilities with its unashamed killing of defenceless animals. (The killing of the fox is justified by its predation of chickens and other livestock.) But Dunsany emphasises the unity with nature that a hunter can achieve: "I think we sportsmen are somewhat nearer to the tides and the growth of trees and the night and the morning, and to whatever we call the plan that orders the planets, than many a man that does more useful things" (47). Moreover, this hunting makes Peridore feel closely tied to the people of his community—tenant farmers, for the most part.

Mrs. Marlin is perhaps an even more potent symbol for closeness with nature than her son. In our first introduction to her, she tells Peridore when the geese will be coming back to the area on the north wind: "'Haven't I seen the north wind?' she said. 'Aye, face to face. And few the secrets he hides from me'" (35). Dunsany even states that the bog had given Mrs. Marlin "whatever powers she had" (98). Later this suggestion is clarified: "There's a power . . . that is hid in the heart of the bog, that is against all their plans [i.e., the plans of the development company]" (131).

An explicitly religious tone enters her dispute with the development company when it is stated that, to her, it would be "sacrilege"

(99) to alter the bog. Her devotion to it is enhanced when her own son, dying of liver failure from drinking too much whiskey, refuses to die in his bed (for that would, in his belief, consign him to hell) but gets up and wanders off "over the bog" (153) to Tir-nan-Og, meaning that he will be young and vibrant forever. Peridore enlists the aid of the local townspeople to hunt for his body, but the treacherousness of the bog foils their efforts.

Whether the supernatural ever comes into play in this novel is an question Dunsany deliberately leaves unanswered. A local doctor, clearly educated in England, suggests that the curses that Mrs. Marlin flings at the company and its employees may be having a psychological effect on the men working there; and, to be sure, all the men from Clonrue leave off working for the company. This element underscores the England/Ireland conflict in the novel. The name of the development company suggests that it is the Irish branch of an English company, a point emphasised by one of the townspeople, who refers to it as "that English company" (179). And yet, the townspeople, although sympathetic to Mrs. Marlin and not wishing the bog to be drained—for, although they and their ancestors have been cutting peat from it since primitive times, they have done so in a manner that does not damage the essential character of the bog—feel that nothing can be done to prevent its destruction: "It's the will of God" (206). This offhand comment suggests the degree to which conventional Christian belief has sided with the forces of civilisation and even mechanisation, as opposed to nature and paganism.

But, in the novel's climactic scene, Mrs. Marlin appears to summon the north wind to unleash a particularly vicious storm that destroys the company's machinery; in the process, the bog itself moves, covering over both the machinery and Mrs. Marlin herself, who has died in the course of events. Did she really summon the storm, or was this merely a fortuitous coincidence? We shall never know.

I have not discussed the element of political violence that underscores *The Curse of the Wise Woman*, for it is not central to the religious theme I am investigating. The novel is set around 1880, when the so-called Land War—a struggle between tenant farmers and landlords—was raging. Indeed, the novel's riveting first scene depicts Peridore's father fleeing from four men who seek to kill him for unspecified actions he has taken; although he escapes and ends up in Paris, he is later killed. This hostility is not extended to his son, who has fervently stayed out of politics. Indeed, at a crucial point in the novel, one of his father's would-be assassins approaches him and says that he can undertake certain actions to put an end to the development company's efforts. Peridore, knowing this would mean the killing of some workers for purposes of intimidation, reluctantly declines the man's offer.

The Catholic/Protestant dichotomy in *The Curse of the Wise Woman* is similarly not something that Dunsany emphasises, and it in fact may be the most disappointing element in it because of the sketchiness of its treatment. The young Peridore, almost seventeen when the novel opens, is attracted to a neighbor, Laura Lanley, and sporadically courts her in the course of the novel. Peridore never declares his own religious affiliation, and only at the end do we learn that their budding romance is nipped in the bud because Laura is a Protestant.

Both *The Blessing of Pan* and *The Curse of the Wise Woman* are written in an exquisitely simple but heartfelt prose that creates an atmosphere of poignant melancholy and sustains it to the end. In both novels, the element of fantasy or the supernatural is reduced almost to the vanishing point; but nevertheless a pervasive sense of the weird infuses both works, making them among the most ethereal of Dunsany's novels. The religious tension that is at the core of both narratives shows how Dunsany was able to employ weirdness—even in a highly attenuated form—to convey profound messages about human life and society, and the ongoing struggles of both faith and secularism in an increasingly mechanised age.

Works Cited

Amory, Mark. *Biography of Lord Dunsany*. London: Collins, 1972.

Dunsany, Lord. *The Blessing of Pan.* London: Putnam, 1927.

———. *The Curse of the Wise Woman.* 1933. London: Collins, 1972.

———. *A Glimpse from a Watch Tower.* London: Jarrolds, 1946.

———. *Patches of Sunlight.* London: Heinemann, 1938.

———. "Romance and the Modern Stage," *National Review* No 341 (July 1911): 827–35.

———. *While the Sirens Slept.* London: Jarrolds, [1944].

Sax Rohmer: The Popular Weird Tale

The work of British writer Sax Rohmer (1883–1959) was once immensely popular, and even now his name conjures up images of bygone bestsellerdom, something on the order of Edgar Wallace or Dennis Wheatley. While a relatively modest proportion of his bountiful work could be said to enter the domain of the weird or supernatural, enough of it does to make all readers and scholars of the genre take account of his writings, whether in the short story or the novel.

Born Arthur Henry Ward in Birmingham, England, on 15 February 1883 (at the age of eighteen he replaced his middle name, Henry, with Sarsfield), Rohmer was the son of Irish parents. His family moved to London in 1885, although he did not begin formal schooling until the age of nine. Rather than attending college, Rohmer decided to take the Civil Service examination, but he failed; he later became a bank clerk, but the drudgery of the work compelled him to resign. It was at this point that he first attempted fiction writing—but his work was uniformly rejected. A brief stint on the staff of a newspaper, the *Commercial Intelligence*, was also unsuccessful. Rohmer then returned more determinedly to the task of fiction writing, and by 1903 he achieved success with the simultaneous acceptance of two stories by leading periodicals of the day. "The Mysterious Mummy" appeared in *Pearson's Weekly Christmas Extra* (26 November 1903), and "The Leopard-Couch" appeared in *Chambers's Journal* on 30 January 1904.

Rohmer did not restrict himself to writing fiction. For a number of years, even after his initial breakthrough into print, he was attracted to the theatre and other performance arts. He wrote much material for a comedian, but the act failed when the comedian developed extreme stage fright. Over the years Rohmer also produced a number of performances in music halls and theatres.

He adopted the pseudonym Sax Rohmer early in his career, but did not apply it to his works of fiction until 1912. He later explained the origin and meaning of the pseudonym as follows: "In ancient Saxon 'sax' means 'blade'; 'rohmer' equals 'roamer.' I substituted an 'h' for the 'a' as a gesture in the direction of phonetics—pretty obscure gesture, I guess" (cited in Van Ash-Rohmer 39). Strangely enough, even his wife, Elizabeth, whom he married in 1909, adopted the pseudonym, becoming Elizabeth Sax Rohmer.

A year after his marriage, Rohmer's first book, *Pause!* (1910), appeared. It was an anonymous collection of essays and sketches, and his second book, *Little Tich* (1911), about a popular comedian of the period, was similarly unrepresentative of the bulk of his published work. But in 1911 Rohmer wrote a series of sketches about the Limehouse district of London, then populated chiefly by Chinese immigrants, and it was in part from this work that he derived the idea of his celebrated villain, Dr. Fu Manchu. Rohmer began writing stories about this evil Oriental, and they were collected in *The Mystery of Dr. Fu-Manchu* (1913). (The hyphen in Fu Manchu was later dropped.) Rohmer attempted to deflect accusations of racism in his portrayal of Fu Manchu and his cohorts by declaring that his depictions were not intended to be as broad-based as they appeared to be:

> Nowadays, I like to think that a Chinese and a Chinaman are not the same thing. When I began writing, "Chinaman" was no more than the accepted term for a native of China. The fact that it has since taken on a derogatory meaning is due mostly to the behavior of those Chinamen who lived in such places as Limehouse.
>
> Of course, not the whole Chinese population of Limehouse was criminal. But it contained a large number of persons who had left their own country for the most urgent of reasons. These people knew no way of making a living other than by the criminal activities which had made China too hot for them. They brought their crimes with them. Naturally, it took our police some time to get their measure. They were dealing with enemies who did nothing in the expected way, who thought differently, who com-

municated with one another in a language that few Englishmen could speak and fewer still could read. (Van Ash-Rohmer 73)

Whether this account sufficiently exculpates Rohmer from charges of racism and stereotyping is highly debatable. The irony, however, as far as his own writing career is concerned is that the popularity of the Fu Manchu stories and novels—they would fill a total of fourteen books, out of the more than fifty that he published in a long lifetime—became a kind of albatross around his neck. Over the next thirty or forty years, there were many occasions when Rohmer wished to write other work but was compelled by economic necessity to churn out more Fu Manchu tales in order to bring in an income.

For our present purposes, we need not take much account of the Fu Manchu volumes, because they are by and large adventure or crime tales without any hint of the supernatural aside from the vague patina of exoticism engendered by the Oriental atmosphere. But Rohmer was always attracted to the supernatural. Although he had renounced belief in religion at an early age, throughout his life he exhibited an interest in spiritualism and occultism; indeed, he believed that one of the houses in which he resided, shortly after World War I, was haunted. Rohmer also briefly joined the Order of the Golden Dawn and a Rosicrucian society. These interests led him to write the nonfiction volume *The Romance of Sorcery* (1914).

What is more, Orientalism was not his chief interest, either in literature or in life; instead, it was Egypt. Rohmer and his wife had first visited Egypt in 1913, and their exploration of the Pyramid of Meydûm on that trip led directly to the writing of *Brood of the Witch-Queen*, serialised in the *Premier* in 1914 but not appearing in book form until 1918. He wrote numerous stories about that ancient land of pyramids and Pharaohs, some of them collected in *Tales of Secret Egypt* (1918) and the much later volume *Egyptian Nights* (1944; published in the U.S. as *Bimbâshi Barûk of Egypt*). If he had had his preference, Rohmer would have written much more about Egypt and much less about the mustachioed Fu Manchu.

Rohmer's literary and personal life underwent some turmoil in the aftermath of World War I. Toward the end of the war he worked in the office of military intelligence, although it is not clear what his actual responsibilities in this capacity were. After the war, on a book tour to the United States, Rohmer engaged in an affair with a young Englishwoman. This affair continued desultorily for years, even after his wife discovered it. Some years later, going alone to the island of Madeira to rest after a bout of overwork, he became involved with an eighteen-year-old Frenchwoman. Elizabeth found out about this affair also and demanded that he spend some time alone in the United States to decide whether he wished to remain with her or not. There was an ultimate reconciliation, and the couple continued in their marriage. In the later 1920s they took frequent trips to the Riviera, as well as another trip to Egypt. On this occasion Rohmer spent a night alone inside the Great Pyramid. Nothing untoward happened—except that he was pelted by large quantities of bat dung.

Although Rohmer was by this time one of the most popular and highly paid writers in the English-speaking world, he was constantly in need of money, thanks in large part to a somewhat extravagant lifestyle. The American magazine *Collier's* was continually dunning him to write more Fu Manchu stories, and he ultimately complied; *Daughter of Fu Manchu* appeared in 1931, the first original book of Fu Manchu (not counting the reprint omnibus *The Book of Fu Manchu*, 1929) since 1917. Five more Fu Manchu books appeared in the 1930s. Meanwhile, Rohmer continued his wide travels, visiting Panama and Haiti among other places.

During War War II Rohmer again worked in military intelligence. After the war, he and his wife moved to the United States, chiefly to avoid the high taxation on wealthy individuals instituted by the new Labour government; moreover, most of Rohmer's markets were now on this side of the water. He continued writing into the 1950s, but his work was chiefly in the mystery or adventure field. He was stricken with Asiatic flu in early 1959. Returning to England, he died on 1 June 1959.

*   *   *

Of Rohmer's prolific output of novels and tales, only a relatively small proportion is of interest to devotees of the weird and supernatural. *The Dream Detective* (1920) features the psychic detective Morris Klaw, who solves his cases by his ability to visualise the last images seen by a dead person. But aside from this supernatural premise, the tales in this volume are orthodox mysteries.

The story collections *Tales of Secret Egypt* (1918), *The Haunting of Low Fennel* (1920), and *Tales of Chinatown* (1922) contain a certain proportion of weirdness. In many cases, Rohmer engages in either the "explained supernatural" (where supernaturalism is suggested, only to be explained away by natural means) or the "ambiguously supernatural" (where doubt remains to the end as to whether the supernatural has come into play or not). In "Breath of Allah," for example, a man thinks he can *see* words coming out of a person's mouth—but this is explained as a hallucination induced by hashish fumes. In "The Whispering Mummy" the mummy's whispers are explained as the result of trickery. But in "The Death-Ring of Sneferu" and "Lord of the Jackals," supernaturalism *may* come into play; indeed, in the latter story it is difficult to account for the sudden appearance of thousands of jackals in any other fashion. Less convincing is "The Haunting of Low Fennel," where the ghostly phenomena are unconvincingly accounted for by an emanation of vapour from the ground.

"Tchériapin" is without question Rohmer's finest weird tale, and it is authentically supernatural—or perhaps pseudo-science-fictional might be a better term. Here the premise is the discovery by a chemist of a formula that allows for rendering any vegetable or organic substance as hard as diamonds. One wonders whether Rohmer was influenced by Robert W. Chambers's tale "The Mask," in *The King in Yellow* (1895), where a somewhat similar petrifying formula is postulated. In any event, the story becomes grimly effective. "The Curse of a Thousand Kisses" fuses horror and poignancy in its suggestion that a hideous old woman is the centuries-old Scheherazade, the victim of a curse.

Brood of the Witch-Queen is Rohmer's most extensive exploration of the supernatural. This account of Antony Ferrara, a seductive young man who turns out to be the son of a "witch-queen" of ancient Egypt, follows the tradition of Egyptian horror set by Richard Marsh's *The Beetle* (1897) and Bram Stoker's *Jewel of Seven Stars* (1903). Although there are scattered mentions of elementals and vampires, the most effective supernatural manifestations—chiefly hallucinations induced by Ferrara upon those who are seeking to eliminate him—are accounted for as a kind of elaborate hypnotism. The novel could have been somewhat more effective if Rohmer had not portrayed Ferrara as purely evil and his antagonists as purely good; and the romance element he includes— Ferrara is seeking to dominate the fetching Myra Duquesne, chiefly to gain control of her fortune—is contrived and conventional. But the novel does succeed in gaining cumulative power as Ferrara's opponents seem repeatedly unable to curtail his supernatural depredations.

Subsequent work by Rohmer in the novel form also featured the supernatural in somewhat lesser degrees. *The Quest of the Sacred Slipper* (1919) implausibly focuses on a slipper of Mohammed whose theft impels its Islamic owners to engage in various supernatural shenanigans to regain it. *The Green Eyes of Bast* (1920) returns us to Egypt, although it is really a mystery novel with supernatural interludes; and its account of a female child born with certain catlike features is unconvincing. Also with an Egyptian substratum is *She Who Sleeps: A Romance of New York and the Nile* (1928), where it is suggested that an ancient Egyptian priestess has awoken from a state of suspended animation, although in the end the supernatural manifestation is dispelled as trickery. Finally, there is *The Bat Flies Low* (1935), a weak occultist novel about a quest for a lamp of perpetual light.

Rohmer was a prodigious plot-weaver and tale-spinner, but there are times when his very facility seems to work against him: there is a distinct sense of the "slick" and the mechanical in much of his work, right down to the level of diction and characterisation. The influence of H. Rider Haggard, Rudyard Kipling, and other writers of mystery and exotic adventure tales is patent, and all too often it seems as if Rohmer is just going through the motions to churn out another tale or serial for the popular magazines. But his authentic enthusiasm for ancient Egypt and his admirable ability to portray landscape, whether in far-flung climes or in his native England, as well as his unfailing skill at compelling narrative, render his work as readable now as it was when it was first written. No one will ever mistake Sax Rohmer for a writer of profound depth or meaning, but as one who can grasp readers' attention and keep them turning the pages he has few equals.

Works Cited

Van Ash, Cay, and Elizabeth Sax Rohmer. *Master of Villainy: A Biography of Sax Rohmer.* London: Tom Stacey, 1972.

Maurice Level and the Grand Guignol

Maurice Level (1875–1926) is the forgotten man of French literature. In spite of having published thirteen novels, dozens of plays, and hundreds of short stories, and being a star contributor to the celebrated Grand Guignol Theatre in Paris, Level is a virtually unknown quantity. He does not appear in any English-language dictionaries or encyclopaedias of French literature—and, incredibly, does not appear even in multi-volume and presumably authoritative French encyclopaedias of French literature. Not a single article has been published about him in an academic journal, and the most basic features of his life are unknown. All we have is his work.

And yet, Level experienced a remarkable popularity in the English-speaking world during the second and third decades of the twentieth century, when two novels, *The Grip of Fear* (1911) and *Those Who Return* (1923), were translated, along with a volume of short stories, first published in England as *Crises* (1920) and, later in the same year, in the United States as *Tales of Mystery and Horror*. (To add to the oddity, Level's stories never appeared in a collection in French.) In 1921, H. P. Lovecraft, who admitted that he had not yet read any of Level's work, wrote a paean to him based solely upon his increasing reputation:

> Nay, I have never read a tale of M. Maurice's, but have yearned to do so ever since beholding the announcement of his book of tales in the reviews a year or so ago. . . . For M. Level I have only the respect most profound—I would that I could create plots as delicious as his! How relieving it is to fly from the pitiful commonplaces of futile, trivial, superficial, ethics-mad, mock-important, sentimental, romantic, false-idea'd, American namby-pamby Sunday-school tales, to something that actually digs under the illusory surface of conventional values & feigned motives, & shakes the real fibres of the human animal! (Letter to Myrta Alice Little 28–29)

Lovecraft goes on here at much greater length, but this should suffice to suggest what an impression Level's mere reputation made on an artist so sensitive to the weird, terrible, and unconventional as Lovecraft.

In "Supernatural Horror in Literature" (1927), Lovecraft's response is somewhat more subdued. In discussing the *conte cruel* ("cruel tale"), "in which the wrenching of the emotions is accomplished through dramatic tantalisations, frustrations, and gruesome physical horrors," he goes on to write: "Almost wholly devoted to this form is the living writer Maurice Level, whose very brief episodes have lent themselves so readily to theatrical adaptation in the 'thrillers' of the Grand Guignol" (53). The overriding fact that Level avoided supernaturalism altogether in his work necessitated such a response, for Lovecraft had considerable doubts as to whether non-supernatural horror, however "gruesome" or extreme, could ever be a legitimate branch of the "weird tale."

As I have mentioned, we know next to nothing of Level's life, except that he studied medicine for a time—a point that becomes evident in a number of his tales. It is unclear when he first became associated with the Grand Guignol Theatre, but his earliest published play appears to date to 1906. The history of the Grand Guignol Theatre has now been charted in a number of volumes,[1] and from them we learn much that is of indirect interest to the study of Level and his work. The theatre was founded in 1897 by Oscar Méténier but taken over two years later by Max Maurey. In spite of its reputation for focusing on death, madness, and eroticism, an average evening's program at the theatre usually included a comedy. (None of the Level stories that have been translated into English are comedies except, perhaps, a single example, the uncollected tale "The Appalling Gift.") Otherwise, the program almost exclusively featured one-act plays, exactly of the sort suited to the intense,

---

1. See Mel Gordon, *The Grand Guignol: Theatre of Fear and Terror* (New York: Amok Press, 1988); Richard J. Hand and Michael Wilson, *Grand-Guignol: The French Theatre of Horror* (Exeter, UK: University of Exeter Press, 2002). The latter volume contains new translations of Level's *Sous la lumière rouge* (as *In the Darkroom*) and *Le Baiser dans la nuit* (as *The Final Kiss*).

tightly constructed plots we find in Level's stories. The theatre's heyday chiefly occurred in the decade or two after World War I, but it declined in the 1930s, especially with the advent of talkies and of horror films; but it continued for decades, not shutting its doors until 1962.

Level was not the most prolific contributor tro the Grand Guignol; that honour goes to André de Lorde, whose overall output includes more than 150 plays, novels, and other work. But Level's plays were among the theatre's biggest hits; one of them was *Sous la lumière rouge* (based on the story translated into English as "In the Light of the Red Lamp"), which premiered in 1911, while *Le Baiser dans la nuit* (based on the story "The Last Kiss") premiered the next year. It would appear that Level wrote his stories first, publishing them in magazines and newspapers (especially the Paris paper *Le Journal*), then adapting them into plays, sometimes with the help of a collaborator. It would seem that few of these plays were actually published; so far as can be ascertained, the following is a complete list of Level's separately published plays:

Le Boulet (with Auguste Monnier). Paris: Ondet, 1906. [The Millstone]
Lady Madeline (with J.-Joseph Renard). Paris: Stock, 1908. [Lady Madeline]
Sous la lumière rouge (with Étienne Ray). Paris: Edition du "Monde Illustré," 1911.
Les Tout-Petits. In *Je Sais Tout* (15 May 1912): 527-35. [The Little Ones]
Les Complices. Je Sais Tout (15 September 1912): 255-62. [The Accomplices]
Le Baiser dans la nuit. In *Le Gosse* by Maurice Level and J. J. Frappa. Paris: Edition du "Monde Illustré," 1913.
Mado. Annales Politiques et Littéraires 77 (1921): 632-36. [Mado]
Le Sorcier. Je Sais Tout (15 February 1922): 33-39. [The Sorcerer]

But there must have been dozens of others. *Lady Madeline* is of interest in being a stage adaptation of Poe's "The Fall of the House of Usher."

The list of Level's published novels runs as follows:

L'Épouvante. Paris: Edition du "Monde Illustré," 1908. [Terror]
Les Portes d'enfer. Paris: Edition du "Monde Illustré," 1910. [The Gates of Hell]

Les Oiseaux de nuit. Paris: Flammarion, 1914. [The Night Birds]

Vivre pour la patrie. Paris: Flammarion, 1917. [To Live for the Nation]

L'Alouette. Paris: Flammarion, 1918. [The Lark]

Mado; ou, La Guerre à Paris. Paris: Flammarion, 1919. [Mado, or the War in Paris]

Le Manteau d'arlequin. Paris: Flammarion, 1919. [The Harlequin's Cloak]

Le Crime. Paris: J. Ferenczi, 1921. [The Crime]

Barrabas (with Louis Feuillade). Paris: J. Ferenczi, 1921. [Barrabas]

L'Ombre. Paris: Flammarion, 1921. [The Ghost]

Les Morts étranges. Paris: J. Ferenczi, 1921. [The Strange Deaths]

L'Île sans nom. Paris: Flammarion, 1922. [The Nameless Island]

La Cité des voleurs. Paris: Flammarion, 1924. [The City of Thieves]

L'Énigme de Bellavista (with Jean Prudhomme). Paris: Tallandier, 1929. [The Enigma of Bellavista]

Le Marchand de secrets (with Jean Prudhomme). Paris: Tallandier, 1929. [The Seller of Secrets]

It is difficult to characterise Level's work, save to say that its relent-less emphasis on crime, hate, vengeance, and their psychological effects constitutes his distinctive contribution to literature. This is the focus of the early novel *L'Épouvante* (1908), translated as *The Grip of Fear*, al-though its French title simply means "terror" or "fright." In this work, a journalist, having stumbled upon an undetected murder, deliberately plants evidence implicating himself as the perpetrator of the crime, merely to experience the thrill of being hunted by the police. The jour-nalist, Onesimus Coche, always imagines that he can reveal the truth to the police if matters go too far; but he finds that his emotions get the better of him as the noose tightens figuratively around his neck. He be-gins to crack under the strain, and it is said of him toward the end: "From the very start Coche had but one enemy: his own imagination."

But accomplished as this novel is, Level's reputation will probably rest on his tales, which if nothing else have all the compactness and "unity of effect" that Edgar Allan Poe believed was the signature feature of the short story. Level's immediate literary influences in this regard were probably Guy de Maupassant (who is cited in *Those Who Return*) and Villiers de l'Isle-Adam, the master of the *conte cruel* whose work preceded Level's by a few decades; but these two writers themselves drew extensively upon the structural perfection of Poe's short stories as models for their own work, and Level manifestly did so as well. Without a wasted word, Level's tales progress from the first scene to the last in a manner that fully exhibits the conflict of emotions that is at their heart, but without the flabby digressions and irrelevancies that often mar even the most accomplished of novels. Level's tales reveal such an economy of means that nothing could be added to or extracted from them without destroying their very fabric.

The emphasis on terror, even if it is of an unambiguously non-supernatural sort, makes the reading of Level's tales at times an excruciating experience. It is not that there is any excess of physical violence involved: "The Last Kiss" is probably the most extreme in this regard, with its unflinching display of the hideous effects of acid when thrown upon a man's (and, later, a woman's) face. "The Kennel" is hideous in its suggestion of a corpse being fed to hungry dogs. But beyond this, the terror in Level's tales is chiefly psychological: the terror of an impoverished prostitute being forced to service the executioner of her lover; the terror of a man coming upon definitive evidence that his lover was buried alive; the terror that a mother feels when she suspects that her new-born baby is the child of a madman. . . . Many of the scenarios Level constructs may seem a trifle contrived and artificial, but his purpose to study the emotional extremes of those who find themselves confronted by madness, guilt, and paranoia.

There is a considerable social element in many of Level's tales—an element that similarly links them to the Grand Guignol's concern for naturalism, a literary movement that emphasised the plight of the out-cast and impoverished and sought to display the harshness and injus-tice of a social fabric built upon radical inequities in wealth and social position. Many of Level's stories feature beggars or other characters on the margins of society who plunge into crime to exact vengeance upon a society that has left them no other means of combating economic inequality. "The Beggar" is prototypical in this regard: a beggar tries in vain to bring help to a man who is being crushed by an overturned cart, but he is driven away by the man's family because they believe he is only looking for a handout. In the end, the beggar can only express a certain wry satisfaction that the man's own family effectively caused his death.

In tales written during and after World War I, Level cleverly adapted his blood-and-thunder style to grim and poignant narratives involving the war. His surprise endings, featuring sudden twists and unexpected dénouements, work well when applied to war scenarios. The deep resentment by the humiliated French at German occupation and brutality is searingly displayed in several tales. It would be interesting to know if any of these were adapted for the Grand Guignol.

The novel translated as *Those Who Return* is a somewhat different proposition. The French title—*L'Ombre*—is particularly difficult to render into English. Its primary meaning is "shadow," but secondarily it can refer to a "shade" (as in shades of the dead), a "ghost," and so on. A suggestion of the supernatural is faintly implicit in the novel, but in reality the "shadows" we are concerned with are the shadows of the past that leave their mark on the present—in particular, on the present-day life of the protagonist, the young Claude de Marbois, who seeks to learn the truth about his beloved mother, who died when he was a child. The sordid tale of crime and illicit love that Claude unearths when he returns to his ancestral home is unfolded skilfully by Level, and with increasing attention to Claude's own psychological instability. In the end, it is not surprising that his mental equilibrium is overwhelmed.

Maurice Level remained a figure of note even after his early death. His play *Le Baiser dans la nuit* was performed as late as 1938 at the Grand Guignol Theatre and was even adapted (loosely and without credit) as an EC comic. But beyond the three volumes already mentioned, none of his work appeared in English in book form subsequent to 1923, and only a few scattered tales appeared in English-language magazines in the later 1920s and 1930s. But among devotees of psychological suspense and the macabre, Level's work has always retained a shadowy interest, and he has refused to fade away. Few authors have displayed greater psychological acuity, greater craftsmanship in the manufacture of short stories, and a more unflinching gaze at the grotesque crimes that human passions are capable of engendering; and few have exhibited those crimes and those passions with loftier artistry.

Works Cited

Lovecraft, H. P. *The Annotated Supernatural Horror in Literature*, ed. S. T. Joshi. New York: Hippocampus Press, 2nd ed. 2012.

————. Letter to Myrta Alice Little (17 May 1921). *Lovecraft Studies* No. 26 (Spring 1992): 26–30.

Irvin S. Cobb and Gouverneur Morris: A Taste for the Weird

In one sense, Irvin S. Cobb (1876-1944) and Gouverneur Morris (1876-1953) could not be more different. Aside from the commonplace similarity of being American short story writers working at roughly the same time period, their lives were as contrasting as the lives of two popular writers could be. Cobb, a resolute Midwesterner in spite of his long residence in New York, attained immense literary and even media celebrity in the course of his life—a celebrity that culminated in 1935, when he was the master of ceremonies at the Academy Awards in Hollywood, where he was embraced and kissed by Claudette Colbert and Shirley Temple. Morris, a scion of a signer of the Declaration of Independence, did attain success as a writer, but abandoned writing in middle age and became a staid bank president. For our purposes, however, their most significant point in common between the two was the fact that a slim but significant sliver of their literary output consisted of powerful tales of supernatural and psychological terror.

It is also striking that, while virtually nothing is known of Morris's life apart from the mere record of his publications, Cobb left an enormous paper trail that has led to numerous biographies, memoirs, and critical studies. Accordingly, the bulk of this essay will be devoted to Cobb's life—a life of fascinating twists and turns, and which led him to long residences in widely scattered locales in the United States.

Irvin Shrewsbury Cobb was born on 23 June 1876, in Paducah, Kentucky, a smallish city of 15,000 people located on the Ohio River in the far western part of the state. He was the second of four children of Joshua and Manie (Saunders) Cobb. In his early years his education alternated between local public and private schools; but his formal education came to an abrupt end in 1892, when his family's financial difficulties (chiefly his father's loss of his job and his subsequent descent into alcoholism) compelled the young Cobb to work full-time. In school he had shown great precocity and the ability to learn quickly; and he also learned much from a family friend, "Uncle" Joel Shrewsbury, from whom his middle name derived. Cobb's readings were wide and diverse, ranging from nineteenth-century literary classics to dime novels. He had also hung around the docks where his father worked, gaining a sense of both the commerce and the romance of the river and his steamboat traffic. Other early interests included birds and reptiles as well as the Native American relics found abundantly in the area; and he was fascinated to hear the stories of the old inhabitants of the town as they reminisced about antebellum days. (As a border state, Kentucky had supporters of both the Union and the Confederate cause.)

All these interests seemed to lead inexorably to his working for the local paper, the *Paducah Daily News*. Beginning as a reporter in 1893, he even attained the lofty position of managing editor in 1895, a position he held for two years. Gradually he felt the need to take his journalistic talents to a larger metropolitan paper, and in 1898 he joined the staff of the *Louisville Evening Post*, where he began a humorous column called "Kentucky Sour Mash," a reference to the bootleg liquor of his state. He also worked as a political reporter, being at the state capitol in Frankfort when the Governor-elect, William Goebel, was assassinated on 30 January 1900.

Cobb had met Laura Baker in 1896, and after several years of persistent courting persuaded her to marry him on 12 June 1900. Soon thereafter the *Paducah Daily Democrat* (later the *News Democrat*) lured Cobb back to his hometown with a higher salary (the sum of $30 a week), and he became managing editor. He continued to support his mother and sisters after his marriage, but he also continued to feel the call of the big-city newspaper. In 1904 he went to the biggest city of all, New York, and by a certain brashness managed to secure a job at the

New York Evening Sun, one of the most distinguished papers of the day. Once established there, he brought his wife and daughter, Elizabeth (born in 1902), to join him. A year later he began an association with the *New York World* that lasted until 1912. Aside from covering such events as the peace conference of the Russo-Japanese War in Portsmouth, N.H., in 1905, he initiated as many as six different humorous columns, most of which ran in the features section on Sunday.

Cobb always maintained that his extensive journalistic writing was good practice for his eventual career as a short story writer and novelist; but he only undertook the latter around 1908, when a colleague, Samuel Blythe, assured him that the *Saturday Evening Post,* one of the best-paying "slick" magazines of the day, would welcome his contributions. One of his earliest stories, "The Escape of Mr. Trimm," appeared in the *Post* in 1909. Soon Cobb was publishing there and in other magazines, including the Munsey magazines, which catered to a popular audience. Cobb, who had been quite thin in his youth, became a corpulent man in his adulthood, and he poked fun at his girth in one of his earliest volumes, *Cobb's Anatomy* (1912). This book, like many of his others during the first decade or two of his career, was published by George H. Doran Company. Cobb had purchased a small house in Yonkers in 1907, and Doran himself became his neighbor in 1909. His first story collection, *The Escape of Mr. Trimm,* appeared in 1913.

Cobb and other reporters were sent to Europe to cover the outbreak of World War I in the later summer of 1914. He set sail on 7 August 1914, proceeding from Liverpool to Belgium. German shelling of the town of Louvain forced him to take cover there for three days; finally he made it to Brussels. But when the Germans took over that city, he tricked the German officials into allowing him wide latitude to explore the region, and his vivid descriptions of the widespread devastation of Belgium brought him considerable celebrity. Later, he and other reporters were detained by the German Army at Beaumont and then taken to Aix-la-Chapelle, in German-controlled Alsace. Cobb and others wrote a letter directly to the Kaiser, stressing the benefits of having American reporters in Germany (the United States was at this time still officially neutral in the conflict); incredibly, the Kaiser acceded to the argument, allowing the reporters to go behind German lines. After some weeks Cobb managed to get to Vaals, in the Netherlands, and then moved on to London, returning home on 1 November. His articles, appearing in the *Saturday Evening Post* and *Philadelphia Public Ledger*, were collected as *Paths of Glory* (1915). He later went on a lecture tour to talk about the war, attracting large audiences.

Cobb wished to return at once to the war front, but illness prevented him: he required an operation for a hernia. He made this unpleasant incident pay immense dividends, for he wrote a long article entitled "Speaking of Operations–," appearing in the *Saturday Evening Post* (6 November 1915), that proved hugely popular; when it was published as a booklet it sold half a million copies.

Cobb continued to write fiction and other matter in immense quantities. The great majority of this work was humour. He initiated a series of tales featuring Old Judge Priest, a no-nonsense judge in Paducah based on an actual individual, William Sutton Bishop, whom Cobb admired. Subsidiary characters—including a sympathetically portrayed black servant of Priest's, Jefferson Poindexter—were also based on figures in Kentucky. A total of forty-two stories and two short novels about Priest appeared in Cobb's lifetime. Cobb—who seemed to model himself on Mark Twain whenever he could, whether it be his fascination with the great rivers of the Midwest or with comic or travel writing—also wrote a number of humorous travel books, the first being *Europe Revised* (1914), followed by a series of books about individual states as part of "The American Guyed Books Series." He also became a popular after-dinner speaker.

But Cobb's literary reputation never recovered from H. L. Mencken's attack on it in various reviews, which were gathered as "The Heir of Mark Twain" and published in Mencken's *Prejudices: First Series* (1919). The opening of the essay testifies both to Cobb's celebrity and to Mencken's disdain of his writing as second-rate and lowbrow:

Nothing could be stranger than the current celebrity of Irvin S. Cobb, an author of whom almost as much is heard as if he were a new Thackeray or Molière. One is solemnly told by various extravagant partisans, some of them not otherwise insane, that he is at once the successor to Mark Twain and the heir of Edgar Allan Poe. One hears of public dinners given in devotion to his genius, of public presentations, of learned degrees conferred upon him by universities, of other extraordinary adulations, few of them shared by such relatively puny fellows as Howells and Dreiser. His talents and sagacity pass into popular anecdotes; he has sedulous Boswells; he begins to take on the august importance of an actor-manager. Behind the scenes, of course, a highly dexterous publisher pulls the strings, but much of it is undoubtedly more or less sincere; men pledge their sacred honor to the doctrine that his existence honors the national literature. . . .

In the actual books of the man I can find nothing that seems to justify so much enthusiasm, nor even the hundredth part of it. His serious fiction shows a certain undoubted facility, but there are at least forty other Americans who do the thing quite as well. His public bulls and ukases are no more than clever journalism—superficial and inconsequential, first saying one thing and then quite another thing. And in his humor, which his admirers apparently put first among his products, I can discover, at best, nothing save a somewhat familiar aptitude for grotesque anecdote, and, at worst, only the laborious laugh-squeezing of Bill Nye. (97–98)

Despite the protestations of Cobb's supporters, Mencken's judgment is fundamentally sound. The fact is that Cobb's brand of writing was, although popular, in no way analogous to the work of Modernists such as Dreiser, Sinclair Lewis, Sherwood Anderson, Willa Cather, William Faulkner, F. Scott Fitzgerald, Ernest Hemingway, and others who would dominate the higher reaches of literature in their time. Cobb was relegated to the status of a "funny man" whose very appearance in a popular magazine like the *Saturday Evening Post* confirmed his mediocrity.

But for quite a time Cobb could, while lamenting his lack of critical esteem, pocket the substantial amounts of money he made from his writing. He spent years renovating an abandoned farmhouse in Westchester county, New York, near the town of Ossining, which he named Rebel Ridge; the work was finally finished in 1921. Cobb did return to the war front in early 1918, and his dispatches were later collected in a more obviously patriotic volume, *The Glory of the Coming*

(1918). He did considerable writing for films from as early as 1917, although none of these were notable successes. Meanwhile he continued to publish story collections throughout the 1920s. Mencken would at least have appreciated Cobb's vigorous opposition to Prohibition and the rise of the Ku Klux Klan in that decade.

In 1922 Cobb gave up his position as staff contributor to the *Saturday Evening Post* to work for *Cosmopolitan,* then a magazine published by William Randolph Hearst and devoted largely to fiction and articles. For the next decade all his stories appeared there; and in 1926, when he parted ways with George H. Doran, his books appeared under the imprint of the Cosmopolitan Book Corporation. By this time his daughter, who had renamed herself Elisabeth, had become a writer herself, publishing her first novel, *Falling Seeds,* in 1927. Another token of Cobb's celebrity was the building of the 200-room Irvin Cobb Hotel in Paducah: it would be difficult to find a similar establishment of the period named after a living author.

But Cobb's finances took a severe hit with the onset of the Depression in 1929; at the same time, his story-writing inspiration appeared to have dried up. He decided to move his family to Los Angeles to pursue film work; surprisingly, he was actually persuaded to appear in films as an actor himself, since both his large girth and his reputation as a humourist were thought to be tailor-made for the movies. His first film appearance had actually occurred as early as 1915, but from 1932 to 1938 he appeared in eleven more films, including the reasonably notable *Steamboat Round the Bend* (1935), starring his good friend Will Rogers. *Judge Priest* (1934), directed by John Ford and weaving together the narratives of a number of Cobb's tales, also starred Will Rogers in the title role. But after *Our Leading Citizen* (1939), based on one of Cobb's stories, was panned, he retired from the film industry.

By this time Cobb was in failing health, and his wife and daughter moved him back to New York. With his fictional pen in abeyance, Cobb turned to autobiography, writing the immense *Exit Laughing* (1941), a long and engaging account of his varied career as journalist, writer, and family man. Irvin S. Cobb died of dropsy on 10 March 1944. His body was cremated, but his ashes were not interred until some months later, when they were placed in a plot in Oak Park Cemetery in Paducah.

Of Gouverneur Morris, all we know is that he was born in 1876, presumably in New York City, to Gouverneur and Henrietta (Baldwin) Morris. He was the namesake and great-grandson of a Revolutionary War hero and signer of the Declaration of Independence. Graduating from Yale in 1898, he began a literary career that extended to at least a dozen novels and four story collections, published between 1901 and 1934. It is the latter that concern us, for nearly every one of these—*The Footprint and Other Stories* (1908); *The Spread Eagle and Other Stories* (1910); *It and Other Stories* (1912); *The Incandescent Lily and Other Stories* (1914)—contain one or more weird tales. Whereas many of Cobb's stories appeared in the *Saturday Evening Post*, Morris was a fixture at another well-paying "slick" periodical, *Collier's*.

Like Cobb, Morris was extensively involved in the film industry. At least eighteen films from 1914 to 1936 were based on novels or stories by Morris, most notably the silent film *The Penalty* (1920), adapted from his 1915 novel and starring Lon Chaney, Sr., as a deformed mastermind who seeks revenge on the doctor who amputated his legs. Morris also co-wrote the screenplay to two other films.

Morris apparently gave up writing in the mid-1930s and, incongruously, became the president of a bank in Monterey, California. Around 1939 he retired to the small town of Coolidge, in northwestern New Mexico. He died in Gallup, N.M., on 14 August 1953.

Cobb and Morris each seem largely known to the weird community on the basis of a single story—Cobb's "Fishhead" (1913) and Morris's "Back There in the Grass" (1911), both of which were reprinted in various anthologies nominally edited by Alfred Hitchcock (actually edited by Robert Arthur). While these tales may in fact be the summit of each writer's work in weird fiction, both wrote a half-dozen or more additional tales that provide further insights into their writing as a whole and their interest in supernatural or psychological horror.

Late in his career, Cobb made clear that he had written a number of tales of this sort and suggested to the publisher Doubleday, Doran that a volume of them be assembled. He referred to "twelve or fifteen of the so-called 'horror yarns' I've done, including such as 'Darkness,' 'The Escape of Mr. Trimm,' 'An Occurrence up a Side Street,' 'The Exit of Anse Dugmore,' 'The Belled Buzzard,' 'One Block from Fifth Avenue,' 'Fishhead,' 'Snake Doctor,' 'The Gallowsmith,' 'Three Wise Men of the East Side,' etc." (letter to Doubleday, Doran, 12 May 1941; quoted in Chatterton 108). This list contains, by today's standards (and even by the standards of Cobb's own day), stories that by no means can be considered "weird" in any meaningful sense, but are largely crime/suspense stories. His output of genuinely weird work constitutes eight stories, including some of those cited in Cobb's letter; of these, only two or three are actually supernatural, while the others can be regarded as tales of psychological terror or suspense. Even some of these are quite close to mere tales of crime, as in "The Escape of Mr. Trimm," really a kind of *conte cruel* in which a criminal experiences a roller-coaster ride of emotions—first the thrill of escaping from impending imprisonment, then the frustration of being unable to remove the cheap metal handcuffs that prevent his attainment of full freedom. Cobb was particularly fond of this story—perhaps because it was virtually his first story of any kind.

"Fishhead," appearing in a Munsey magazine, the *All-Story Cavalier*, in early 1913, had the distinction of being praised in a brief letter to the editor by the young H. P. Lovecraft: "It is the belief of the writer that very few short stories of equal merit have been published anywhere during recent years. It is easy to imagine with what genuine regret the editors to whom it was submitted declined to print it" (letter to the editor, *All-Story Cavalier*, 8 February 1913; *H. P. Lovecraft in the Argosy* 34). That last sentence refers to the fact that the story had been rejected by several editors, including George Horace Lorimer of the *Saturday*

Evening Post, who remarked: "It pains me to send back one of the best written stories I have seen in years." Editors at *Everybody's Magazine* ("I don't know when a short story has impressed me more strongly or more unpleasantly") and *Redbook* ("readers aren't educated up to raw beef yet") also praised the story but were apparently afraid to print it, until finally Robert H. Davis of the *Cavalier* accepted it (Lawson 89). (For Lovecraft, there were a number of ironies here. First, the repeated rejection of a story because it was too grisly echoes the rejection of such tales as "In the Vault" and "Cool Air" by Farnsworth Wright of *Weird Tales,* who became hesitant to publish such work after the May–June–July 1924 issue of the magazine was banned in the state of Indiana because it had contained "The Loved Dead," a story about a necrophile nominally written by C. M. Eddy, Jr., but extensively revised by Lovecraft. Another such story, "The Rats in the Walls," faced similar rejection as being "too horrible"—and the editor who delivered this opinion was . . . Robert H. Davis.)

It is easy to see why Lovecraft enjoyed the story: it broached the idea of a fish-man hybrid of the sort that he would elaborate upon years later in "The Shadow over Innsmouth" (1931). That story was also probably influenced both by another tale of a fish-man, Robert W. Chambers's "The Harbor-Master" (1897; included as the first five chapters of the episodic novel *In Search of the Unknown* [1904]), and by Algernon Blackwood's "Ancient Sorceries" (in *John Silence–Physician Extraordinary* [1908]), a tale of a small town in southern France all of whose inhabitants turn into cats at night. Lovecraft was also no doubt impressed with the vivid depiction of the almost primitive rural topography, expressly set at a lake on the border between Kentucky and Tennessee, a locale no doubt well known to Cobb. Lovecraft may have gained tips from this story about how to draw upon his own knowledge of the history and topography of New England in his later tales. "Fishhead" was in fact based on a "short descriptive essay for a newspaper column" (Chatterton 121), but this item has not come to light.

Another story that undoubtedly influenced Lovecraft is Cobb's other overtly supernatural story, "The Unbroken Chain," which appeared in the September 1923 issue of *Cosmopolitan*. Then as now, the issue came out at least a month before its cover date, and Lovecraft received a copy of the issue from Frank Belknap Long in early August, at the very time he was writing "The Rats in the Walls."[1] The tale—dealing with a Frenchman who, because he has an infinitesimal amount of African blood in him, experiences a flash of ancestral memory when he is struck by a train (recalling an ancestor who was killed by an onrushing rhinoceros) and cries out in an obscure African language—clearly foreshadows Lovecraft's use of the same device when the American businessman Delapore, appalled by the realisation that his family practised cannibalism for centuries, utters words successively in old English, Latin, Gaelic, and a primitive "ape-cry" (letter to Frank Belknap Long, 8 November 1923; *Selected Letters* 1.258).

If we are repulsed at the apparent racism of Cobb's story,[2] we should be aware that throughout his life Cobb spoke out against racism and championed the achievements of African Americans. We have already seen how he portrayed the black companion of Judge Priest, Jefferson Poindexter, with unfailing sympathy and sensitivity, and how he lamented the rise of the Ku Klux Klan in the 1920s. Upon his return from Europe in 1918, he delivered numerous speeches lauding the bravery of black soldiers on the front (Lawson 164). In his newspaper columns he spoke courageously and sarcastically against prejudice against both non-whites and women:

> All men are born free and equal. That immortal statement, you will re-call, was penned and adopted by gentlemen largely engaged in owning slaves. Yet nonetheless it is true that all men are born equal unless they

---

1. Lovecraft to J. Vernon Shea (8–22 November 1933), *Letters to J. Vernon Shea, Carl F. Strauch, and Lee McBride White* 179.

2. It is interesting to note that the avowed racist Lovecraft has actually eliminated the racist element when he adapted the motif in "The Rats in the Walls." Here the protagonist is an unmistakable Caucasian who draws upon his own (white) family heritage when he regresses along the evolutionary scale.

happen to be Indians or negroes or Chinamen or Japanese or Hindoos or Mexicans, in which case it would have been much better for them if they had not been born at all. Likewise all men are born free and equal unless they happen to be born women, in which case they rank with the habitual criminals and the congenital idiots. (Cited in Lawson 71)

Anita Lawson tells of how a black servant of the Cobb family, named Uncle Rufus, told the boy of ghosts and devils:

When not running errands, he [Rufus] remained inside the one room shack that was all that remained of Dr. Saunders' slave quarters. Like Mandy [another servant], he fed and entertained the children who visited him, offering them sweet potatoes and hoe cakes. But visits to Rufus were most thrilling because of the tales he told of "hoodoos," ghosts, devils and "ha'nts." After an evening visit the children would be afraid to go from his cabin to the main house unless Mandy lighted the way with a lantern from the porch. Rufus' stories were so frightening that Cobb claimed to be a grown man before he could enter a darkened room without tensing in expectation of "Old Raw Haid and Bloody Bones" or some other gruesome phantasm, but the excitement was so enjoyable that the children always went back for more. (13)

This anecdote suggests the source of the story "Darkness," which deals with a man who is so afraid of the dark that he lives for decades with all the lights on in his house, day and night. The story also deals with the perennial issue of blood feuds in rural Kentucky. Cobb addressed the issue on at least one occasion, speaking of feuding families, "not one of those sanguinary feuds of the mountains, involving a whole district, . . . nor yet a feud handed down as a deadly legacy from one generation to another until its origin is forgotten . . . but a shabby, small neighborhood vendetta affecting two families only" (*Back Home* 70). This is exactly the sort of feud that leads to death and horror in "Darkness."

Somewhat related to "Fishhead" is "Snake Doctor," which depicts a man who seems to have an uncanny relationship with snakes. But it is very clear that no kind of physical transformation is at play here. Moreover, the story—which tells of a man who suspects the "snake doctor" of having an affair with his wife, and who dies when he thinks he has been bitten by a snake in the snake doctor's house, a snake that proves to be stuffed—is clearly derived from Ambrose Bierce's classic tale of psychological horror, "The Man and the Snake," where a man is terrified to death by a toy snake. Nevertheless, Cobb seemed proud that the story won the O. Henry Memorial Award Committee's first prize for best short story of 1922.

Another superb tale of psychological terror, "The Gallowsmith," may have had its inspiration from a hideously botched hanging of a black man in 1896—a man actually known to Cobb (Lawson 24). In the story, a seemingly phlegmatic "gallowsmith"—that is, a self-styled expert in the technique and mechanics of hanging—finds himself unwontedly disturbed by the cursing of a condemned man whose execution he mishandles. The conclusion of the story may seem a bit contrived—analogous to those of Cobb's partial contemporary, O. Henry, whose work Cobb admired—but it is a fitting capstone to a narrative of cumulative psychological horror.

The element of contrivance is particularly notable in "Faith, Hope and Charity," the last of Cobb's weird tales—a somewhat predictable but still effective tale of comeuppance where three escaped prisoners all suffer the most horrible deaths they can envision. This story in particular reveals the creaking of the short story machinery that justifiably condemned Cobb to second-rate status in American literature.

The one instance where Cobb combined his patented humour with weirdness is "The Second Coming of a First Husband." The humour is perhaps a bit broad and obvious, but succeeds well in its basic purpose.

Gouverneur Morris's weird work largely follows the pattern of Cobb's—predominantly consisting of tales of psychological suspense, with one or two notable tales of supernatural horror. Preeminent among the latter, of course, is "Back There in the Grass" (1911), an incredibly chilling and innovative narrative that broaches the idea of a hideous race of miniature human beings on a remote Polynesian island. Perhaps making a nod to Robert Hichens's classic "How Love Came to Professor Guildea" (1900), which finds terror in the paradoxical notion of a ghost that has fallen in love with a living human,

"Back There in the Grass" shows the effects of such unwholesome affection both upon the "womankin" whom a white man has captured and upon the white man himself. The fact that the man keeps his foot-high inamorata as a "kind of pet," and that his (white) fiancée is about to arrive, only augments the terror and pathos of the scenario.

This tale is representative of Morris's work in that it depicts the emotional effects of extraordinary or unusual situations upon the human psyche; most of his other weird tales, however, do so in a generally non-supernatural manner. Hence, "The Crocodile" (1905) presents a powerful portrayal of gloom and depression as a man goes into permanent mourning over the death of his wife, so that his son grows up in an atmosphere of unrelieved melancholy. There is a hint of supernaturalism toward the end, as the ghost of the dead wife seems to make an appearance; but the bulk of the tale focuses on the crippling of both the father's and the son's emotions even as the latter finds some fleeting moments of happiness upon his marriage to a sprightly young woman who unexpectedly enters his life.

"The Footprint" (1907) and "The Bride's Dead" (1908) are Nietzschean tales of survival in remote places. The latter in particular contrasts the physical strength of the brutal Farallone with the psychological strength of the young woman whom he hopes to wrest away from the weak-spirited man she has married; but in the end it is the woman who outlasts him. But although she remains true to her husband, she makes her contempt for him known at the end.

"The Execution" in some ways echoes Cobb's "The Gallowsmith" in focusing on the emotional trauma of state-sanctioned murder. Here the embodiment of almost ruthless courage is the mother of a young man sentenced to death, who escapes and returns to his home, only to suffer an unexpected comeuppance at the hands of his own blind, crippled father.

An uncollected story, "Derrick's Return" (1923), is uncharacteristic in that it is something of a religious (or perhaps anti-religious) fable. The morality of the tale may be a trifle obvious and the element of fantasy may be slight or superficial, but its very anomalousness in Morris's output makes it fully worth seeking out.

Both Irvin S. Cobb and Gouverneur Morris attained celebrity in their day, but it failed to endure beyond their lifetimes. There is much to be said for the view that, like many other short story writers of the period (preeminently O. Henry), their tales are at times too artificial and too neatly resolved to be fully realistic; but Cobb's sensitive portrayal of the people and landscape of his native state, and Morris's intense focus on the emotions of people enmeshed in tormenting circumstances, both work well in their weird work, and it is no accident that it is that work that largely causes them to be remembered today. Devotees of weird fiction have always been keen on resurrecting exemplary stories from past decades or centuries, and as a result many writers who would otherwise have faded from literary history retain a foothold in public consciousness as a result of the scattered weird tales they wrote over a career that may have been devoted to writings of a very different sort. Cobb and Morris fit that paradigm perfectly, and their weird output retains a vitality that allows it to live, while their abundant mainstream work falls into oblivion.

Works Cited

Chatterton, Wayne. *Irvin S. Cobb*. Boston: Twayne, 1986.

Cobb, Irvin S. *Back Home*. New York: George H. Doran, 1912.

Lawson, Anita. *Irvin S. Cobb*. Bowling Green, OH: Bowling Green State University Popular Press, 1984.

Lovecraft, H. P. *H. P. Lovecraft in the Argosy*. Ed. S. T. Joshi. West Warwick, RI: Necronomicon Press, 1994.

———. *Letters to J. Vernon Shea, Carl F. Strauch, and Lee McBride White*. Ed. S. T. Joshi and David E. Schultz. New York: Hippocampus Press, 2016.

———. *Selected Letters*. Ed. August Derleth, Donald Wandrei, and James Turner. Sauk City, WI: Arkham House, 1965–76. 5 vols.

Mencken, H. L. "The Heir of Mark Twain." In *Prejudices: First Series*. New York: Alfred A. Knopf, 1919. 97–104.

Bran Mak Morn and History

Robert E. Howard's fascination with history was of long standing. Aware of his own position as the son of pioneering settlers in Texas, Howard saw his family's saga of cultivating the wilderness echoed in the titanic struggles of ancient peoples to maintain their cohesiveness in primitive lands where both a hostile natural environment and the inroads of opposing, perhaps decadent civilisations must be combated. In none of his cycles of heroic fantasy was this complex interplay of nature and civilisation more vividly expressed than in his Bran Mak Morn stories.

It is well known that the figure of Bran Mak Morn, a Pict who waged an ultimately futile struggle against the might of the Roman legions and other such foes as the Celts, the Norsemen, and the Saxons, had fascinated Howard from an early period. A fragmentary play, *Bran Mak Morn*, dates to as early as 1922-23, while the four completed tales involving Bran—"The Lost Race" (written 1924-25), "Men of the Shadows" (written 1925-26), "Kings of the Night" (probably written in 1930), and "Worms of the Earth" (probably written in late 1931)—extend over much of Howard's mature writing career. Other tales such as "The Dark Man" (probably written in 1930) and "The Children of the Night" (1930) involve Bran or the Picts tangentially, as do lesser, fragmentary works. Rarely in Howard's work do we find the richness of historical setting, the struggle of barbarism against civilisation, and the epic sweep of history portrayed so poignantly as in the Bran Mak Morn stories.

Recent scholarship has determined that Howard's initial knowledge of the Picts almost certainly derived from G. F. Scott Elliot's *The Romance of Early British Life* (1909) (see Burke-Louinet 344). Where he derived his knowledge of the Romans is less certain, but the wide availability of histories of the Romans even in Howard's remote locale makes it clear that he had a tolerable familiarity with the overall course of Roman history, especially as it impinged upon the Celts, the Picts, and other barbarian races in northern Europe and, especially, the British Isles.

A brief account of the Roman occupation of Britain will be a useful preliminary to our study of the historicity of the Bran Mak Morn stories. Although the Phoenicians and the Greeks appear to have traded with the inhabitants of Britain (as pottery remains attest), the Romans did not become aware of the British Isles until Julius Caesar's war with the Gauls in the 50s B.C.E. In 55 B.C.E. Caesar invaded Britain, but his "conquest" of the island was superficial; he did, however, establish Cassivellaunus, a leader of a Celtic tribe, the Belgae, as a client king. But Caesar's domestic troubles, culminating in the Roman civil war that ended the republic and ended his life in 44 B.C.E., prevented his devoting further attention to this remote region of the Roman world. Caesar's lasting contribution was the conquest of Gaul and his rendering it a loyal component of the Roman realm.

With the end of the civil wars and the establishment of the Roman Empire in 27 B.C.E. by Augustus, Roman expansionism came to the fore. The emperor Claudius personally led an invasion of Britain in 43 C.E., with a force of 40,000 men. By this time the southeastern portion of England came under firm Roman rule. The British queen Boudicca (formerly spelled Boadicea) waged a strong rebellion in 61, but the island was ultimately subdued, largely through the efforts of the governor, C. Suetonius Paulinus, and the capable general Cn. Julius Agricola, whose biography was written by Tacitus. Wales was subjugated in 78. The Romans ventured into Scotland in 84, defeating the Picts at the battle of Mons Graupius—a location not clearly identified, but probably near the site of present-day Aberdeen. But the Picts were never subjugated by the Romans. The Romans built their celebrated wall, named after the emperor Hadrian, in 122–28, along the river Tyne. A second wall, the so-called Antonine Wall, was built in 142 miles farther north, at the Firth of Forth, but it was soon abandoned.

In 197, when the Roman governor of Britain, Clodius Albinus, took troops away from England in an attempt to become emperor, the Picts stormed Hadrian's Wall; but it was quickly rebuilt and the Romans drove the Picts back into Scotland. Around 296 the Roman leader Carausius declared himself emperor of Britain and independent of Rome. The Celts and the Picts used this occasion to disrupt the government. At this time the south and east coasts of Britain were attacked by Saxons from northern Europe, and the emperor Diocletian ordered the construction of forts along the eastern, or Saxon, shore.

In the course of the fourth century C.E. Roman forces gradually withdrew from Britain. In 367, Britain was attacked simultaneously by Celts from Ireland, Picts from Scotland, and Saxons from Europe, and Hadrian's Wall was breached. In 410 the emperor Honorius issued his celebrated decree stating that the local Roman forces would henceforth be responsible for their own defence. Roman control of Britain was, in effect, ended.

In the course of the four centuries of Roman rule, the Romans generally stationed three legions (about 5000 men each) in Britain: one, the VI Victrix, at Eboracum (York); another, the XX Valeria Victrix, at Deva (Chester); and a third, the II Augusta, at Isca Silurum (Caerleon-on-Usk in southern Wales). A fourth legion, the IX Hispana, mysteriously disappeared around 119 C.E.—certainly a fruitful basis for a story by Howard or Lovecraft! But current scholarship believes that the legion either suffered a humiliating defeat and was disbanded, or was transferred to Noviomagus, a region along the Rhine river.

Some of the smaller details of Howard's portrayal of the Romans are inaccurate—not surprisingly, as he never claimed to be an authority on Roman history. In "Worms of the Earth" we are introduced to Titus Sulla, "military governor of Eboracum" (85); later he is referred to, more accurately, as "governor of this province" (92). Howard no doubt coined the name as an allusion to L. Cornelius Sulla, the general who marched on Rome in 81 B.C.E., became a dictator, and voluntarily retired to private life in 79, dying later that year. Sulla's actions are generally regarded as the initiation of the civil wars that led to the downfall of the Roman republic. Sulla's tyrannous behaviour is presumably meant to be reflected in Titus Sulla, but the cognomen Sulla is not found in the later Roman empire, as A. H. M. Jones and his colleagues have established in *The Prosopography of the Later Roman Empire* (1971–92), a compilation of all proper names found in the empire from 260 to 641 C.E. Similarly, the Roman general in "Kings of the Night" is named Marcus Sulius, a name not attested anywhere in Roman history. (The closest we have is a P. Suillius Rufus, a consul under Claudius.) In general, Howard appears to be unfamiliar with the customary nomenclature of the Roman aristocracy, featuring a praenomen (e.g., C. or Gaius), a nomen (the *gens* or family name; e.g., Julius), and the cognomen (e.g., Caesar). Only plebeians or slaves had only two names (Titus Sulla, Marcus Sulius), and they would not be likely to have been put in positions of authority as Howard depicts them.

In "Men of the Shadows" Howard refers in passing to "a rich merchant of Corinium" (16), a well-established Roman city on the site of present-day Cirencester. But throughout his Bran Mak Morn stories he refers to Britain, or some unspecified region thereof, under the curious designation Alba (see, e.g., "The Lost Race" 175). Britain was never called Alba either by the Romans or by any other known peoples; Howard perhaps meant to write Albion, an ancient designation for Britain found in Pliny's *Natural History*. In "Men of the Shadows" the narrator (a Roman soldier) refers to some of his cohorts as "Romans from Latinia" (5), an apparent error for Latium, the region around Rome and one of the earliest settled by the Romans. The inhabitants of the area were called *Latini*, thereby perhaps accounting for Howard's error.

The precise historical setting of the Bran Mak Morn tales is a matter of debate, as Howard does not always provide enough clues for an exact dating. A synopsis of a Bran Mak Morn story clearly establishes Bran's period as "between 296 A.D. and 300 A.D." (245), and Howard well knew that this period—when the usurper Carausius' rebellion had been suppressed—was a critical one in Roman history, both in Britain and on the Continent, when "Goths and Vandals and Franks massed along the Rhine" (245). But in the actual Bran Mak Morn stories, precision of dating is much harder to ascertain. When, in "Men of the Shadows," the wizard (presumably the same Gonar found in "Worms of the Earth") presents a broad spectrum of Pictish, Celtic, and Roman history, several important events are cited. The wizard first envisions "the Celtic Brennus, whose Gallic hordes had sacked Rome" (28). There were in fact two Gallic chieftains named Brennus, one who sacked Rome in either 390 or 387 B.C.E. (it was he who made the celebrated cry *Vae victis!* [Woe to the conquered]), and another who overran Macedonia in 279 B.C.E. Howard is clearly thinking of the first, and admitted in a letter that Bran was named after him (339). The wizard now shows "the face of both a demi-god and a degenerate" (28) who proves to be Julius Caesar, and then a battle in which Roman "legions shatter[ed] the hordes of Caractacus" (28)—more properly spelled Caratacus, a Celt who attempted to resist the Roman's invasion of Britain in 43 C.E. and was eventually captured in 51. The wizard continues his evocation of the past, depicting the slow decadence of the Romans and the increasing power of the German and other barbarians on the periphery of the Roman empire.

At this point the wizard's account switches to the future, and he thrillingly depicts Rome's downfall: "The Vandal's foot spurns the Forum. A savage horde marches along the Via Appia. Yellow haired raiders violate the Vestal Virgins. And Rome falls!" (29). These are the events of 455 C.E., when Rome was sacked by the Vandals led by Gaeseric. Rome's official downfall occurred in 476 C.E., when the last Roman emperor, Romulus Augustulus, was deposed. All this does not help greatly in dating the events (if they can be so called) of "Men of the Shadows," and there is no evidence to place the events either before or after the rebellion of Carausius (296 C.E.). As for the epic battle between Romans and the combined forces of the Picts, Britons, Gaels, and Northmen in "The Kings of the Night," this too is difficult to date precisely within the course of Roman history, given the lack of specific historical details in the story. We have seen that Celts, Picts, and Saxons attacked Britain in 367, and this date is certainly conceivable for the events in "The Kings of the Night," even if it contradicts the chronology for Bran Mak Morn established in the synopsis. There are similarly too few historical indicators in "Worms of the Earth" and "The Lost Race" to date the events in those tales precisely.

On the broader question of Howard's understanding of the history of the Picts, Celts, and other tribes that sought to battle Rome for supremacy in Britain, the historical evidence is far less clear. Given the paucity of written records (and, in the case of the Picts, their complete absence), our understanding of the movements of these tribes must come almost exclusively from archaeology. In recent decades many assumptions common to previous centuries—and absorbed by Howard, Lovecraft, and other writers of the period—have now come into question. In particular, Howard appears to have envisioned a tripartite sequence of migration, with the Picts as the first tribe to come to Britain, followed by two different Celtic tribes, the Gaels (who drove the Picts north into Caledonia [Scotland] and west into Wales), and the Cymri, who drove the Gaels northward and established themselves in the South.

Archaeological evidence does not appear to corroborate this scenario. It is now believed that the first group to come to Britain were the so-called Windmill Hill people, who crossed over from Europe around 3000 B.C.E. A second group, the Beaker Folk, came from northern Europe sometime between 2500 and 2000 B.C.E. During the Bronze Age in Britain (c. 2000 to 1000 B.C.E.), a group now known as the Wessex Culture came to southwest Britain from the Continent, soon spreading over the entire island. The Celts were a large group that dominated northern and central Europe, and they appear to have been the last prehistoric invaders of Britain. The Beaker Folk and the Wessex Culture may have been Celts. The first we hear of them in the historical record is in Caesar's *Gallic War*, when he notes that a Celtic tribe named the Belgae had crossed the English Channel at some time prior to his writing and settled the southern regions of Britain. It is otherwise very difficult to match the numerous tribes mentioned by Caesar and other Roman writers—the Iceni, the Brigantes, the Catuvellauni, the Coritani, and numerous others—with specific Celtic groups as revealed by archaeology.

Where the Picts fit into this picture is by no means clear. Their name is derived from the Latin *Picti*, meaning "painted men," referring to the Picts' habit of body tattooing. We have seen that they first appear in the historical record in their defeat by the Romans at the battle of Mons Graupius (78 C.E.). How much earlier they had come to Britain is unclear. There is no evidence that they were the first inhabitants of Britain or that they were driven north by the Celts; it is simply a fact that, by the first century C.E., they were well ensconced in Scotland, and, although occasionally joining forces with the Celts against the Romans, were largely independent of, and hostile to, the Celts.

The history of the Picts that Howard presents in "Men of the Shadows" and "The Lost Race" contains a number of curious features. In the latter tale we learn that the Picts "came from the south. Over the islands, over the Inland Sea" (179), i.e., the Mediterranean Sea, reflecting Howard's belief that the Picts had originated in southern Europe and spread all over the continent. After a battle between two kings, the defeated group "set sail for the far-off cliffs that gleamed white in the sunlight" (180), i.e., the cliffs of Dover. Finding "a race of red-haired barbarians, who dwelt in caves" (180), the Picts drove them back into the forest, only to be driven back themselves by the invading Celts. The Picts mingled with the red-haired giants and became "a race of monstrous dwarfs" (180), retreating to caves and caverns and initiating legends of the "little people." This history is largely duplicated in "Men of the Shadows," although Howard oddly notes there that the Celts "came from the North" (26), driving the Picts into Scotland and Wales. Here Howard suggests that it was the Picts who were responsible for the construction of Stonehenge, "the great rampart they had built not far from Corinium" (12), echoing the poem at the beginning of the story: "Stonehenge of long-gone glory / Sombre and lone in the night, /

Murmur the age-old story / How we kindled the first of the Light" (4). Howard repeats the assertion in "The Dark Man" ("Our stone circles rose to the sun," 162). But Stonehenge was almost certain constructed—or, at any rate, begun—by the Beaker Folk, as early as 2500 B.C.E., with modifications by other peoples down to about 1400 B.C.E. (Lehmberg 9); it is unlikely that the Picts had anything to do with the site.

Several Howard scholars have noted that this history of the Picts becomes altered in later stories, notably "Worms of the Earth," where it is noted that it is the "worms" themselves—the half-human aboriginal inhabitants of Britain—who were driven into caves by the Picts. (The existence of the "worms" was anticipated in "The Children of the Night," where a group of "Things" conversing in a "hissing, reptilian speech" [223] are seen.) Rusty Burke and Patrice Louinet are probably correct in believing that this alteration was a result of Howard's coming into contact with H. P. Lovecraft. Howard had noted that in Lovecraft's "The Rats in the Walls" (reprinted in *Weird Tales* for June 1930) a character in the south of England, through hereditary memory, had used some Gaelic. Howard interpreted this as suggesting Lovecraft's adherence to a minority view that the Gaels had retained control over the south of England over the Cymri. Lovecraft had in fact carelessly pillaged the Gaelic from Fiona Macleod's "The Sin-Eater," and it was he who pointed out to Howard that the Picts were unlikely to have been the source of the legendry of the "little people," but rather that the source was a pre-Aryan Mongoloid group whom both the Picts and the Celts had driven out. In this Lovecraft was echoing the views of Margaret A. Murray, who in *The Witch-Cult in Western Europe* (1921) put forth the hypothesis that this pre-Aryan race was the source of both the legends of the "little people" and of the witch cult. Murray's theory is now regarded as an historical fantasy, but Lovecraft was attracted to it because it appeared to lend a scholarly imprimatur to the theory of the "little people" expounded in the horror fiction of Arthur Machen a generation earlier.[1] (Machen is

---

1. Another small influence of Lovecraft on Howard in "Worms of the Earth" may

cited by name in "The Little People" [1928], a fragment written before Howard's communication with Lovecraft. This item continues to depict the Picts themselves as the source of the "little people," with the added suggestion that the Picts have continued to exist to the present day.)

Howard's most egregious lapse in historical accuracy was his constant citation of Norsemen as occasional collaborators with the Celts and the Picts against the Romans. Their most celebrated appearance is in "Kings of the Night," when the wizard Gonar must summon King Kull of Valusia to lead the reluctant Norsemen into battle after the death of their king, Rognar. There is certainly no recorded instance of Norsemen or Vikings doing battle with the Romans; indeed, these peoples do not show up in the historical record until the late eighth century C.E., when intermittent invasions by Danes upon the eastern shore of Britain began. A century later, in 878, King Alfred defeated the Danes, but the respite was only temporary, as a second wave of Scandinavian invasion of Britain began around 980. I am compelled to believe that Howard's inclusion of the Norsemen in his Bran stories was a deliberate distortion of history in order to lend added weight to the struggles of barbarian tribes against the seemingly invincible power of Rome.

We now come, at last, to the ambiguous figure of Bran Mak Morn. Although Howard readily admitted that Bran was for him a symbol of resistance to the power of the Romans, it should not be believed that this scenario simplistically echoes Howard's customary preference for barbarism over civilisation, found elsewhere in his fiction and in his

---

be worth pointing out. When the worms destroy the Tower of Trajan, we are given Bran's reaction: "The worms of the earth! Thousands of vermin digging like moles far below the castle, burrowing away the foundations—gods, the land mass must be honeycombed with tunnels and caverns—these creatures were even less human than he had thought . . ." (120). This passage is a direct echo of one in Lovecraft's "The Lurking Fear" (1922; reprinted in *Weird Tales*, June 1928), in which a colony of moles have undermined the foundations of the Martense house in upstate New York: "'My God! . . . Molehills . . . the damned place must be honeycombed . . . how many . . .' . . . God knows how many there were—there must have been thousands" (Lovecraft 370, 372).

copious correspondence with Lovecraft. In fact, Bran strives to be a civilising force, seeking to pull the Picts out of the slough of barbarism. As early as the play *Bran Mak Morn* we see Bran lamenting the fact that "The Picts are savages" (236); he goes on to state: "I must make them civilized. They are wolves and I must make them men. . . . I do it because the welfare of the nation is my sole ambition" (236). This conception is directly echoed in "Men of the Shadows," when Bran Mak Morn faces off against the ancient wizard, as the Roman narrator reports:

> And I was vaguely aware that it was but another phase of the eon-old warfare. The battle between Old and New. Behind the wizard lurked thousands of years of dark secrets, sinister mysteries, frightful nebulous shapes, monsters half hidden by the fogs of antiquity. Behind the chief, the clear strong light of the coming Day, the first kindling of civilization, the clean strength of a new man with a new and mighty mission. The wizard was the Stone Age typified; the chief, the coming civilization. (19)

At this point it is worth considering Joseph A. McCullough V's theory that Bran is a Christ figure, and that the saga of Bran Mak Morn can be seen as the "story of a failed messiah." There is good reason to doubt this interpretation, especially in light of Howard's professed agnosticism. McCullough reads the sentence "The battle between Old and New" in the above passage as an allusion to the Old and New Testaments, but the context makes this interpretation extremely implausible. McCullough and others put great emphasis on the crucifixion scene that opens "Worms of the Earth," seeing in it a symbol both of "Bran's damnation" and also "the damnation of the entire Pict race." But this is also a highly strained interpretation. In the first place, the crucifixion of Jesus was by no means symbolic of his damnation (!), but rather a necessary stage (in the Christian tradition) in his ascension to godhead. More importantly, crucifixion was—as Howard surely knew from his readings in Roman history—a very commonplace punishment for criminals, and if any symbolism is to be attached to it, it is a sort of passing contempt for the lowly status of the condemned. This is exactly what we find in the opening of "Worms of the Earth," where the crucifixion of a Pict is depicted as the acme of Roman arrogance. When Titus Sulla languidly remarks, "You see, emissary of Pictland, how swiftly Rome punishes the transgressor," Bran retorts: "I see . . . that the subject of a foreign king is dealt with as though he were a Roman slave" (88).

The notion, propounded by McCullough and others, that Bran's summoning the "worms of the earth" to avenge the execution of the Pict is symbolic of Bran's damnation of himself and his people is similarly open to objection. It is indeed remarked by the witch Atla, at the end of the story, that "you have brought them [the worms] forth and they will remember! And in their own time they will come to you again!" (127), perhaps suggesting that the worms will be the ultimate destroyers of the Pict nation; but this scenario is directly contradicted by several of the other Bran stories, in which it is clearly stated (as Howard knew—or believed—the historical record indicated) that the Picts would be ultimately destroyed by the Celts, Romans, Saxons, and other invaders of Britain. As Bran states at the end of "Men of the Shadows":

> For what we could not keep by battle, we have held by cunning for years and centuries unnumbered. But the New Races rise like a great tidal wave and the Old gives place. In the dim mountains of Galloway shall the nation make its last fierce stand. And as Bran Mak Morn falls, so vanishes the Lost Fire—forever. From the centuries, from the eons. (29–30)

This is echoed directly in "The Dark Man," where it is stated that "Bran Mak Morn fell in battle; the nation fell apart" (162). In other words, it is Bran alone who holds the race together; once he is gone, the Picts cannot survive. There is no suggestion anywhere in the Bran cycle that Bran himself is somehow the cause of the Picts' ultimate demise.

If, however, Bran wishes the Picts to become civilised—indeed, in the *Bran Mak Morn* play he provocatively notes, "A hard, thankless task it is to raise the Pict nation out of savagery and bring it *back* to the civilization of our fathers" (236; my emphasis)—would they not become just like their hated foes, the Romans? Not exactly, because the Romans of Bran's era have already been reduced to a decadence—gluttony, sexual aberrations, and the like—that augurs their own passing. In "Worms of the Earth" Bran speaks scornfully of his stay in Eboracum disguised as a Pict emissary: "Rome is courteous to barbarian ambassadors, they give us fine houses to live in, offer us slaves, pander to our lusts with women and gold and wine and games, but all the while they laugh at us" (91). It may be worth noting here that, in contrast to the assertion of Marc A. Cerasini and Charles Hoffmann, who claim that "Howard's knowledge of Roman civilization undoubtedly came from the works of historians whose Christian leanings biased their judgments of the Empire's role in shaping the ancient world," there is nowhere any indication in the Bran saga that "the Romans murdered Christ [or] oppressed Judea" (20). The scriptural record is too clear that Pontius Pilate crucified Jesus only reluctantly, and at the vociferous insistence of his Jewish enemies. What galls Howard most about the Romans is not their relations with the Christians but the arrogance they habitually display against their barbarian foes, especially their supreme confidence in their military might: as Cormac of Connacht ponders in "Kings of the Night," before the great fight with the Roman legions, "He had never fought Romans before, knew nothing of their arrogant self-confidence, of their incredible shrewdness in some ways, their incredible stupidity in others" (59). The fact that, in this story, it takes the supernatural appearance of Kull of Valusia to defeat the Romans suggests that Howard well knew that the Romans were not easily beaten.

The great virtue of the Bran Mak Morn cycle is not in any fancied resemblance to Christian myth but in its poignant etching of the inexorable march of history, where "New" replaces "Old" without any heed as to the cultural supremacy of the new over the old. The grand sweep of history that we find in such documents as "The Hyborian Age" is rendered intimate and personal in Howard's tales of a single figure, Bran Mak Morn, who strives to civilise his people but knows in his heart that the effort is foredoomed to failure. In one of the most poignant passages in all Howard's work, the wizard testifies to this in "Men of the Shadows":

The glory of the Nameless Tribe is vanished; like the snow that falls on the sea; like the smoke that rises in the air. Mingling with past eternities. Vanished the glory of Atlantis; fading the dark empire of the Lemurians. The people of the Stone Age are melting like hoar-frost before the sun. Out of the night we came; into the night we go. All are shadows. A shadow race we are. Our day is past. (27)

Is it too much to believe that Howard was hinting that our own civilisation is headed toward an ultimate oblivion in the face of some newer and more vigorous race, only to be overwhelmed in its turn by a race newer still?

Works Cited

Burke, Rusty, and Patrice Louinet. "Robert E. Howard, Bran Mak Morn and the Picts." In Robert E. Howard. *Bran Mak Morn: The Last King.* 2001. New York: Ballantine, 2005. 343–60.

Cary, M., and H. H. Scullard. *A History of Rome.* 3rd ed. New York: St. Martin's Press, 1975.

Cerasini, Marc A., and Charles Hoffman. *Robert E. Howard.* Mercer Island, WA: Starmont House, 1987.

Chadwick, Nora. *The Celts.* Harmondsworth: Penguin, 1970.

Hammond, N. G. L., and H. H. Scullard ed. *The Oxford Classical Dictionary.* 2nd ed. Oxford: Clarendon Press, 1970.

Howard, Robert E. *Bran Mak Morn* [play]. In *Bran Mak Morn: The Last King.* 2001. New York: Ballantine, 2005. 235–36.

———. "The Children of the Night." In *Bran Mak Morn: The Last King.* 2001. New York: Ballantine, 2005. 217–32.

———. "The Dark Man." In *Bran Mak Morn: The Last King.* 2001. New York: Ballantine, 2005. 131–66.

———. "Kings of the Night." In *Bran Mak Morn: The Last King.* 2001. New York: Ballantine, 2005. 33–75.

———. "Letter to H. P. Lovecraft, circa January 1932." In *Bran Mak Morn: The Last King.* 2001. New York: Ballantine, 2005. 338–40.

———. "The Lost Race." In *Bran Mak Morn: The Last King.* 2001. New York: Ballantine, 2005. 169–85.

———. "Men of the Shadows." In *Bran Mak Morn: The Last King.* 2001. New York: Ballantine, 2005. 3–30.

————. "Synopsis." In *Bran Mak Morn: The Last King.* 2001. New York: Ballantine, 2005. 245–46.

————. "Worms of the Earth." In *Bran Mak Morn: The Last King.* 2001. New York: Ballantine, 2005. 85–127.

Jones, A. H. M., et al. *The Prosopography of the Later Roman Empire.* Cambridge: Cambridge University Press, 1971–92. 3 vols. in 4.

Lehmberg, Stanford E. *The Peoples of the British Isles: A New History: Volume 1: From Prehistoric Times to 1688.* Belmont, CA: Wadsworth Publishing Co., 1992.

Lovecraft, H. P. *Collected Fiction: A Variorium Edition.* Volume 1: 1905–1925. New York: Hippocampus Press, 2015.

McCullough, Joseph A., V. "Robert E. Howard, Christianity, and the Saga of Bran Mak Morn." Sword & Sorcery website (http://www.swordandsorcery.org/bran-mak-morn.asp)

The Novels of Donald Wandrei

It is commonly said that everyone has one novel in them—the novel of his or her own life. Donald Wandrei had two novels in him, but the autobiographical novel proved to be the second, and much the better, of the two. Within a span of less than three and a half years, from the fall of 1929 to the beginning of 1933, Wandrei—then just beginning his career as a writer of horror and science fiction tales—produced two novels, *Dead Titans, Waken!* and *Invisible Sun,* the former of which appeared in quite different form as *The Web of Easter Island* (1948) and the latter of which remained unpublished until 2011.

On 9 September 1929, Wandrei told his correspondent of nearly three years, H. P. Lovecraft: "I . . . am now working on a story of age-old horror" (MTS 240–41). He immediately asked Lovecraft for the Latin versions of the phrases "Devil's Highway" and "God's Highway," suggesting that he had already drafted the opening chapter. The next surviving letter to Lovecraft does not occur until 26 June 1930, at which time Wandrei gives more details about his novel, which he now names *Dead Titans Waken: A Mystery of Time and Spirit:*

> As the title probably suggests, it is a romance of terror and horror, commencing near the locale of Stonehenge and concluding on Easter Island. This is the novel which I began in New York last summer, and which I mentioned to you at the time. The novel has great possibilities, if I can successfully achieve a rather stupendous feat in handling so long a work. I have many incentives to keep me at it—the sheer pleasure of creating, my father's failing health, necessity of improving my financial condition, and the interest of some three publishers who express their willingness to consider the novel when completed. With time, energy, and a little luck, I may be able to complete it by the early part of August. (MTS 252)

In October Wandrei announces that the novel was "completely halted" by his father's several operations and by his graduate work at the University of Minnesota, but that it is nevertheless "more than three-quarters done" (MTS 260). In this same letter, Wandrei notes that a chapter from it, "slightly changed," would be appearing in *Weird Tales* as "Something from Above." If so, then the novel underwent significant revision in fourteen months before Wandrei deemed it complete, for nothing remotely like "Something from Above" appears in the finished version of *Dead Titans, Waken!* Indeed, it is difficult even to conceive how the plot of "Something from Above"—involving two groups of extraterrestrial entities, one from Saturn and one from even farther gulfs of space, battling for control over an anti-gravitational element called Seggglyn—could in any way have been a part of *Dead Titans, Waken!* as we now know it.

It is not clear exactly when in the interval between October 1930 and the very end of 1931 Wandrei completed the novel: he merely tells Lovecraft on 6 January 1932, that the novel "was done a week ago." In any case, although he acknowledges "at least two major weak spots," he is nevertheless so anxious to get it off his hands that he has already sent one copy to publishers and one of the two carbons to Lovecraft, with instructions that he pass it on to August Derleth and Clark Ashton Smith. Wandrei never names the "three publishers" who had expressed interest in it some years before, but it appears to have been sent only to one publisher—Harper & Brothers—where it was rejected. Wandrei regrettably ignored Clark Ashton Smith's sensible suggestion of submitting it to *Weird Tales* as a serial.[1]

Dead Titans, Waken! is clearly a first novel—perhaps as much of a "practice" novel as Lovecraft deemed his own first attempt at lengthy narrative, *The Dream-Quest of Unknown Kadath*. While Wandrei manages well enough to sustain interest from beginning to end, and more

---

1. See Clark Ashton Smith to Donald Wandrei, 6 April 1932 (ms., Minnesota Historical Society [hereafter abbreviated MHS]).

significantly to conceive of a plot sufficiently complex to require a novel for its exposition, the writing on the whole is somewhat clumsy and—in spite of the length of time during which it was being worked on—occasionally seems a little hasty. Nevertheless, it is scarcely a work of which any writer need be ashamed.

Perhaps the novel's greatest interest lies in its foreshadowing of Wandrei's later work. Clearly, it anticipates his later shift toward min-gling horror and science fiction. It is noteworthy that the final chapters contain the core of what would become Wandrei's most celebrated sci-ence fiction tale, "Colossus" (*Astounding,* January 1934)—the notion that our own universe is merely an atom in some incalculably larger super-universe, and that it is possible to break through to this vaster realm.

The Web of Easter Island was dedicated to Lovecraft; the first version bears no dedication, but the influence of Lovecraft nevertheless hangs heavy over it. The incomprehensible gibberish uttered by various hu-man characters—an echo of the speech of the titans—is clearly modelled upon the R'lyehian language introduced by Lovecraft in "The Call of Cthulhu" (1926). Indeed, if one removes the first three letters of the word "septhulchu," one sees a very elementary anagram of "Cthulhu." Wandrei's use of the documentary style—filled with letters, diaries, newspaper clippings, and the like—also reflects Lovecraft's similar usage in "The Call of Cthulhu" and "The Whisperer in Darkness." One wonders, in fact, whether Wandrei's omission of the story "Something from Above" (however it would have fit into the novel) reflects his sense that *Dead Titans, Waken!* already owed too much to Lovecraft; for that story, with its account of a strange meteorite falling on a plot of farmland, is clearly derivative of "The Colour out of Space."

Lovecraft's own reaction, when he first read *Dead Titans, Waken!,* was what might be termed reservedly enthusiastic. Although noting numerous points that might require revision, especially in terms of psychological motivation and adequate emotional preparation for the horrors depicted, Lovecraft nevertheless felt that "The novel as a whole is a great piece of work." Clark Ashton Smith's reaction was still more enthusiastic:

Your novel came o.k., and I have read it with immense pleasure. The plot seems all right to me, and I do not see that it calls for any structural modifications. My only suggestion is, that the wording might be touched up in places, in the earlier chapters. The later chapters are superior in style, it seems to me—especially where they are written in the first person. The tale is full of imaginative ideas; and some of the descriptions of strange phenomena—the changeability of the pitted image, etc.—might stand considerable amplification.[2]

Writing to Derleth, Smith was somewhat more blunt: "I got a very favorable impression of the general plot, but found the style uneven, especially in the earlier chapters. The later ones, especially those written in the first person, seemed much more adequate."[3] Lovecraft, too, opened up somewhat more to Derleth:

... the chief criticism I give it is that the first & second halves are atmospherically incompatible. He began by surrendering to the popular "action" tradition, but grew cosmic & poetic after he got started into earth's bowels. In the first part bizarre horrors are introduced without adequate emotional preparation, but later on the cosmic vision gets really tremendous at times—so that I extracted a whale of a wallop from the performance as a whole, & wish I could have written it myself! (Lovecraft to August Derleth, 21 January 1932; *Essential Solitude* 443)

Lovecraft was right in remarking to Derleth that the novel would face difficulties in securing a book publisher; indeed, after his initial submission, Wandrei appears to have lost interest in *Dead Titans, Waken!* and shelved it. By this time he had already begun work on his second novel-length work, *Invisible Sun.*

The revision of *Dead Titans* did not occur until the mid-1940s. In February 1946 Wandrei—evidently responding to Derleth's wish for horror or science fiction novels for Arkham House—is suggesting some possible new titles for the novel, since he had come to dislike his original. He rattles off a whole list of them: *They Will Come Again; They Who*

---

2. Clark Ashton Smith to Donald Wandrei, 1 March 1932 (ms., MHS).

3. Clark Ashton Smith to August Derleth, 24 February 1932 (ms., Wisconsin Historical Society [hereafter abbreviated WHS]).

Enter; The Web of Easter Island; They Shall Wake Again; In Their Power; To Haunt the Future.[4] Incredibly, Wandrei's preference was for *To Haunt the Future,* but no doubt Derleth prevailed upon him to choose the one we know. It is not clear when actual revision commenced, but by February 1947 Wandrei states that the Web "bubbles along,"[5] noting that he had already written 15,000 new words of text. By the end of April, Wandrei is on the "last few pages" of the revision and claims to have written 35,000 words of new text. He asserts that "The novel is a good 300 percent better than it was," but there is reason to question his judgment.

The major revisions in the novel—aside from mere rewriting of existing prose, which indeed is extensive throughout—are as follows:

Chapter III of *Titans*—a nearly unaltered interpolation of the story "A Fragment of a Dream" (1926)—has been placed as Chapter XII of *Web.* The context, therefore, is radically changed: whereas in *Titans* the "dream" occurs as a result of the train accident in which Carter Graham is involved, in *Web* it is the product of Graham's concluding battle with the titans on Easter Island.

Much of Chapter V of *Titans* has been dropped, and an entirely new chapter (now Chapter IV) inserted into *Web.* This is the chapter in which Dan Farrell pilfers the green statuette and takes it with him in an attempt to cross the Atlantic to America (in a seaplane in *Titans,* on a ship in *Web*). In the newer version Wandrei has added a painfully coy and purportedly risqué love element on board the ship. Many readers have noted that this chapter simply does not fit in the narrative, and indeed much of it is occupied with a romance that has no bearing whatever on the plot. And yet, Wandrei actually thought this chapter much superior to its predecessor: "I particularly like the new chapter, which is rather sexy but completely motivated whereas the chapter I discarded rambled all over and had no real reason to be in the book."

The most significant change, perhaps, is that Graham's diary—

---

4. Donald Wandrei to August Derleth, 22 February 1946 (ms., WHS).
5. Donald Wandrei to August Derleth, 11 February 1947 (ms., WHS).

which in *Titans* occupies the entirety of Chapters X, XI, and XIII—is now reduced to a single chapter (X) in *Web*. Even this chapter is narrated with far greater sobriety and more tempered emotionalism than its original (especially with the entire omission of the interpolated piece, "Myrna"—an adaptation of the then unpublished prose poem "The Delirium of the Dead"—in which Graham relates his youthful love of a woman who dies and whose grave he subsequently violates out of grief). To my mind the newer version fails to bring Graham to life, even though it may harmonise somewhat better with his persona as a sober scientist. Chapters XI, XII, and XIII of *Web* are not presented in diary form—again, in my view, to their detriment. Evidently Wandrei did not agree, in 1947, with Clark Ashton Smith's dictum that these first-person passages represented some of the most vivid writing in the novel.

In regard to stylistic changes, one can again make good arguments that the earlier version on the whole stands up better than the later one. By 1947 Wandrei had for some years ceased to be a practicing writer, and perhaps his rustiness shows. It is true that some stylistic infelicities—especially in the later portions—have been eliminated; but on the other hand, some quite vivid passages have been unwisely omitted. Consider the following passage from *Titans*, where Graham recounts his emotions when reading of the history of the world over the 500,000 years from his own time to the time in which he finds himself after battling the titans:

> . . . I read most of all as a traveller marooned in time, desolate in the midst of plenty, and with gravely wise companions wherever I turned, lonely in the heart of the highest civilization humanity had ever achieved, and aching with the burden of old griefs and irrecoverable years, of vanished cycles and an oblivion that had plundered me of my rightful life in the days when the world was young.

Whatever one's judgment about the relative merits of *Dead Titans, Waken!* and *The Web of Easter Island*, we can all find an interest in a novel begun by a twenty-one-year-old in the vigor of budding authorship who, when he completed it some months prior to his twenty-fourth birthday, was already a seasoned veteran of the pulps.

Invisible Sun is a different proposition altogether. The existence of this novel had been known for decades, but there was doubt as to whether it was completed or, if it was, whether the manuscript survived. As it happens, both the original handwritten draft and the final typescript are intact, and we are now in a position to assess both its strengths and its defects.

Wandrei began the novel very shortly after he returned to New York from Minneapolis in August 1932; in contrast to his long and apparently sporadic work on *Titans*, Wandrei finished *Invisible Sun* in a matter of months, from September 1932 to January 1933. This time Wandrei sent the completed work to Derleth first—presumably because, as a mainstream writer, he might be more astute in judging this mainstream novel than pure fantaisistes like Lovecraft or Smith—and Derleth's adverse judgment of it was at least partly responsible for Wandrei's permanent shelving of the work. It was, however, like *Titans*, submitted to a publisher (unspecified) immediately upon completion, but was evidently rejected.[6]

Wandrei supplies the motivation of the work a few months before he began writing it:

> For a long time I have been germinating a second novel, semi-autobiographical, partly based on experiences I have heard of, as an excursion into what might be called the poetry of realism. I think I shall begin work on it shortly. God knows it will be an arduous and exhausting task, since I want it to be without question the best and most mature work that I have yet done. I feel that the time is about ready—far enough away from experience so that the work will not be one-sided, and yet not so far that the fire and the intensity will have burned low.[7]

Wandrei expresses the core of the novel in Chapter LI, when Sven discusses the plot of the novel he himself is working on:

---

6. ". . . the original is now in the hands of the first prospective publisher . . ." Donald Wandrei to August Derleth, 1 February 1933 (ms., WHS).

7. Donald Wandrei to August Derleth, 11 July 1932 (ms., WHS).

I start with a situation, the most important in the protagonist's life, that is, my purpose begins there though the situation actually concludes the novel. No, I won't tell you what the situation is. We'll assume that the hero is Mr. X. The great crisis of his life is Y, a decision, we'll also assume, to drop out of sight and go to some remote place to live in oblivion the rest of his days. When X is making this decision, all the influences of his past experiences would be brought to bear. In the white heat of extremity, the extraneous parts of his life would be shorn away, but everything that contributed to his decision or that would be affected by it would stand out clearly in his mind, or at least they would form an undercurrent in his thoughts. These past experiences would come as flashes of memory, pictures of old occurrences, but they would probably be in a sort of confused flux. . . . The novel would begin with the first and earliest of these experiences bearing on the crisis, but each scene or memory picture, for the sake of unity and art again as well as life, would be presented immediately, as it happened when it was in the process of happening, and with no hint of the catastrophe which I, as the artist, know already. An apparent irrelevance might be presumed by the reader during the early pictures and episodes, in that they might seem disconnected, but as he read on, he would begin to see the design above the threads.

This, in essence, is *Invisible Sun.*

Taking these two passages together, we can assume that the basic thrust of the novel is the attempt to explain how Drew Gordon came to fall in love with Helione Forrest and, when she jilted him, killed her. Within this simple scenario Wandrei adds a mass of detail about Drew's upbringing, so that the reader can understand what led him to his final act.

It would be an engaging exercise to trace all the autobiographical elements in *Invisible Sun.* We shall touch upon only the highlights here; many are perhaps lost in oblivion, given the relative absence of documentary evidence regarding Wandrei's early life. First and foremost, does Helione have a real counterpart? She appears to be based loosely upon Barbara Fawcett Craigie, whom Wandrei mentions in 1927 as "one of the two friends I have made at the university." Wandrei does not elaborate on his relations with Craigie in any correspondence I have seen, but Richard L. Tierney states that at some point in his life he "came within an ace of marrying" (xix) her, although this probably occurred years after the writing of *Invisible Sun*, perhaps around 1947. However, extensive correspondence from Craigie to Wandrei survives, and it becomes clear from this that the two of them are becoming very close; but then Craigie wrote Wandrei a poignant letter (postmarked 25 September 1929) in which the subtext is that Wandrei should seek someone else upon whom to bestow his "friendship," since the two of them share few interests in common. One is led to believe that Wandrei was already infatuated with Craigie, and that she was attempting to restrain him or keep her distance from him, because she felt at this time that a serious relationship between the two of them would lead to disappointment. However, Craigie and Wandrei continued meeting until at least 1931; a definitive break may have come about the next year. Several of Craigie's known characteristics correspond with those of Helione Forrest: she was habitually late, she tended to gossip, and she was obliged to take care of numerous siblings, often yearning for a place of her own.

The other friend mentioned by Wandrei is Hjalmar Björnson, an Icelander who "writes . . . in a rugged, saga-like fashion" and who is clearly the model for Sven. Björnson published a few pieces in the *Minnesota Quarterly* during Wandrei's involvement with that magazine (run by students of the University of Wisconsin), but beyond this we do not know much about him. The character of Pudge is very likely based upon Ed Meyroth. He and Wandrei were initially friendly around 1931, but they later became heated adversaries; Meyroth actually married Barbara Craigie sometime before 1944, but the marriage did not go well and they separated in 1946. It was around this time that Barbara re-established contact with Wandrei, leading to their contemplated marriage. A photograph of Meyroth, taken on Memorial Day 1931, depicts Meyroth as decidedly pudgy. Wandrei and Barbara are also in the picture.[8]

---

8. The photo is in the archives of the Minnesota Historical Society. I am grateful

Many other details in the novel—some significant, some trivial—echo Wandrei's own life. He himself had entered the University of Minnesota at the age of sixteen. He had had horrific problems with his teeth. His mother cooked "excellent meals" for him. He had witnessed a fall of red snow in January 1926—an incident that he cited in a number of his tales. Wandrei had been profoundly influenced by Arthur Machen's *The Hill of Dreams*, of which he owned the rare "blue paper" edition of 1922; and it could well be said that that novel's sensitive portrayal of the struggling writer inspired *Invisible Sun's* minute depictions of Drew's moods and sentiments.

Drew's discovery of Clark Ashton Smith's *Ebony and Crystal* from an ad in a pulp magazine (clearly modelled on *Weird Tales*) is a faithful echo of Wandrei's own discovery of Smith's work in 1924. In a letter to Lovecraft he notes: "In three months—the summer I read 'Ebony and Crystal' and 'The Hill of Dreams'—my ideas underwent a complete revolution, and I walked to the opposite side of the fence, changing from a half-materialistic scientist to a romanticist and idealist and aesthete" (MTS 81). At the very time he wrote the above passage in April 1927, Wandrei had already conceived of some unspecified novel and stated: "I am going to devote a chapter of my novel to Smith . . ."

In responding to one of Derleth's criticisms of *Invisible Sun,* Wandrei asserted that the episodes in Chapters VI and VII "are exact and faithful reproductions of the most frightful experience I ever had." The allusion is to the callous reaction of two women following the death of a little girl in a fire, leading to Drew's violent misanthropy and misogyny. Wandrei goes on to remark:

> I have never had any faith in people because, as a result of that experience, all possibilities of respect for human beings were destroyed in me before they ever had a chance to develope [sic]. You yourself can realize what

---

to Dwayne H. Olson for supplying me with a photocopy of it.

a profound shock such a series of events would have had for any sensitive mind, young or old.[9]

Richard L. Tierney reports Wandrei telling him "that at age seven he had been devastated when a fire originating in a chocolate shop had burned down the St. Paul Public Library." Whether the incident related in Chapters XIII–XV—when Drew as a teenager develops a crush on a librarian but is shattered when she marries another man—is real is not clear, but one suspects that it might be. Wandrei reports working for a year and a half (presumably during high school) at the St. Paul Public Library and the Hill Reference Library (*MTS* 29).

But the interest of *Invisible Sun* lies not in how many correspondences with Wandrei's own life there may be, but in its lapidary prose, its vividness of incident, its emotive power, and its cumulative effectiveness. Some passages may perhaps be awkwardly written, some incidents clumsy and unintentionally comical, but as a whole *Invisible Sun* is a moving human document that fully sustains Wandrei's attempt to create a "poetry of realism." Certainly the most arresting passages— aside from the bold depictions of sexual activity—are the several instances where Wandrei uses the still new device of stream-of-consciousness to convey an interior monologue. Two passages in particular—Helione's lengthy reflections in Chapter LII, leading to a startling but subtly expressed masturbation fantasy, and Drew's concluding swirl of thoughts, as the varied incidents of his entire life pass through his mind in the course of his murder of Helione—rank, to my mind, among the finest passages in Wandrei's entire oeuvre.

It does not appear, however, as if the early responses to the novel were very enthusiastic. Derleth in particular expressed severe criticism of the novel, much of it evidently focusing on the amount and nature of the sexual episodes. Incredibly, the ordinarily prudish Lovecraft defended these episodes:

---

9. Donald Wandrei to August Derleth, 1 February 1933 (ms., WHS).

Regarding the repulsiveness of the latter scenes—to which, amusingly enough, the otherwise none too squeamish Comte d'Erlette is inclined to object—I do not think that they form any breach of artistry. It is the business of the artist to relate whatever is significant in reality; & if this rottenness truly typifies an important stratum of contemporary youth, it is certainly of grave significance as a social tendency. Nothing is gained by whitewashing or sentimentalising. What is essentially beastly & inartistic in life must be bestially and harshly shewn. Blame life, not the artist. The loathsome lives of the swine portrayed in this novel, if they are indeed a widespread & characteristic phenomenon, are logical results of the so-called "new morality" which proceeds from the abandonment of harmonic patterns & aesthetic values in the art of living. Our younger generation now glorify fornication, adultery, & sodomy. Next will come a worship of incest—with brothers & sisters, parents & children, glorying in a warmer tie now despised by "old-fashioned prejudice"—the frenzied maenad & the goat of the Sabbat. A beautiful world, with beautiful trends, is that world of anti-Puritanism which our young friend [Frank] Belknap [Long] exalts so passionately! You have shewn it as it deserves to be shewn! (Lovecraft to Donald Wandrei, [27 February 1933]; MTS 321)

Wandrei's purpose in his depictions of sex may not exactly have been what Lovecraft states here, but no doubt he was gratified that at least one reader did not find them overdone or cheaply titillating.

Nevertheless, even though Wandrei disagreed with the bases of many of Derleth's criticisms, his negative reaction—along with that of a New York couple, the Overbys—persuaded Wandrei to abandon any plans to revise and market his novel. "Three critics of the four I chose have now seen the thing and unanimously disagree, but unanimously ripped the thing to pieces. I have already junked it."[10] Certainly, Wandrei would have had difficulty securing its publication in 1933, if only because of the sexual episodes; but Invisible Sun does not deserve its sixty-five-year oblivion.

A final note on Wandrei's use of the pseudonym, Carrol Amworth. He is a little vague on the subject, but explains some aspects of the matter to Derleth: "I have decided to publish under a pseudonym, and

---

10. Donald Wandrei to August Derleth, 18 February 1933 (ms., WHS).

henceforth continue publishing part of my work under the nom-de-plume, part under my own name, for a variety of reasons too long to go into."[11] Possibly Wandrei was planning to use the pseudonym for "mainstream" work and his real name for his horror and science fiction writing, since he had already become widely known for that work.

Wandrei's two novels are both flawed, but both powerful in their own ways. *Invisible Sun* reveals a marked improvement in technique and emotional maturity from *Dead Titans, Waken!*, and it is unfortunate that adverse reaction dissuaded Wandrei from continuing work on it and from completing any new work in the novel form. By the mid-1930s he had found his niche as a prolific writer of science fantasies for the pulps, and—although in the later 1930s he did write several plays, including one, *Love to Murder*, which he describes as a "mystery drama" (MTS 390) with elements of satire—he did not make any concerted effort to return to mainstream writing. By the early 1940s he had virtually given up writing altogether, producing in the remaining four and a half decades of his life only a handful of short stories and some poems. But the two novels in this volume both display, in their very different ways, a literary promise that for many and complex reasons was never fully realized. Both should be read as much for their insights into Donald Wandrei's life and mind as for their own intrinsic virtues.

Works Cited

Lovecraft, H. P., and August Derleth. *Essential Solitude: The Letters of H. P. Lovecraft and August Derleth*. Ed. David E. Schultz and S. T. Joshi. New York: Hippocampus Press, 2008. 2 vols.

Lovecraft, H. P., and Donald Wandrei. *Mysteries of Time and Spirit: The Letters of H. P. Lovecraft and Donald Wandrei*. Ed. S. T. Joshi and David E. Schultz. San Francisco: Night Shade, 2002. [Abbreviated in the text as MTS.]

Tierney, Richard L. "Introduction." In *Colossus: The Collected Science Fiction of Donald Wandrei*. Minneapolis: Fedogan & Bremer, 1989. ix–xxix.

---

11. Donald Wandrei to August Derleth, 24 January 1933 (ms., WHS).

III. Some Contemporaries

Science and Superstition: Fritz Leiber's Modernisation of Gothic

In his historical treatise "Supernatural Horror in Literature" (1927), H. P. Lovecraft spoke of the development of weird fiction in the century after Edgar Allan Poe, who revolutionised the field with his intense focus on psychological realism:

> The best horror-tales of today, profiting by the long evolution of the type, possess a naturalness, convincingness, artistic smoothness, and skilful intensity of appeal quite beyond comparison with anything in the Gothic work of a century or more ago. Technique, craftsmanship, experience, and psychological knowledge have advanced tremendously with the passing years, so that much of the older work seems naive and artificial; redeemed, when redeemed at all, only by a genius which conquers heavy limitations. (80–81)

In letters Lovecraft spoke somewhat less sanguinely about the advances made in weird fiction in his day. Disappointed by the trite and hackneyed products served up regularly by such pulp magazines as *Weird Tales*, Lovecraft came to feel that an entirely new methodology must be used in order to create a "willing suspension of disbelief" in regard to the supernatural phenomena presented in weird fiction. Lovecraft well knew that such tropes as the vampire, the werewolf, and the ghost had become virtually played out, at least in their traditional forms, by the radical advance of scientific knowledge in the course of the nineteenth century; accordingly, he believed, "The time has come when the normal revolt against time, space, & matter must assume a form not overtly incompatible with what is known of reality—when it must be gratified by images forming *supplements* rather than *contradictions* of the visible & mensurable universe" (*Selected Letters* 3.295–96).

Lovecraft himself implemented his principles by the extensive use of the most up-to-date findings of science, with the result that such things as the psychic vampire in "The Shunned House" (1924) and the witch in "The Dreams in the Witch House" (1932) bear little resemblance to their Gothic predecessors. But in other ways Lovecraft tended to look backward: his richly textured prose style, however scientifically precise it could be in such works as *At the Mountains of Madness* (1931), always retained a certain whiff of Poesque extravagance, while his incorporation of contemporary social, political, and cultural artifacts, although far from non-existent (see Joshi, "Topical References"), did little to persuade readers that his tales of horrors arising from the depths of New England history had any direct relevance to modern concerns.

It was left to Lovecraft's late disciple Fritz Leiber to bring the weird tale full-fledged into the contemporary world. In his works of the late 1930s and 1940s, both in the short story and the novel, Leiber emphatically showed how the horror tale could be used to highlight central issues in contemporary social life, from rapid and perhaps uncontrolled urbanisation to the growth of religious scepticism, and from the psychological tensions of modern life to the devastation of a world war. The pinnacle of this achievement was the novel *Conjure Wife* (1943), but traces of its development can be found in a wide variety of tales written before and after that landmark work. And once Leiber had set the pattern, other writers such as Ray Bradbury and Richard Matheson elaborated it in their own novels and tales, ultimately planting the seeds of the horror "boom" of the 1970s and 1980s, when Stephen King, Ramsey Campbell, Peter Straub, and numerous others completed the revolutionising of Gothic tropes for a modern readership.

Some, perhaps much, of Leiber's concurrent work in other genres can also be seen, even if somewhat more indirectly, as harbingers of this modernisation. While the Fafhrd and Gray Mouser stories might seem like harmless excursions into literary and historical nostalgia, their very lightness of tone—frequently highlighted by sardonic humour and self-parody—betray a modern consciousness that has little in common with the lofty bombast of the heroic fantasy tradition. Leiber's science fiction is even more emphatically modern in its breathtaking extrapolations from present-day science. Even in so early a work as *The Dealings of Daniel Kesserich*, written in 1936 but not published until 1997, we find some hints of Leiber's later work. Set in a small town in California where, as the narrator remarks, the people "remain superstitious witch-fearers and witch-burners" (20), we encounter the enigmatic figure of Daniel Kesserich, a scientist of whom one character notes: "I tell you their attitude toward Kesserich was that of a medieval serf toward a black magician, a puritan scullery girl toward a so-called witch" (56). Leiber is well aware that, to the scientifically untutored, the abstruse findings of modern science—relativity, quantum theory, even hypnosis—are little different from the black magic practiced by mediaeval alchemists. In fact, Kesserich has found a means for "overcoming the limitations of the human mind" (70) by going backward and forward through time.

Leiber was also aware that the horror tale was almost inherently a backward-looking genre because of its emphasis on, and utilisation of, such ancient elements of myth, superstition, and folklore as the vampire, the ghost, and the werewolf. He appears quite early on to have wrestled with the quandary of how to update these venerable tropes so that they could still have relevance and emotive power in a twentieth century that had come close to relegating them to the dustbin of intellectual and cultural history. In the late essay "My Life and Writings" (1975) Leiber discusses at length his motivations for writing horror fiction:

> Now, looking back at those days [the early 1940s], it seems to me obvious that I found the supernatural horror story easier to write because its structure and dynamics were simpler and closer to my own experience. The success of such a story depended on creating in the reader a feeling of strange and lonely terror, and that was something I could do. The essential elements were a weird phenomenon, a carefully slow and poetic build-up, and a sensitive protagonist to experience the terror, and then escape to tell the tale. . . . I found artistic capital in my extended childhood fears of the dark and violence, the unexpected and unknown, to which a strong curi-

osity added the necessary spice of wonder. Such stories didn't show up my limited social development, while the memories of a lonely childhood were a storehouse of suitable atmospheric material, in which the early-absorbed language of *Macbeth, King Lear* and *Hamlet* was not the least useful treasure. (59-60)

This passage, strikingly similar to several in Lovecraft's essays and letters (and remember that Lovecraft, too, had a "lonely childhood" and "limited social development"), does not directly address the issue of modernising the weird tale, although some hints are there. And in spite of Leiber's suggestion that his language in these early tales was directly or indirectly derived from Shakespeare, the one thing that strikes us about his works of the 1940s is their aggressively modern language, ranging from a deft imitation of hard-boiled crime fiction in "The Automatic Pistol" to Camus-like existential angst in "Smoke Ghost" and numerous other tales.

Curiously, an appropriate place to begin the study of Leiber's modernisation of Gothic is "Spider Mansion" (*Weird Tales*, September 1942), a tale that remained uncollected until it was gathered in the posthumous volume *The Black Gondolier* (2000). This flamboyant and histrionic tale—set in a hackneyed haunted mansion (to which the narrator comes, predictably enough, in a thunderstorm), an evil dwarf-turned-giant, a prototypical lady-in-distress (the hapless wife of the giant), and suitably bombastic language ("'You'll rot forever, eternally embalmed in hell,' were the first words I heard" [133]), and, to cap it all, a giant spider—is exquisitely balanced on the verge of self-parody, or, more precisely, a parody of the Gothic conventions that Leiber had plainly recognised as stale conventions more suitable to evoke a smile than a shudder. It is very likely that he wrote this tale—a tale written *after* "The Automatic Pistol" and "Smoke Ghost" had already been published—with *Weird Tales* in mind, perhaps even as a test to see whether the readers of that venerable pulp magazine could sense that they were being deliberately teased. There is some doubt as to whether many of them saw through the joke.

What is remarkable is that "The Automatic Pistol" had itself appeared in *Weird Tales* two years earlier, in the May 1940 issue. This striking tale of a handgun that exacts vengeance for the death of its owner shows Leiber's adeptness in mastering the hard-boiled style pioneered by Dashiell Hammett and Raymond Chandler during the years of Prohibition and the Depression ("Well, the years kept passing and the bootlegging business stayed good except that the hijackers became more numerous and Inky got a couple of chances to show us what a nice noise his automatic made" [128]); but more significantly, it likens the pistol itself to a witch's familiar. When one of the characters, Glasses, makes this allusion, another, No Nose, finds himself puzzled, as he does not know what a familiar is; so Glasses explains:

> "Well, No Nose, the Devil used to give each witch a pet black cat or dog or maybe a toad to follow it around and protect it and revenge injuries. Those little creatures were called familiars—stooges sent out by the Big Boy to watch over his chosen, you might say. The witches used to talk to them in a language no one else could understand. Now this is what I'm getting at. Times change and styles change—and the style in familiars along with them." (133–34)

That final sentence is the key: in updating the myth of the familiar, Leiber has not only spurned the use of a conventional animal (and recall that Lovecraft's familiar in "The Dreams in the Witch House"—a tale that Leiber, as we shall see, greatly admired—is Brown Jenkin, a relatively conventional rat, albeit with tiny humanlike hands), but an animate entity altogether. In our mechanised age only a thing of steel can achieve the intimacy with its owner that formerly resided in living creatures.

Of "Smoke Ghost" (*Unknown Worlds*, October 1941) it is difficult to speak in small compass. This mesmerising tale is virtually the prototype of the urban horror story, and its influence upon a long line of writers from Bradbury to Ramsey Campbell to Clive Barker is patent. Leiber has testified in "My Life and Writings" that "Smoke Ghost" was a "modern-setting supernatural horror story" (59), while in the autobiographical essay "Not Much Disorder and Not So Early Sex" he notes that it was his "first strong supernatural story" and that it was inspired by riding the elevated trains in Chicago, which "introduced and wedded me to Chicago's lonely and dismal world of roofs" (281). In "Smoke Ghost," the protagonist, Catesby Wran, appears to see a cloudy, smoky figure on the roof of a building as he rides the elevated. He had earlier discussed the matter of ghosts with his secretary, Miss Millick, and when she states that she had once seen "a thing in white" coming out of a closet in the attic bedroom, Wran counters significantly:

> "I don't mean that kind of ghost. I mean a ghost from the world today, with the soot of the factories on its face and the pounding of machinery in its soul. The kind that would haunt coal yards and slip around at night through deserted office buildings like this one. A real ghost. Not something out of books." (109)

Wran continues to draw out the sociopolitical implications of such a modern ghost:

> "Just picture it. A smoky composite face with the hungry anxiety of the unemployed, the neurotic restlessness of the person without purpose, the jerky tension of the high-pressure metropolitan worker, the uneasy resentment of the striker, the callous opportunism of the scab, the aggressive whine of the panhandler, the inhibited terror of the bombed civilian, and a thousand other twisted emotional patterns." (110)

Wran's first glimpse of the entity emphatically places it within the context of a modern age far different from the aristocratic castles of old-time Gothic fiction, the never-never-land of Poe's fictional topography, and even from the witch-haunted Arkhams and Innsmouths of Lovecraft's invented New England:

> There was a particular sea of roofs he had grown into the habit of glancing at just as the packed car carrying him homeward lurched around a turn. A dingy, melancholy little world of tar-paper, tarred gravel, and smoky brick. Rusty tin chimneys with odd conical hats suggested abandoned listening posts. There was a washed-out advertisement of some ancient patent medicine on the nearest wall. Superficially it was like ten thousand other drab city roofs. . . . Unconsciously it came to symbolize for Catesby Wran certain disagreeable aspects of the frustrated, frightened century in which he lived, the jangled century of hate and heavy industry and total wars. (112)

It is significant both that Wran is himself an advertising executive (what more modern function can there be?) and that, after he has seen the smoke ghost several times, he consults that modern substitute for the priest, a psychiatrist. And yet, Wran is convinced that there are no such things as ghosts: "Science and common sense and psychiatry all go to prove it" (111). When faced with the undeniable reality of the ghost, all Wran can do is to worship it: "I will obey you. You are my god. . . . You have supreme power over man and his animals and his machines. You rule this city and all others. I recognize that" (122–23). The smoke ghost is the symbol for the industrialised world that, paradoxically, has simultaneously banished conventional spectres from modern consciousness through the advance of science and, by means of the psychological pressures it places upon human life lived in accordance with the unnatural rhythms of machinery, reintroduced them in a different form. As Wran had noted at the outset, "It's a rotten world . . . Fit for another morbid growth of superstition. It's time the ghosts, or whatever you call them, took over and began a rule of fear. They'd be no worse than men" (111).

It is debatable whether Leiber's "The Hound" (*Weird Tales*, November 1942) has any relation to Lovecraft's identically titled tale of 1922; one rather doubts it, since Lovecraft's histrionic and deliberately overwritten story of ghouls, stolen amulets, and supernatural revenge seems leagues—or centuries—away from Leiber's brooding account of a modern werewolf. In this tale of David Lashley, an employee in a clothing store who appears to be plagued by an immense and ferocious-looking dog, Leiber definitively transfers the locus of supernatural terror from the exterior world to the interior—that is, to the world of our inmost fears and neuroses. It is significant that Lashley, in wondering whether the entity haunting him is some kind of werewolf, has to "read up on such things at the library, fingering dusty books in uneasy fascination" (187). The stock image of the werewolf is now consigned to out-of-date treatises that contain only the musty products of those long ages of pre-scientific delusion: "what he had read made them seem innocuous and without significance—dead superstitions—in comparison with this thing that was part and parcel of the great sprawling cities and chaotic peoples of the Twentieth Century" (187). That century features the "endlessly varying howls and growls of traffic and industry" (187)—the only modern equivalent of the werewolf's cries.

A friend of Lashley's, Tom Goodsell, delivers a somewhat pedantic lecture on the difference between ancient and modern ghosts. "The supernatural beings of a modern city?" he notes. "Sure, they'd be different from the ghosts of yesterday. Each culture creates its own ghosts" (190). Goodsell notes that it is the very triumph of modern science in banishing fears of conventional supernatural entities that has unleashed modern terrors of a very different sort: "We began by denying all the old haunts and superstitions. Why shouldn't we? They belong to the era of cottage and castle. They can't take root in the new environment. Science goes materialistic, proving that there isn't anything in the universe except tiny bundles of energy. As if, for that matter, a tiny bundle of energy mightn't mean anything" (190). But what is the effect on the human psyche?

> "Meanwhile, what's happening inside each one of us? I'll tell you. All sorts of inhibited emotions are accumulating. Fear is accumulating. Horror is accumulating. A new kind of awe of the mysteries of the universe is accumulating. A psychological environment is forming, along with the physical one. Wait, let me finish. Our culture is ripe for infection. . . . How would you know when the infection had taken place? . . . Why, they'd haunt us, terrorize us, try to rule us. Our fears would be their fodder. A parasite-host relationship. Supernatural symbiosis. Some of us—the sensitive ones—would notice them sooner than others. Some of us might seem them without knowing what they were. Others might know about them without seeing them." (191)

In regard to the specific existence of a werewolf, Goodsell remarks:

> "Yes, I think there'd be werewolves among our demons, but they wouldn't be much like the old ones. No nice clean fur, white teeth and shining eyes. Oh, no. Instead you'd get some nasty hound that wouldn't surprise you if you saw it nosing at a garbage pail or crawling out from under a truck. Frighten and terrorize you, yes. But surprise, no. It would fit

into the environment. Look as if it belonged in a city and smell the same. Because of the twisted emotions that would be its food, your emotions and mine. A matter of diet." (191)

Leiber is careful not to render the existence of the werewolf entirely psychological: other characters see it, or sense it, sometimes even before Lashley himself does. Accordingly, the werewolf becomes not simply a product of Lashley's own perturbed psychological state—something suggested earlier in the story by reference to his recollection of a cartoon from World War I in which a wolf was portrayed as symbolic of "war, famine, or the ruthlessness of the enemy" (188)—but a supernatural symbol of the fears that haunt our war-torn age.

"The Dreams of Albert Moreland" (in *Night's Black Agents*, 1947) carries forward the connexion between war and the supernatural that "The Hound" had only hinted at. This tale, aside from expressing Leiber's long fascination with chess, renders the outbreak of World War II a cosmic event that could spell nothing less than the unraveling of the entire fabric of the universe. Beginning pointedly in "the autumn of 1939" (169), the tale recounts the recurring dreams of Albert Moreland, who finds himself playing on an immense chessboard and comes to believe that "He had traced a frightening relationship between the progress of the game and of the War" (182). In one significant passage Leiber fuses interior and exterior horror by seeing in modern psychological trauma, caused both by the war and by the frenetic and neurosis-producing tempo of industrialised life, a reflection of the dissolution of the cosmos:

> As I walked the streets I felt myself inundated by an omnipresent anxiety, and I sensed taut, nervous misery in each passing face. For once I seemed able to look behind the mask which every person wears and which is so characteristically pronounced in a congested city, and see what lay behind—the egotistical sensitivity, the smouldering irritation, the thwarted longing, the defeat . . . and, above all, the anxiety, too ill-defined and lacking in definite object to be called fear, but nonetheless infecting every thought and action, and making trivial things terrible. And it seemed to me that social, economic, and physiological factors, even Death and the

War, were insufficient to explain such anxiety, and that it was in reality an upwelling from something dubious and horrible in the very constitution of the universe. (179)

With "The Girl with the Hungry Eyes" (1949) Leiber all but completes his transformation of Gothic horror icons into something balefully credible in the modern world. This well-known tale of a woman who, not in herself but only in her photographed image as seen on billboards and other advertising, exercises a fatal sexual lure upon the men who see it is distinguished by its tight-lipped, Hemingway-esque prose ("But the Girl isn't like any of the others. She's unnatural. She's morbid. She's unholy" [228]), and in its suggestion that the girl is a vampire very different from the conventional sort ("There are vampires and vampires, and the ones that suck blood aren't the worst" [240]). In the end the narrator—the photographer who discovered the girl and, to his abiding regret, caused her image to be broadcast to the world—becomes aware of what she symbolises:

> I realized that wherever she came from, whatever shaped her, she's the quintessence of the horror behind the bright billboard. She's the smile that tricks you into throwing away your money and your life. She's the eyes that lead you on and on, and then show you death. She's the creature you give everything for and never really get. She's the being that takes every-thing you've got and gives nothing in return. When you yearn towards her face on the billboards, remember that. She's the lure. She's the bait. She's the Girl. (241)

There is more to this than just the false promises of advertising: what is involved is a far deeper, broader psychic vampirism as formerly repre-sented by such mythological entities as the Lorelei or the Sirens—the "eternal feminine" whose temptations are ineluctably seductive to males of a certain temperament, especially those of such "limited social development" as Leiber.

As noted earlier, *Conjure Wife*—first published in *Unknown Worlds* (April 1943) and in book form in 1953—is the acme of Leiber's updat-ing of Gothic tropes, in this case the tropes of witchcraft, voodoo, and sorcery. Leiber has stated in "Not So Much Disorder" that the novel was loosely based upon his experiences at Occidental College in Los Angeles (348), but that he transferred to setting to a fictitious college in New England, Hempnell College, so that the scenario could be geographically closer to the source of American witchcraft traditions. On the face of it, the central plot of the novel—a group of faculty wives practicing witchcraft in order to advance their husbands' careers—might seem comical, something on the order of Alice Hoffman's novel *Practical Magic* (1995), the basis of a popular film. But in Leiber's hands the plot becomes the vehicle for compellingly dramatic action, complete with a striking twist at the climax, and more significantly a textbook instance of the modernisation of Gothic tropes.

Leiber's chief concern is the matter of convincingness. He is well aware that his readers are likely to be, in the overwhelming main, skeptical of the notion that actual witchcraft has come into play—or, rather, that the witchcraft practiced by the quartet of wives has actually been supernaturally efficacious in its stated purpose. Of the hundreds of thousands of witches persecuted in the Middle Ages and Renaissance, including those in Salem, a certain percentage may well have believed that they were witches and that their magic rituals—ranging from herbal potions to the practice of the Black Mass—did indeed produce the effects they sought; but no one believes that they were gifted with supernatural powers. It is, accordingly, vital to Leiber's purpose that both Norman Saylor (whom Leiber himself, in "Not So Much Disorder," describes as "a cocksure anthropology [actually sociology] professor . . . intent on promoting the scientific outlook and eradicating superstition from the world" [348]) and his wife, Tansy, are profound skeptics. The most that Norman can admit—after he has inadvertently discovered that Tansy is practising some kind of conjure magic derived from "an old Negro conjure doctor" (7) whom Norman had interviewed years before in the course of some research—is the following:

> "And what is superstition, but misguided, unobjective science? And when it comes down to that, is it to be wondered if people grasp at super-

stition in this rotten, hate-filled, half-doomed world of today? Lord knows, I'd welcome the blackest of black magic, if it could do anything to stave off the atom bomb." (18)

This is the same kind of sociopolitical rationalisation of the supernatural—superstition as the product of the multifarious terrors and psychological pressures of modern existence—that we have seen in Leiber's short stories. But Tansy herself, even though she admits that "I've always felt that women were more primitive than men, closer to ancient feelings" (17), is said to be a sceptic: "But Tansy was so sane, so healthily contemptuous of palmistry, astrology, numerology and all other superstitious fads. A hardheaded New Englander. So well versed, from her work with him, in the psychological background of superstition and primitive magic" (10).

Once the fact of Tansy's attempts to practice magic is revealed, the question, both for Norman and for the reader, is whether Tansy's magic has actually worked or whether she is merely a neurotic. In spite of some hints of the former—Norman himself ponders, early in the novel, "Ever since he had married her, his life had been luck, luck, luck!" (4); and later, "there was . . . something magical and frightening" (5) about his professional success—both Norman and the reader clearly opt for the latter at the start. Tansy confesses that "the things I did . . . well, they seemed to work . . . at least most of the time" (14); this hesitation and equivocation seem to clinch the psychological explanation of Tansy's actions, for if her magic really had supernatural force, why did it not work all the time? (We later realise that the magic of the other wives, often directed against Tansy's own magic and in support of their own husbands, has on occasion negated Tansy's efforts.) Norman, when faced with this notion of other faculty wives engaged in witchcraft, can only laugh at the idea:

> Norman smiled. That had been an odd notion Tansy had let slip toward the end—that Evelyn Sawtelle and Harold Gunnison's wife and old Mrs. Carr were practicing magic too, of the venomous black magic variety. And not any too hard to believe, either, if you knew them! That was the sort of idea with which a clever satirical writer could do a lot. Just carry it a

step further—picture most women as glamor-conscious witches, carrying on their savage warfare of deathspell and countercharm, while their reality-befuddled husbands went blithely about their business. (24)

The rest of the novel is a systematic onslaught on the reader's scepticism so that the only alternative left is to assume that supernatural magic is actually being practised—but Leiber is compelled to use the most austere elements of logic and reason to effect this contra-rational result. His chief weapon is the law of probability. Given a certain series of actions, what is the most plausible explanation of them? If that explanation is conventionally regarded as supernatural, should it be rejected on that count alone? Would it not be more rational to accept the supernatural in lieu of clutching at such implausible straws as extreme coincidence or widespread psychological trauma?

As soon as Tansy gives up her magic, odd—and generally bad—things begin to happen to Norman. A young woman in love with him falsely accuses him of seducing her. A disgruntled student tries to kill Norman with a gun. Norman himself seems to be losing control, speaking recklessly in class and jeopardising his position. Harvey Sawtelle, a stodgy and elderly professor in Norman's department, wins the chairmanship over him. Leiber dares us to reject the most obvious relation of cause and effect here—that Tansy's abdication of magic has allowed her rivals to gain power so that their husbands are vaunted over Tansy's. To be sure, all these disparate events could be coincidence—but how likely is it that they could all have happened in such a short period of time? Gradually Norman himself seems to be coming around to the supernatural view, especially when the their cat, Totem, is apparently killed by a stone dragon that had formerly rested on the roof of one of the college buildings. At this point Norman confesses, "Sorcery *is*. . . . Something has been conjured down from a roof. Women are witches fighting for their men. Tansy was a witch. She was guarding you. But you made her stop" (89). But that is not quite the end of the matter. Later Norman wonders whether even witchcraft might be encompassed within the bounds of a wider conception of science:

. . . was it not likely that all self-destructive impulses were the result of witchcraft? Those universal impulses that were a direct contradiction to the laws of self-preservation and survival. To account for them, Poe had fancifully conceived an "Imp of the Perverse," and psychoanalysts had laboriously hypothesized a "death wish." How much simpler to attribute them to malign forces outside the individual, working by means as yet unanalyzed and therefore classified as supernatural. (107)

Here again the principle of probability ("was it not likely . . ."; "how much simpler . . .") is put to use. And yet, Norman cannot quite bring himself to admit the supernatural even in this quasi-scientific manner. Even when he himself begins a succession of magic rituals to counter those of his enemies, he is still maintaining that he only "pretend[s] to believe in black magic in order to overawe three superstitious, psychotic women who had a hold on his wife's mental life" (173)—in other words, that all this magic was merely of psychological origin and that its efficacy, if indeed it was efficacious, operated purely on a psychological level, just as a man who is told that he is the object of a curse might well fall ill if he believes that curses are real. Norman elaborates this conception with a certain sheepishness at his own credulity:

> What a ludicrous picture it was . . .: a woman who half believed in witchcraft driven mad by three women who perhaps believed fully in witchcraft or perhaps not at all, their schemes opposed by a husband who believed not at all, but pretended to believe to the full—and was determined to act in every way in accord with that belief. (174)

In this context it is significant that Norman initially uses "the modern science of symbolic logic" (173) to come to Tansy's aid: symbolic logic, the pinnacle of Western philosophical rationalism, would seem just about as far from witchcraft and sorcery as anything could be, and yet it does prove fruitful (along with certain elements of superstition, such as the use of mirrors, potions, a piece of thread tied into an intricate knot, and the like) in combating the ultimate source of the evil, the aged Mrs. Carr, who had sought to usurp Tansy's young body while hoping to entice Norman to kill her own body with Tansy's soul trapped within it.

Conjure Wife once again suggests that ancient superstition, far from being banished by scientific rationalism, has only gone underground, remaining as potent as ever and perhaps all the more powerful for its apparent defeat by reason. Norman Saylor is at the outset presented as a "modern husband" (1), and a telling metaphor regarding his house is also made at the beginning: "Today's washable paint covered last century's ornate moldings" (2). The modern age may cover over the superstitions of the past, but this superficial coating only conceals and does not eradicate. Ironically, Saylor and his colleagues are themselves referred to as witches, "performing the necessary rituals to keep dead ideas alive, like a college of witch-doctors in their stern stone tents" (3). In one of his classes Norman states that "we're modified anthropoid apes inhabiting night clubs and battleships" (35)—a brilliant simile that underscores how the retention of primitive superstition has gone hand in hand with spectacular technological progress.

It may be wondered whether any literary influences can be detected in *Conjure Wife*. Leiber has testified to his great admiration for one of Lovecraft's later narratives, "The Dreams in the Witch House" (1932), a skilful fusion of ancient myth with modern science. In that tale, a witch of the seventeenth century, through the use of advanced mathematics, has managed to find a way to travel through time and extend her baleful influence well into the twentieth century. Leiber, in the essay "Through Hyperspace with Brown Jenkin: Lovecraft's Contribution to Speculative Fiction" (1966), speaks of the tale as "Lovecraft's most carefully worked out story of hyperspace-travel" (91) and points to its possible influence upon such later works as William Sloane's *To Walk the Night* and Ward Moore's *Bring the Jubilee*. While, of course, time travel is not involved in *Conjure Wife*, Leiber may well have seen in Lovecraft's tale a clever means of updating an ancient superstition, and he has chosen to do very much the same, albeit in a quite different direction.

By the early 1950s, as Leiber himself has acknowledged ("Not So Much Disorder" 358-59), a multiplicity of factors was pushing him away from supernatural fiction toward science fiction; but by this time his modernisation of Gothic had already been fully accomplished. Although he would return on numerous occasions to the purely weird—especially in the novel *Our Lady of Darkness* (1977), an exhaustive expansion of the core idea of "Smoke Ghost"—his subsequent work would only add further depth and nuance to the radical modernisation of Gothic that he had effected in the course of the 1940s.

Leiber's influence upon the development of the modern weird tale, as on the development of the sword-and-sorcery tale and the genre of science fiction, is evident. His use of aggressively modern urban settings, his ingenious adaptation of primitive myth to modern contexts, and his use of the supernatural to highlight contemporary social, cultural, and political concerns have made a permanent impact upon the field and furnished a model for some of the most noted writers who followed him. It is, to choose only one example, difficult to imagine Ramsey Campbell's tales of urban horror (specifically in *Demons by Daylight* and *Dark Companions*) without reference to Leiber's. Campbell has now made an eloquent tribute to his debt to Leiber in the article "All the Ghosts That Made Me":

> The urban supernatural stories of Fritz Leiber, then (with Robert Aickman) the greatest living writer in the field, had given me a direction. Long before the invasion of everyday settings by the supernatural had become a cliché of the genre, Fritz was writing stories in which the supernatural arose from the everyday setting. What Chicago and, later, San Francisco were for him, Liverpool already was for me, and I needed only to use his example to help me draw on my experience of my home town and be true to myself. (432)

It is fitting that the most distinguished contemporary practitioner of weird fiction should, in this fashion, acknowledge Leiber's influence upon his own work; for it was Leiber who was largely responsible in rescuing the supernatural tale from irrelevance in an age of factories, advertising, and atom bombs; it was he who showed that these very elements of modernity could themselves serve as the sources of new supernatural traditions that would carry the weird tale into the twentieth and twenty-first centuries.

Works Cited

Byfield, Bruce. *Witches of the Mind: A Critical Study of Fritz Leiber.* West Warwick, RI: Necronomicon Press, 1991.

Campbell, Ramsey. "All the Ghosts That Made Me." In *Ramsey Campbell, Probably: On Horror and Sundry Fantasies.* Ed. S. T. Joshi. Harrogate, UK: PS Publishing, 2002. 432–35.

Joshi, S. T. "Topical References in Lovecraft." In *Lovecraft and a World in Transition: Collected Essays on H. P. Lovecraft.* New York: Hippocampus Press, 2014. 289–307.

Leiber, Fritz. "The Automatic Pistol." In *Night's Black Agents.* 235–40.

———. *Conjure Wife.* 1943–53. New York: Ace, 1981.

———. *The Dealings of Daniel Kesserich.* New York: Tor, 1997.

———. "The Dreams of Albert Moreland." In *Night's Black Agents.* 169–84.

———. *Fafhrd & Me.* Ed. John Gregory Betancourt. Newark, NJ: Wildside Press, 1990.

———. "The Hound." In *Night's Black Agents.* 185–99.

———. "My Life and Writings." In *Fafhrd & Me.* 55–64.

———. *Night's Black Agents.* Rev. ed. New York: Berkley, 1978.

———. "Not Much Disorder and Not So Early Sex: An Autobiographic Essay." In *The Ghost Light.* New York: Ace, 1991. 251–365.

———. "Smoke Ghost." In *Night's Black Agents.* 109–23.

———. "Spider Mansion." In *the Black Gondolier.* Seattle: Midnight House, 2000. 121–39.

———. "Through Hyperspace with Brown Jenkin: Lovecraft's Contribution to Speculative Fiction." 1966. In *Fafhrd & Me.* 85–96.

Lovecraft, H. P. *The Annotated Supernatural Horror in Literature.* Ed. S. T. Joshi. New York: Hippocampus Press, rev. ed. 2012.

———. *Selected Letters.* Ed. August Derleth, Donald Wandrei, and James Turner. Sauk City, WI: Arkham House, 1965–76. 5 vols.

Master and Pupil: August Derleth and Ramsey Campbell's First Book

Ramsey Campbell has frequently testified to the invaluable assistance that August Derleth lent him in the earliest stages of his literary career, especially in the revision of the stories that comprised his first book, *The Inhabitant of the Lake and Less Welcome Tenants* (1964), which was published by Derleth's Arkham House when Campbell was only eighteen. Now, with the publication not only of the complete surviving correspondence between Campbell and Derleth, as well as an expanded edition of *The Inhabitant of the Lake* (which includes additional stories written around the time that book was assembled), we can come close to a definitive charting of the early relationship between these two men—a relationship in which Derleth generously took on the role of an accomplished professional of the literary trade and Campbell revealed himself as a precocious novice who quickly absorbed the lessons he was receiving on an almost daily basis.

The final contents of *The Inhabitant of the Lake* include ten stories. They are as follows. (Dates of composition—taken from the afterword to the expanded edition—and word counts are supplied.)

The Room in the Castle [November 1961; 6800 words]
The Horror from the Bridge [1962?; 10,000 words]
The Insects from Shaggai [April/May 1962; 9300 words]
The Render of the Veils [April 1962; 4600 words]
The Inhabitant of the Lake [June–July 1962; 13,000 words]
The Plain of Sound [1962; 4400 words]
The Return of the Witch [late 1962; 5000 words]

The Mine on Yuggoth [September 1962; 4800 words]
The Will of Stanley Brooke [late 1962; 2500 words]
The Moon-Lens [January 1963; 5600 words]

The expanded edition includes the following stories:

The Box in the Priory [1960; 3500 words]
The Tomb-Herd [early 1961; 4000 words]
The Face in the Desert [1961; 2600 words]
The Horror from the Bridge [first draft] [1961; 10,000 words]
The Tower from Yuggoth [1961; 9700 words]
The Insects from Shaggai [first draft] [late 1961; 9300 words]
The Church in High Street [1961; 5800 words]

Campbell's very first letter to Derleth, dated 16 August 1961, announced that "I have recently been attempting a number of pastiches of the Lovecraft Mythos" and asked Derleth to read some of them (3). By this time, "The Tower from Yuggoth" had already been accepted by a British fanzine, *Goudy*, edited by Pat Kearney, and it appeared in its second issue (1962). Derleth somewhat officiously responded:

> I should say at the outset that we had better see your pastiches of Lovecraft Mythos stories because a) the Lovecraft material is copyrighted and so protected and b) the approval of Arkham House is necessary before any copyrighted material can be released for publication. This is a necessary provision, of course, because if we did not enforce it scores of cheap imitations would flood the market, reflecting unfavorably on Lovecraft and his work. (4)

Derleth's claims to ownership of the "Lovecraft Mythos" were largely fantasy, and he was unable to acknowledge that his own pastiches—whether it be the tales in *The Mask of Cthulhu* (1958) and *The Trail of Cthulhu* (1962) or, worse, the "posthumous collaborations" with Lovecraft gathered in *The Watchers out of Time and Others* (1974)—were themselves among those that "reflect[ed] unfavorably on Lovecraft and his work."

Derleth asked Campbell to send his stories in a group. It took some time for Campbell to type them, as they existed only in autograph manuscripts. He finally sent them on in a letter dated 10 August 1961, but this letter is clearly misdated and was probably written on 10 September. (A subsequent letter of 24 September noted that the stories were "on their way to you" [11].) In his letter of 6 October 1961, Derleth reported having read two of the stories; he didn't specify which ones, but he did declare that "I do think them competent." But he went on to make the momentous suggestion:

> . . . there is one alteration I think you should definitely make; . . . and that is to remove your stories from the Lovecraft milieu. I mean, keep the Gods, the Books, etc., but establish your own place. This would give the stories vastly more authenticity as an addition to the Mythos rather than pastiche pieces, and it might then be possible for us to consider their book publication in a limited edition over here.
>
> What I suggest you do is establish a setting in a coastal area of England and create your own British milieu. This would not appreciably change your stories, but it would give them a much needed *new* setting and would not, in the reader's mind, invite a direct comparison with Lovecraft, for in such a comparison they would not show up as well as if you had your own setting and place-names for the tales. (15)

Campbell quickly replied on 9 October, stating his eagerness to come up with a British locale for his tales: "it will, I should think, necessitate some research into the history and geography of the region I pick, and therefore some little time should pass before the revised version of the tales is completed" (16). Campbell initially thought that the Devon-Cornwall region would be a possible locale, but of course he ultimately set his tales in the Severn valley.

In his letter of 18 October 1961 Derleth already all but accepted a volume of Campbell's tales: "I have finally found time to read your stories consecutively, and, without at this time making a firm commitment, I do think you have a potential Arkham House book here" (18). Derleth repeated his criticism that Campbell should relocate his stories to England, and also that Campbell should do less summarising and more narrating. He then offered specific criticisms of "The Box in the Priory," "The Tomb-Herd," "The Tower from Yuggoth," and "The Horror from the Bridge." It is only in his letter of 22 October that Campbell told Derleth that he was only fifteen years old.

Of the tales Derleth read at this juncture, several do indeed betray the flaws that Derleth perspicaciously identified. "The Box in the Priory," a story about Byatis (an entity glancingly cited in Robert Bloch's "The Shambler from the Stars"), is set in Arkham; and, aside from a glancing citation (180) of "Elder Gods" (inventions of August Derleth, who wanted a set of "good" deities to oppose the "evil" Old Ones), features a surprise ending—where a "snake-like thing . . . as wide as a human body and impossibly long, had been merely the face-tentacle of the abomination Byatis" (*I* 182)—taken either from Lovecraft's "The Shunned House" (1924) or from his ghostwritten tale for Harry Houdini, "Under the Pyramids" (1924; published as "Imprisoned with the Pharaohs"), where what appears to be an entity of moderate size proves to be only a tiny portion of an incalculably larger creature.

"The Tomb-Herd" is set in Kingsport (the Massachusetts city that Lovecraft identified with Marblehead in "The Festival" [1923]) and features a protagonist with the transparently Lovecraftian name Richard Dexter. Aside from a curious reference to Zothique (*I* 185)—a continent of the far future around which Clark Ashton Smith wove an entire cycle of tales—the tale draws from a number of Lovecraft stories, including "The Rats in the Walls" and "The Call of Cthulhu." Even the throw-away line "I read of what Azathoth had resembled *before* that monstrous nuclear chaos had been bereft of mind and will" (*I* 187) reminds us of the line in "The Whisperer in Darkness" that reads: "I learned whence Cthulhu *first* came . . . and I started with loathing when told of the monstrous nuclear chaos beyond angled space which the *Necronomicon* had mercifully cloaked under the name of Azathoth" (*CF* 2.520–21). Campbell also errs in coming up with the implausible-sounding name Asquith Place, which does not evoke New England but rather the British prime minister H. H. Asquith. And as for the conclusion of the tale, Campbell attempts to invest the narrative with a kind of existential horror—"And I think of those stains of which which I found at the last—*those stains on my own face and hands*" (*I* 191)—that not only evokes "The Whisperer in Darkness" again ("For the things in the chair . . . were the face and hands of Henry Wentworth Akeley" [*CF* 2.538])—but also "The Shadow over Innsmouth," where the protagonist discovers that he is related to the hideous hybrid creatures in that decaying Massachusetts backwater.

"The Tower from Yuggoth" continues the excessively close pastiche of Lovecraft's stories by coming up with a narrator named Edward Wingate Armitage (derived from Edward Derby of "The Thing on the Doorstep," Nathaniel Wingate Peaslee of "The Shadow out of Time," and Dr. Henry Armitage of "The Dunwich Horror") and also by being set in the year 1929. (There are some chronological difficulties in the story, as it is declared that Armitage was born in 1879 [*I* 221] and enrolled at Miskatonic University in 1916 [*I* 223], at which time he is said to be eighteen years old [*I* 225].) Once again a tissue of Lovecraftian elements, the story is a kind of mirror-image of "The Whisperer in Darkness": whereas in Lovecraft's tale the fungi from Yuggoth have come to the Earth to mine an element they cannot find on their native planet, here Armitage finds a tower, built by the fungi, that allows him to transport himself to Yuggoth. There are imitations of "The Dunwich Horror" as well as of *The Case of Charles Dexter Ward* (in the form of letters in archaic language found by Armitage).

"The Horror from the Bridge" may be of the the most interest among these very early tales. The story was based on entry 217 in Lovecraft's commonplace book: "Ancient (Roman? prehistoric?) stone bridge washed away by a (sudden and curious?) storm. Something liberated which had been sealed up in the masonry years ago. Things happen" (*CE* 5.233). Set in the imaginary Massachusetts town of Healyville, it focuses on a character named Philip Wentworth. This name may have been derived from the "posthumous collaboration" "Wentworth's Day," in *The Survivor and Others* (1957). Although the story is heavily indebted to "The Dunwich Horror," there is a major difficulty in reconciling it to that tale. Philip Wentworth is said to have been the "Miskatonic University librarian" (*I* 209) in 1900 and appears to have retained that function in 1931; but if so, what happened to Henry Armitage, who was the librarian who defeated the Whateley clan in "The Dunwich Horror"? Campbell actually makes note of the fact that "1928 was a particular year of horror, with inexplicable occurrences in many places" (*I* 211), but never cites Armitage.

Matters become more curious when we consider the similarly titled "posthumous collaboration" "The Horror from the Middle Span," which was based on the identical commonplace book entry but was manifestly written *after* Campbell's story. On 21 October 1965 Derleth told Campbell: "If I can find time I'll do another short Lovecraft tale from one of the HPL notes or dreams, but that depends" (256). He did write the story sometime thereafter, including it in his anthology of original tales, *Travellers by Night* (1967); but he made no acknowledgment to Campbell that he might well have been inspired by Campbell's story to write his own.

Campbell asked Derleth why he had said nothing about "The Face in the Desert," to which Derleth responded somewhat opaquely on 25 October 1961: "I said nothing about THE FACE IN THE DESERT because I didn't need to say anything about it" (24). By this Derleth meant that the story did not explicitly use Mythos trappings, even though its setting in the Arabian desert in the year 1930 clearly evokes Lovecraft's "The Nameless City." Once again Campbell attempts to invest the tale with existential horror out of "The Shadow over Innsmouth" when he has the narrator come upon a set of stone pillars in the desert, on the top of one of which "I glimpsed a loathsome and foetal replica forming at the centre of the translucent bulb—a ghastly but recognisable likeness to my own face" (*I* 198). Derleth, however, rejected this story for *Inhabitant*, remarking in a letter of 20 July 1963 that "it's just out of place here" (127). In his letter of 25 July he added that it is "certainly the weakest story in the book" (128). Weak or not, we may find that it is less irrelevant to the contents of *Inhabitant* than some other stories that made their way into that volume.

On 1 November 1961 Campbell announced the completion of a new story, "The Insects from Shaggai." He delayed sending it to Derleth until he had revised it several times, and he may not have sent it in until he mailed the entire manuscript of *Inhabitant* to Derleth on 11 March 1963. I cannot find a specific comment by Derleth on the story, but it is one of Campbell's stronger tales of this period, so presumably Derleth felt it worth keeping in the book. The title, of course, is derived from the title of one of Robert Blake's stories, "Shaggai," as cited in "The Haunter of the Dark" (1935). The first draft is set in Arkham and Ipswich (it is not clear whether, at this juncture, Campbell was aware that Ipswich was a real town in Massachusetts), but at least it appears to take place in the present day, if the mention of a "sports car" (*I* 246) can be taken as a hint in that direction. The history of the insects from Shaggai found in the tale is manifestly an imitation of the history of the Old Ones related in *At the Mountains of Madness*.

Derleth expressed an interest in using a story by Campbell in his original anthology *Dark Mind, Dark Heart* (1962); but he made clear that such a story would not appear in Campbell's collection. By 22 January 1962 Derleth was expressing impatience with Campbell, stating that "If I am to see a story for possible inclusion in my new anthology of hitherto unpublished horror tales—DARK MIND, DARK HEART—I must see it posthaste" (39). Campbell thereupon submitted a revised version of "The Tomb-Herd." Derleth, in his letter of 7 February 1962, said that he still found the story not quite satisfactory, but went on to say that he would use the story on two major conditions: 1) that the title be changed to "The Church in High Street"; and (2) that he be allowed a free hand to "alter and delete as I see fit" (41). Campbell naturally acceded to these requirements, for the prospect of appearing in an Arkham House volume at the age of sixteen was too good to pass up. Campbell, however, must have known that in England the common usage is not "High Street" (equivalent of "Main Street" in the

United States) but "the High Street."

Campbell's version of the revised version of "The Tomb-Herd" does not survive, so all we have is Derleth's rewrite, which duly appeared in *Dark Mind, Dark Heart.* The one thing that can be said for it is that Derleth's revisions are relatively seamless, for it is difficult now to detect what the one author wrote and what the other. The story is, of course, now set in the Severn valley area that Campbell had chosen as the British equivalent for Arkham, Kingsport, Dunwich, and Innsmouth. Derleth himself had suggested this region in his letter of 18 October 1961, in reference to "The Horror from the Bridge," since the bridge in question was said to be of Roman origin. Campbell did not specifically reply to this suggestion, but on 19 November 1961 he reported:

> I had some trouble inventing fictitious names for towns in the region, but finally came up with the following: Brichester, Camside, Temphill (originally 'Temple Hill', according to one of my tales), Severnhill and Goatswood (the last title may be good for the location of a tale about Shub-Niggurath, if ever I get round to it—there wasn't ever a story written about this deity by any author, was there?) I hope these all sound authentic. (28)

"Severnhill," of course, was later modified to Severnford.

By this time Campbell was already revising the stories that would actually be included in *Inhabitant.* In this same letter he wrote:

> I've completed the second draft of the BOX IN THE PRIORY, editing out the summaries, and also adding in dialogue where possible. Since I didn't come across any references in my research to priories in the Severn Valley region, while I did find frequent ones to castles, I decided to play safe and call the story, instead, THE ROOM IN THE CASTLE. (28)

The story, aside from being set in Severnford and (at Derleth's suggestion) noting the existence of a copy of the *Necronomicon* at the British Museum instead of at Miskatonic University in Arkham, contains considerably greater dialogue than his earlier stories—one instance of how Campbell took up Derleth's suggestion of telling instead of showing. But it still cannot be said that the story is a notable success; aside from a citation of a "curiously-figured star-shaped stone, which . . . would keep off the power of Byatis" (*I* 18)—an idea derived from Derleth's comical use of these items (taken from *At the Mountains of Madness*) as talismans against the Old Ones—we are regaled by the sight of the dreaded god destroyed by gasoline (petrol), in the manner of the hydrochloric acid that the protagonists of "The Shunned House" use to eliminate the psychic vampire in that tale.

"The Horror from the Bridge" is now set in Clotton, but still takes place in the chronologically remote period of 1931, thereby lessening its immediacy of effect. Here again we find a mention of the "seal of the Elder Gods" (*I* 33), and the tale remains heavily reliant on "The Dunwich Horror." Instead of whippoorwills serving as psychopomps, Campbell substitutes nightjars (*I* 28); and instead of the backwoods New England dialect that Lovecraft used to good effect in his tale, Campbell introduces a character who speaks in lower-class British dialect ("I was just goin' up to bed w'en I 'eard these shots an' yells down be the river" [*I* 39]).

"The Insects from Shaggai," now set in Brichester, remains fairly close to the first draft. "The Mine on Yuggoth" is not notably different from "The Tower from Yuggoth," with the requisite changes made to the name of the protagonist (now Edward Taylor) to make it sound less obviously Lovecraftian, and to the setting (now Brichester). Derleth had been irritated that the original version of the story had been published in *Goudy*, which proved to be uncopyrighted, although the editor had informed Campbell that it would in fact be registered for copyright. When he got a copy of the magazine, Derleth fulminated (letter of 14 May 1962):

> I turned at once to your story, and I am sorry to say that THE TOWER FROM YUGGOTH is now in the public domain. The magazine is not under copyright, no sort of notice was published with your story that could be construed as a legal protection, and your story can now be lifted and reprinted by anyone who elects to do so. This is very foolish publishing, and I hope you will not again be so foolish as to permit such printing of a story without copyright. (61)

But Campbell altered "The Mine on Yuggoth" sufficiently from its predecessor that Derleth felt justified in including it in *Inhabitant.*

Campbell stated in his letter of 26 April 1962 that he was "working on a new Mythos tale" (57), "The Render of the Veils." A month later he asked Derleth if it would be all right to let Jack Chalker use the story in his fanzine *Mirage;* but Derleth, still angry over the *Goudy* matter, made pretty clear what his views were: "The book editor's point of view is simply this: why shd. I pay for the privilege of publishing this if the author can give it away to a fanzine?" (64). It is not clear when Derleth actually read the story; he may have done so only when he received the full manuscript of *Inhabitant* from Campbell. At this time the collection was actually titled *The Render of the Veils* [*and Other Stories?*]; but Derleth, after reviewing the manuscript, declared that "the second most weak story is the one you have chosen for your title story, THE RENDER OF THE VEILS; so this must be altered" (128). (The weakest story, which Derleth rejected outright, was "The Face in the Desert.")

And yet, "The Render of the Veils" has several points to recommend it. It may be the first Cthulhu Mythos story in which Campbell does not seek to imitate Lovecraft's dense prose idiom. There is a more contemporary tone to this tale than is present in many of Campbell's earlier stories; and although it is based on an entry in Lovecraft's commonplace book (no. 204: "Disturbing conviction that all life is only a deceptive dream with some dismal or sinister horror lurking behind" [*CE* 5.232]) and features Campbell's invented book of forbidden lore, *The Revelations of Glaaki,* the story is much less of a Lovecraft pastiche than many other tales of this period.

That cannot be said for "The Inhabitant of the Lake," the longest of Campbell's early Mythos tales. This novelette roughly echoes "The Whisperer in Darkness" in its epistolary format, and much information on *The Revelations of Glaaki* (which, we now learn, extends to eleven volumes) and on the "god" Glaaki itself is provided. Campbell leaves himself open to amusement at his own expense when he depicts the baleful god as actually dwelling in a placid-seeming lake in the middle of England; just as Lovecraft, writing probably in a conscious parody of his own style and manner in the ghostwritten tale "The Horror in the Museum," depicts an explorer who brings back the actual god Rhan-Tegoth from the frozen wastes of Alaska and locks him up in a large box in the basement of a museum. There may be something of parody— or, more precisely, a fairly obvious in-joke—in Campbell's devising of a new "god," Daoloth, surely derived from the name of his correspondent and publisher.

"The Plain of Sound" was conceived as early as late 1961:

> I have another story waiting to be written after these have been rewritten: the basic plot being about some shunned region in the Brichester-Camside area whence unplaceable sounds are said to emanate. The sounds eventually are discovered to be *beings* from some other dimension where matter itself exists only as sound, and where matter of our sort is known only as an odor. I think I could make something worthwhile of this idea. (30)

But he began writing it only in mid-July 1962. Derleth read it only when he read the manuscript of Campbell's book, remarking:

> As a general criticism, I have to point out that your endings tend to fall down. THE PLAIN OF SOUND, for instance, which is a good, interesting story, comes up with a weak ending. "I saw what it took from its victims," as you have it, is a let-down; it is simply not enough, at least, for this old pro; we cannot imagine that "it" took anything sufficiently horrible to drive Tony insane. (128)

The basic thrust of the story is a novel one—"Sounds in this area *are equivalents of matter in another dimension*" (I 118)—and there is nothing corresponding to it in Lovecraft's work. Campbell does not seem to have altered the ending after receiving Derleth's criticism, for the final line remains: "I saw what it took from its victims! *I saw what it took from its victims!*" (I 122), which could indeed be subject to the criticism of excessive vagueness. And yet, in some senses this ending echoes that of Lovecraft's *At the Mountains of Madness*, where Danforth, seeing something that the narrator (William Dyer) does not see as they are flying away from the mountains of madness, utters all manner of cryptic phrases evidently reflecting his apocalyptic vision. Campbell's protagonist does much the same: "He speaks of 'the snailhorns,' 'the blue crystalline lenses,' 'the mobility of the faces,' 'the living flame and water,' 'the bell-shaped appendages,' and 'the common head of many bodies'" (*I* 122).

"The Return of the Witch" is the most peculiar story in *Inhabitant* in that, in spite of the citation of the *Revelations of Glaaki*, there is nothing notably Lovecraftian about it. Campbell dates the story to late 1962 (*I* 288), although in his own bibliography he places it as the first story of 1963 (*Core of Ramsey Campbell* 24). He declares that the story is based on commonplace book entry no. 99 ("Salem story—the cottage of an aged witch—wherein after her death are found sundry terrible things" [*CE* 5.225]), but in fact the tale focuses on a writer, Norman Owen, who moves into a house formerly occupied by a suspected witch, Gladys Shorrock; in the course of the story the soul of Gladys possesses the body of the writer, or at least coexists with his own soul.

Campbell has declared that he was struck by how similar the story was to Henry Kuttner's "The Salem Horror" (*Weird Tales,* May 1937), a story that Campbell had never read before its appearance in Derleth's anthology *Tales of the Cthulhu Mythos* (1969). It deals with a writer who similarly unleashes the spirit of a witch, Abigail Prinn, who had died in 1692, and is in fact a close pastiche of Lovecraft's "The Dreams in the Witch House." One detail in Campbell's story—where Norman finds that he has transported a wooden chest from a dream into the real world—echoes a similar detail in Lovecraft's story, where the protagonist, Walter Gilman, brings back a spiky image that, in a dream, he had broken off a railing.

"The Will of Stanley Brooke" is similarly only tangentially Lovecraftian, and perhaps not Lovecraftian at all. This story is also apparently not discussed in the Campbell-Derleth correspondence. Campbell dates it either to late 1962 (*I* 289) or 1963 (*Core of Ramsey Campbell* 24). Here the idea is that Stanley Brooke, dying of cancer, makes a new will in which all his assets and effects are to be given to a man, William Collier, who proves to be his exact double. In the end Collier is killed by Brooke's lawyer. Are we to assume that Collier is the revived body of Brooke? More pertinently, where exactly is the Lovecraft influence? Campbell himself states: "The theme derives from Lovecraft's 'The Festival', although at the time I didn't realise it did" (*I* 289). I am not certain of the purport of this remark, but my own feeling is that Campbell was (perhaps unconsciously) thinking of *The Case of Charles Dexter Ward*, where Joseph Curwen's colleague in alchemy, Simon Orne, departs from Salem and comes back as his own son, Jedediah, to deflect attention from the fact that he does not seem to age appreciably even with the passing of decades.

The final tale of *Inhabitant*, "The Moon-Lens," is set in Goatswood and fulfils Campbell's early wish to write a story specifically about Shub-Niggurath, which in his view had rarely been done. On 4 December 1961 he wrote to Derleth: "I don't recall stories solely about Shub-Niggurath, though I used him quite often in THE DWELLER IN DARKNESS" (29). (The reference is to Derleth's story "The Dweller in Darkness" [*Weird Tales*, November 1944].) Campbell declares that the story was based on commonplace book entry no. 189 ("Ancient necropolis—bronze door in hillside which opens as the moonlight strikes it—focussed by ancient lens in pylon opposite?" [*CE* 5.231]), and the story follows this plot-germ closely; but the scenario where the protagonist, wishing to get from Goatswood to Brichester, is tricked into staying overnight in a hotel is manifestly adapted from "The Shadow over Innsmouth."

We can now return to the issue of the title of Campbell's collection. As mentioned, he had wished to call it *The Render of the Veils*. His argument went as follows: "the story carrying this title is probably the best in the book, and the name of the collection might also be symbolic of my writing—'rending the veils' by the 'revelations' contained in the tales" (79 [2 September 1962]). Derleth, even before reading the title story, expressed reservations:

> Our new bulletin is on press. In it I announced your book under the
> title of THE BOX IN THE PRIORY, which I have to confess I like as a ti-

tle considerably better than THE RENDER OF THE VEILS, which isn't Lovecraftian but rather more like Bloch's THE OPENER OF THE WAY. There is still plenty of time in which to settle on a title. The RENDER is just a trifle too pretentious for my taste, suggests the mystic rather than the dreadful or terrible, and I should think we would want to avoid that and make its appeal more frankly Lovecraftian. (99 [7 March 1963])

In my estimation Derleth is correct; Campbell, however, continued to defend his title. The book could not be called *The Box in the Priory* because Campbell had changed the title of that story to "The Room in the Castle," and this story was never considered as a potential title for the book. But, as we have seen, when Derleth actually read "The Render of the Veils," he felt that its weakness (in his judgment) disbarred it from being suitable for the title of the collection.

On 3 August 1963 Campbell suggested *The Inhabitant of the Lake* as a title, since it was "pretty Lovecraftian" (132). Derleth was noncommittal, replying: "Well, we'll come up with something. It can be an inclusive title, needn't be taken from a story in the book. Something like UNWELCOME TENANTS or THE INHABITANT OF THE LAKE AND OTHER UNWELCOME TENANTS, which I like a little better than just the story title alone" (134). Campbell expressed enthusiasm for the latter title, and that seemed to settle the matter. But then Derleth announced in a postcard of 4 February 1964: "Incidentally, because of my erroneous instructions to the artist for the jacket, the title of your book is now THE INHABITANT OF THE LAKE AND LESS WEL-COME TENANTS, instead of OTHER UNWELCOME T." (169). The artist in question was Frank Utpatel, who did not only the dust jacket art but also a map of the Severnford-Brichester area for the endpapers. It was only fifty years later, in his augmented edition of the book, that the originally agreed-upon title was restored. Campbell, who believed that the erroneous title was taken from Derleth's own forthcoming book, *Colonel Markesan and Less Pleasant Persons* (1966), has remarked dryly: "I felt few tenants could be less welcome than Glaaki" (*I* 290).

Interestingly, as early as 12 October 1961 Derleth advised his young correspondent (17): "Yes, I would advise signing your stories

Ramsey Campbell—it's a good author's name, and it will avoid confusion with John Campbell" (i.e., the science fiction writer and editor John W. Campbell, Jr.). Derleth continued to press Campbell on the matter, especially when it came to the publication of "The Church in High Street" in *Dark Mind, Dark Heart*; but Campbell was insistent: "Unless you're really against it, I would prefer to retain the initial in 'J. Ramsey Campbell'. Without the initial the name sounds to me rather *bare*—and no other combination of my names sounds at all inspiring" (46 [22 February 1962]). Only years later did Campbell feel that the "J." was unnecessary.

Campbell's early Cthulhu Mythos stories are not only heavily indebted to Lovecraft but, as he came to realise later, to Derleth. For the fact is that Campbell largely swallowed (as most other writers and critics up to that time did) Derleth's erroneous interpretation of the Lovecraft Mythos: in his view, benign "Elder Gods" were in a battle for supremacy against "evil" Old Ones (Cthulhu, Yog-Sothoth, etc.), with such ridiculous talismans as the star-stones cited in many of Derleth's stories. The bleak cosmic vision of Lovecraft's tales was largely beyond Derleth's comprehension; for him, Lovecraft's "gods" really were gods, and they could only be battled with the weapons of black magic—incantations, "forbidden" books, and the like. Campbell unwittingly adopted many of these Derlethian principles in his own Mythos tales, and it is a credit to his native talents as a writer that they remain as vigorous and entertaining as they are.

But the remarkable thing about Campbell is that, well before the appearance of *The Inhabitant of the Lake* in the spring of 1964, he was already moving beyond the Lovecraft influence to write stories that reflected his own ideas, moods, and conceptions. Derleth did accept a number of these for his various anthologies of the 1960s, such as "The Stone on the Island" (included in *Over the Edge*, 1964) and "The Cellars" (included in *Travellers by Night*, 1967). Others he rejected, such as "The Childish Fear" and "An Offering to the Dead." The first draft of "The Interloper," one of the more striking tales in Campbell's second story collection, *Demons by Daylight* (1973), was written so early as August 1963. It is not clear whether Campbell actually sent this story to Derleth, although he expressed a desire to do so. Derleth did have the good judgment to accept the revolutionary Mythos tale "Cold Print" for *Tales of the Cthulhu Mythos*. Indeed, *Demons by Daylight* was largely completed by 1968, and Derleth had sent a contract for it in November of that year; it was only his increasing ill health that prevented the volume from appearing in his lifetime. By this time Campbell was well on the way to being the writer we know today—the author of hundreds of tales and a score of novels that have ushered in a new era in weird writing and raised its author to the pinnacle of literate weird fiction.

Works Cited

Campbell, Ramsey. *The Inhabitant of the Lake and Other Unwelcome Tenants.* Hornsea, UK: PS Publishing, 2011. [Abbreviated in the text as *I.*]

Campbell, Ramsey, and August Derleth. *Letters to Arkham: The Letters of Ramsey Campbell and August Derleth, 1961–1971.* Ed. S. T. Joshi. Hornsea, UK: PS Publishing, 2014.

Campbell, Ramsey, with Stefan Dziemianowicz and S. T. Joshi. *The Core of Ramsey Campbell: A Bibliography and Reader's Guide.* West Warwick, RI: Necronomicon Press, 1995.

Lovecraft, H. P. *Collected Essays.* Ed. S. T. Joshi. New York: Hippocampus Press, 2004–06. 5 vols. [Abbreviated in the text as *CE.*]

———. *Collected Fiction: A Variorum Edition.* Ed. S. T. Joshi. New York: Hippocampus Press, 2015. 3 vols. [Abbreviated in the text as *CF.*]

Thomas Ligotti's *The Nightmare Factory*

Sometime in 1986, as a cocksure young critic chiefly devoted to promoting the work of H. P. Lovecraft and some of his worthier disciples, I received a review copy of a not particularly well-produced book from Silver Scarab Press called *Songs of a Dead Dreamer*, by a writer I had never heard of, Thomas Ligotti. In spite of an enthusiastic introduction by Ramsey Campbell (who, I suspected, was paying a tribute to friendship rather than to literary quality), I quickly dismissed the book as yet another of the seemingly endless array of "fan fiction" that has brought such disrepute to the field of supernatural horror. I have no idea what happened to my copy of this book—probably I gave it away to someone in a casual moment. What folly!—Imagine what I could now get for this book on eBay!

It was only some years later, and chiefly through the urging of Stefan Dziemianowicz, that I was tempted to probe Ligotti's work again. I was at work on a book called *The Modern Weird Tale*, a broad survey of selected writers of supernatural fiction since Lovecraft, and was strongly advised to give Ligotti some consideration. I obtained the Robinson edition of *Songs of a Dead Dreamer* and began reading. Its first story, "The Frolic," electrified me, and I was a Ligotti devotee for life.

One of the disadvantages of being a practising critic, in this or any other field, is that one falls into so inveterate a habit of reading analytically that the sheer *pleasure* of reading tends to be slighted. It does not help that, in the course of one's professional obligations, one is generally forced to read a considerable quantity of mediocre work. But Ligotti gave me the first genuine *frisson*—in the literal sense of the term—that I had received in years. His work made me realise why I had become a student of weird fiction to begin with—it was to experience that indescribable sensation of being *unnerved*. The purpose of supernatural fiction, I am convinced, is not to horrify or frighten, as such; it is to *make one uneasy*. The very best of Lovecraft, Blackwood, Machen, Aickman, Campbell, and T. E. D. Klein has this quality; and the best of Ligotti has it too. When reading his work, one enters a universe as distinctive and idiosyncratic as Tolkien's or Peake's: a world we half recognise as our own, but one that has been rendered insane—or, perhaps, a world whose latent insanity has finally been brought to the surface by a skilled hand.

The Nightmare Factory—an omnibus collecting Ligotti's first three story collections, *Songs of a Dead Dreamer*, *Grimscribe* (1991), and *Noctuary* (1994)—must take its place among the cornerstone volumes of any library of contemporary weird fiction. Without the least violence of diction, Ligotti is capable of suggesting that the world, the universe, is *awry* in some hideous way that we fail to grasp only because of our deliberate blindness. His prose style can at times be as tortured and metaphor-laden as M. P. Shiel's, but it is a vital, indispensable vehicle for his conveyance of a world where nightmare has replaced reality: purely on the level of prose, no one in modern weird fiction equals or even approaches him. (At the same time, Ligotti sometimes becomes so enamoured of his own gift for language that he lapses into preciosity and self-indulgence—a fault particularly on display in the prose-poems that conclude *Noctuary*.)

Much of Ligotti smells of the study: he is among the most well-read writers in the history of supernatural fiction. He has frequently stated that it is the earlier, more mystical works of Lovecraft, rather than the later, more scientifically rationalised narratives, that have influenced him: hence, "The Last Feast of Harlequin," although resonant of "The Shadow over Innsmouth" (1931), in reality draws more from "The Festival" (1922). It is my contention that "Nethescurial" is an extraordinarily oblique pastiche of "The Call of Cthulhu." "The Tsalal," the capstone of *Noctuary*, draws subtly upon Poe's *Narrative of*

Arthur Gordon Pym. In a field such as ours, this bookishness may not be such a bad thing: Ligotti scorns the notion that weird fiction, and perhaps all fiction, is some kind of "treatment of life" (as Lovecraft himself said as he was entering his "realistic" phase): the writer is a demiurge, creating a universe that may or may not connect with the "real" world at his whim.

Perhaps the most heartening thing about Thomas Ligotti is the very fact that so unconventional a writer could have attained the kind of celebrity he has. Emerging from the small press (and retaining his devotion to it), consciously eschewing explicit gore, refusing to fill his works with "sympathetic" characters to whom the more naïve sorts of readers feel they need to identify, and, most courageous of all, declaring flatly that the "horror novel" is a virtual oxymoron to which he has no desire to devote his talents, Ligotti has nonetheless managed to achieve a status that goes well beyond a mere cult following. After writing the three volumes gathered in *The Nightmare Factory*, Ligotti appears to have experienced a period of uncertainty as to the direction he wished his literary career to take; but with *My Work Is Not Yet Done* (2002), a scintillating volume whose title story is of short novel length, Ligotti has wondrously regained his focus. The title of this book may well be prophetic, and it is certain that we have not heard the last of this most unclassifiable of writers.

Caitlín R. Kiernan and Sensuous Prose

If I were a creative writer (which, mercifully, I am not) and stumbled upon the work of Caitlín R. Kiernan, I would be inclined simply to give up and find another line of work. Kiernan is so much better than anyone writing imaginative fiction today that it has become something of an embarrassment. She is the best in her field at so many things—best in the exquisite modulation of her prose; best in the sensitive portrayal of the complex and at times contradictory motivations of humans, quasi-humans, and non-humans; and, most of all, best in the compelling evocation of fear, terror, loneliness, pain, tragedy, and heartbreak. In little over two decades of writing she has generated ten or eleven novels and seven or eight story collections, along with several separately published short novels. So she combines a gratifying productivity along with an impeccable standard of merit, and we can expect her to maintain that fusion of quality and quantity for many years to come.

One of the many distinctive qualities of her work—perhaps more readily visible in her story collections than in her novels—is her effortless mastery of a multiplicity of genres. In her body of fiction we have stories of supernatural horror, science fiction, fantasy, even some noir or hard-boiled crime tales—and, more provocatively, a melding of these and other genres into something beyond description or classification. This wide range again distinguishes her from her peers. Who can match it? Strangely enough, the only writer I can think of is the venerable William F. Nolan, who in every other regard is about as antipodal to Kiernan as any writer can possibly be. Or perhaps we have to go all the way back to the *fons et origo* of weird fiction, Edgar Allan Poe, who revolutionised the tale of supernatural and psychological horror, who all but founded the detective story, and who even engaged in cosmic fantasy (if his nonfiction treatise *Eureka* can be so classified).

There is, in addition to a diversity of genres, a matching diversity of tone and ambiance. It may be true that, in general, an overriding atmosphere of melancholy pervades all her narratives, but she is eminently able to vary the mood when the opportunity arises. In part, this variation is the product of the shifting or blending of genres Kiernan effects. Who would have expected her to write in the tough, hard-boiled manner of Hammett and Chandler? But in "The Maltese Unicorn" she brilliantly turns the trick; and noir elements are also present, along with much else besides, in the short novel *Black Helicopters* and the noir/cyberpunk hybrid "Hydraguros."

But it is those tales that touch on heartbreak and the regret for lost lives, lost loves, and lost happiness that most move us. "Pony" is a vignette dedicated to love, sex, apple orchards, and stone walls. It was later incorporated into what I still regard as her most accomplished and evocative novel, *The Red Tree* (2009), although the award-winning *The Drowning Girl* (2012) is a close second. A prose poem like "A Child's Guide to the Hollow Hills" can be contrasted with the brooding stream-of-consciousness of the science fiction tale "A Season of Broken Dolls," which in turn is contrasted with the steampunk mode of "The Steam Dancer (1896)."

Kiernan's tales also display the dynamic and imaginative manner in which its author engages with the work of her predecessors. Peter Penzoldt, in *The Supernatural in Fiction* (1952), chastised H. P. Lovecraft for being "too well read," by which he meant that Lovecraft had absorbed so many of the great writers of weird fiction before and during his lifetime that it sometimes became difficult to know what was Lovecraft's own imaginative creation and what was some conscious or unconscious recollection of something he had read. The criticism is, to my mind, unjust; for, like Shakespeare, Handel, and so many other creative artists, Lovecraft almost always transmuted what he borrowed from others, so that it became distinctively his own.

And we can say very much the same, to an amplified degree, for Kiernan's work. The very title of *Beneath an Oil-Dark Sea* (the second volume of her best short fiction) looks back to Homer and his "wine-dark sea," perhaps by way of Robert Aickman, who used that phrase for the title of one of his more memorable stories. The opening story, "Bradbury Weather," trumpets itself as a homage to Ray Bradbury, but it is so much more than that. Even the author of *The Martian Chronicles* might have been challenged to feature the extraordinary union of clutching horror and inexpressible poignancy that we find in this slowly building narrative. A later story, "The Melusine (1898)," may also betray a Bradbury influence in its use of the carnival theme—but of course that theme is not owned by Bradbury, and this tale is more an echo of Kiernan's own fascination with the figure of the mermaid and analogous entities.

Other tales make nods to other writers—but only as a way of acknowledging their work as a springboard for the release of Kiernan's own imagination. Are we to think of "In the Dreamtime of Lady Resurrection," with its vivid second-person narration, as an evocation of the Frankenstein motif? The author candidly acknowledges "Untitled 17" as a tribute to Angela Carter's *The Company of Wolves*, while "The Sea Troll's Daughter" harks all the way back to *Beowulf*—an offshoot of her writing the novelisation of that ancient text following the 2007 film. "One Tree Hill," although vividly summoning up the spectral depths of New England history and topography, is a nod to T. E. D. Klein's expansive novel *The Ceremonies* (1984), itself an homage to Machen, Lovecraft, and other classic weird fictionists.

Lovecraft, indeed, is a writer to whom Kiernan has returned time and again—and her imaginative elaborations of this writer far predate her relocation from the South to Lovecraft's native city of Providence, R.I., in 2008, as attested by several short stories and the novel *The Daughter of Hounds* (2007), a riff on Lovecraft's concept of ghouls. Ghouls in fact become the focus of "The Peddler's Tale," which is also one of the few successful attempts to draw upon Lovecraft's early dreamland fantasies modelled on the work of Lord Dunsany. It is worth noting that Lovecraft himself did not incorporate ghouls in these early dreamland tales; they first entered his fiction in the real-world stories "The Hound" (1922) and "Pickman's Model" (1926), and the ghouls—along with the enigmatic painter Richard Upton Pickman—only came to the dreamworld by way of the dreamland fantasy *The Dream-Quest of Unknown Kadath* (1926-27). "The Peddler's Tale" is quite a bit darker and more evocative than most of Lovecraft's generally mediocre Dunsany pastiches—and no one could say of this tale that it is a mere pastiche.

Pickman himself is the focus (even though he never actually appears in the narrative) of "Pickman's Other Model," whose deliberately old-fashioned prose and manner of narration, using Lovecraft's patented method of the documentary style, paradoxically reveals Kiernan's own sophistication—her awareness of the ambiguities inherent in the historical record and the mysteries that may lurk beyond and behind bland newspaper reports and film reviews.

There is a vaguely Lovecraftian air to "As Red as Red," a rumination on certain historical features found in "The Shunned House" (1924), while "Fish Bride" and "Houndwife" infuse Lovecraft's "The Shadow over Innsmouth" and "The Hound" with a plangency those narratives consciously lack, as Kiernan teases out the emotive ramifications of their horrific scenarios. But her tales are by no means lacking in terror; the single sentence "The hound bays" toward the end of the latter is balefully potent.

Literature is not the only fount of inspiration that Kiernan has drawn upon. "The Ape's Wife" is a half-parodic, half-touching tribute to the film *King Kong*—but here the inherent absurdity of that scenario is shorn away and the implacable plangency of the interspecies love story is brought to the fore. "In View of Nothing" is a science fiction tale that presents a tip of the hat to the music of David Bowie.

Kiernan's well-known scientific training—she was trained in vertebrate palaeontology and has written learned papers on the subject—infuses much of her work, but she is careful not to let pure science overwhelm any narrative, even those science fiction tales set in the far future where scientific advance has perhaps rendered the distinction between human and non-human ambiguous at best and meaningless at worst. In this sense, "The Ammonite Violin" is representative. It is not, indeed, a science fiction tale—far from it. Instead, it features a complex interplay of science (ammonites—a kind of extinct mollusc—are inlaid into the wood of a violin), crime, loss, and art.

But, more than any other feature of her work, it is Kiernan's prose that keeps us coming back to her over and over again, like a crazed drug addict desperate for his daily fix. Her prose is *sensuous* in the best sense of the much-abused term. By this I do not refer to the frequent erotic episodes in Kiernan's work—episodes whose languorous panache make her one of the more stimulating sex writers of our time. Many of her sexual scenarios involve lesbianism, although there is some token heterosexual sex here and there; and Kiernan's penchant for depicting sexual congress with aliens, androids, and other anomalous entities adds a distinctive flavour to much of her writing.

But that is not what I mean by calling her prose sensuous. Even in those passages whose subject-matter is perfectly chaste, her prose beckons us with a lapidary manipulation of rhythm and sense that conveys so much more than what is written on the page. Consider a paragraph chosen almost at random from "Pony":

> A thousand variations on a single moment. It doesn't matter which one's for real, or at least it doesn't matter to me. I'm not even sure that I can remember anymore, not for certain. They've all bled together through days and nights and repetition, like sepia ink and cheap wine, and by the time I've finally caught up with you (because I always catch up with you, sooner or later), you're standing at the low stone wall dividing the orchard from the field. You're leaning forward against the wall, one leg up and your knee pressed to the granite and slate as if you were about to climb over it but then forgot what you were doing. The field is wide, and I think it might go on forever, that the wall might be here to keep apart more than an old orchard and a fallow plot of land.

What a deft intertwining of topographical description, pensive reflections on past and present, and dreamlike wistfulness! And yet, how different is this prose-poeticism from the tough-guy (or tough-gal?) style of "The Maltese Unicorn" ("It's the sort of self-righteous bushwa so many grifters hide behind. They might stab their own mothers in the back if they see an angle in it, but, you ask them, that's jake, cause so would anyone else"). Again, diversity of genre produces diversity of style, tone, and mood.

In "Galápagos" Kiernan has written: "There are sights and experiences to which the blunt and finite tools of human language are not equal." This may be true, even a truism; but, just as Lovecraft, for all his use (and overuse) of words such as "unnamable" and "indescribable," sought to portray his outré images and conceptions to the best of his considerable ability, Kiernan uses all the rhetorical tools available to her to make the reader grasp the bizarre, terrifying, at times ineffable scenes she has so carefully orchestrated. I will cite only one example and let it serve for the whole. "Tidal Forces" is an incredible fusion of cosmicism and body horror, and the almost inconceivable nature of the weirdness of this scenario is summed up in one imperishable sentence: "I think there are galaxies trapped within her eyes."

The more we learn about Kiernan, the more we see that there is an inextricable fusion between her life and her work. This is no doubt true for any author, but in Kiernan's case there seems to be something more going on; and that is why readers will appreciate the story notes, brief and laconic as some of them are, found in this book. We learn, for example, that "And the Cloud That Took the Form" is an expression of her *ouranophobia*—a fear of the wide-open sky. "The Beginning of the Year without a Summer," beyond its many other virtues, betrays the disenchantment of a Southerner for the cold winters and less than invigorating springs of rock-ribbed New England. It becomes evident that Kiernan's life experiences enter into, and even in some mysterious way engender, the most distinctive features of her work, and future biographers and critics will be kept busy tracing the interrelations between the two.

Caitlín R. Kiernan does not care to be called a "horror writer," and with good reason: that term is far too crude and blunt to convey even a fraction of all the diverse elements that make her work unique. Perhaps she wishes to be a writer of what Lovecraft called "weird fiction"; or maybe she prefers Aickman's coinage "strange stories." These terms seem sufficiently broad and ambiguous to encompass the multiplicity of tones, moods, manners, and motifs that make up Kiernan's short fiction, and in *Beneath an Oil-Dark Sea* you will find the full range of her work amply displayed. Her output to date has already placed her at the head of her field; she has nothing more to prove. Any subsequent work can only augment her achievement.

Acknowledgments

"Establishing the Canon of Weird Fiction," first published in *Studies in Weird Fiction* (Spring 2005).

"Some Notes on Ambrose Bierce": "I. Bierce as Political Satirist," first published as the introduction to Bierce's *Fall of the Republic and Other Political Satires* (University of Tennessee Press, 2000). "II. Bierce as Fabulist," first published as the introduction to *The Collected Fables of Ambrose Bierce* (Ohio State University Press, 2000). "III. What Happens in 'The Death of Halpin Frayser,'" first published in *Studies in the Fantastic* No. 2 (Winter 2008-09).

"A Triumvirate of Fantastic Poets: Ambrose Bierce, George Sterling, and Clark Ashton Smith," first published in *Extrapolation* (Summer 2013).

"Gertrude Atherton: Death and Women," first published as the introduction and afterword to Atherton's *The Caves of Death and Others* (University of Tampa Press, 2008).

"Bram Stoker: *Dracula and Others*," first published as the introduction to Stoker's *Five Novels* (Barnes & Noble, 2006).

"Mary E. Wilkins Freeman: The Domestic Ghost," previously unpublished.

"E. Nesbit: Lying Awake in the Dark," previously unpublished.

"Edna W. Underwood: Dear Dead Women," first published as the introduction to Underwood's *Dear Dead Women* (Tartarus Press, 2010).

"Things in the Weeds: The Supernatural in Hodgson's Short Stories," first published in *William Hope Hodgson: Voices from the Borderland*, ed. Massimo Berruti, S. T. Joshi, and Sam Gafford (Hippocampus Press, 2014).

"M. R. James and the Classic Ghost Story," first published as the introductions to James's *Count Magnus and Other Ghost Stories* (Penguin, 2005) and *The Haunted Dolls' House and Other Ghost Stories* (Penguin, 2006).

"Some Notes on Lord Dunsany": "I. The Pegāna Mythos," first published as the introduction to Dunsany's *The Complete Pegāna* (Chaosium, 1998); "II. Jorkens," first published as the introductions to Dunsany's *The Collected Jorkens* (Night Shade Books, 2004-05; 3 vols.); "III. Christianity and Paganism in Two Dunsany Novels," first published in *Critical Essays on Lord Dunsany*, ed. S. T. Joshi (Scarecrow Press, 2013).

"Sax Rohmer: The Popular Weird Tale," first published as the introduction to Rohmer's *Brood of the Witch-Queen* (Centipede Press, 2013).

"Maurice Level and the Grand Guignol," first published as the introduction to Level's *Tales of the Grand Guignol* (Centipede Press, 2011).

"Irvin S. Cobb and Gouverneur Morris: A Taste for the Weird," previously unpublished.

"Bran Mak Morn and History," first published in *Two-Gun Bob: A Centennial Study of Robert E. Howard*, ed. Benjamin Szumskyj (Hippocampus Press, 2006).

"The Novels of Donald Wandrei," first published as the afterword to Wandrei's *Dead Titans, Waken! and Invisible Sun* (Centipede Press, 2011).

"Science and Superstition: Fritz Leiber's Modernisation of Gothic," first published in *Fritz Leiber: Critical Essays*, ed. Benjamin Szumskyj (McFarland, 2007).

"Master and Pupil: August Derleth and Ramsey Campbell's First Book," first published in *Ramsey Campbell: Critical Essays on the Modern Master of Horror*, ed. Gary William Crawford (Scarecrow Press, 2014).

"Thomas Ligotti's *The Nightmare Factory*," first published in Stephen Jones and Kim Newman, ed. *Horror: Another 100 Best Books* (Carroll & Graf, 2005).

"Caitlín R. Kiernan and Sensuous Prose," first published as the introduction to Kiernan's *Beneath an Oil-Dark Sea* (Subterranean Press, 2015).

Index